PRESSURE ON EDUCATION

For my parents
Rose and John Brynin

Pressure on Education

MALCOLM BRYNIN

Avebury

Aldershot · Brookfield USA · Hong Kong · Singapore · Sydney

Published by
Avebury
Ashgate Publishing Limited
Gower House
Croft Road
Aldershot
Hants GU11 3HR
England

Ashgate Publishing Company
Old Post Road
Brookfield
Vermont 05036
USA

British Library Cataloguing in Publication Data

Brynin, Malcolm
    Pressure on Education
    I. Title
    370.941

ISBN 1 85628 339 9

Printed and Bound in Great Britain by
Athenaeum Press Ltd, Newcastle upon Tyne.

Contents

Acknowledgements

The support of the Economic and Social Research Council is gratefully acknowledged. I am especially grateful to many people within education who have contributed time and information to make some of the following possible, and to previous colleagues at the University of Leeds, where this project started. I very much appreciate the time and effort given, apparently without demur, by friends and colleagues in the ESRC Research Centre at the University of Essex: Nick Buck and Andrew Clark for reading and advising on early drafts of different chapters; Louise Corti, Ann Farncombe, Charanjit Singh and Rachel Smith for help in presentation; and Terry Tostevin in the Research Centre's library for assistance in checking references. I am also grateful to John Treble at the University of Bangor for volunteering helpful comments on two of the chapters, and to my close friend, Steve Jordan, at McGill University, Montreal, for support and advice in depth. Finally, I would like to thank my wife, Terri, for managing to steer clear of much of this project for at least some of its preparation for the much greater and harder task of running a school. Unfortunately, working in an education system which currently forces many heads to work long evenings and at weekends - doing things such as checking the budget entries for stationery, searching for a supply teacher at the right price, preparing briefing material for governors - leaves little time for discussion of the fundamentals of education, which may in many homes such as ours be reduced to a quick word over breakfast. Presumably it's all to the good. But despite the impediments I believe our views on education are much the same, so this book is hers too.

Introduction

.... many academics do not grasp the subversive features of the intellectual milieu in which they are living. How long will the traditionalists maintain their pose of benevolent neutrality? Until the bomb comes in through the window? (Cox, 1972, p5)

While for many commentators education is an explosive matter, the interests of most people are far more prosaic - a desire for high grades, parental concern over behaviour at a particular school, teacher frustration with pay or promotion prospects. Yet 'British education... is widely regarded to be in a state of crisis' (Green, in DCS, 1991, p6). All political persuasions have played their part in the establishment of the crisis agenda. Whether the accusation is underprovision (right-wing lack of resourcing) or overprovision (left-wing concern for quantity over quality), a politically symbiotic relationship appears to develop - though it is the Right's image of rescue from crisis that predominates: 'Baker on the schools revolution. NOTHING WILL STOP US NOW (*Daily Mail*, 15.9.87). Only three years later the hyperbole was beginning to falter. 'Mrs Thatcher has ordered her Education Secretary to a crisis meeting today. John MacGregor will be confronted by a Premier determined to put new drive into the Government's classroom revolution' (*Daily Mail*, 17.10.90). In the meantime, the language of fundamentalism passes down the power structure to the committee set up to establish the English curriculum. The new curriculum 'should bring about revolutionary change in the schools, and indeed have some influence on our national character' (Cox, 1991, p152). But can the character of tens of millions of people really be so influenced by one working group on the teaching of English?

One of the effects of the crisis is to transfer attention away from what young people may or may not want out of education, or hope to be as actors within education. Concern attaches to outcomes alone (what can young people produce). Again this is reflected in the language of change. At the worst, young people are redesignated as parts of the body,

1

sometimes even by those defending them from other depredations. This, for instance, is Pedley, arguing that competition between children is damaging.

> Such incentives, whether rewards or punishments, act like purgatives on lazy bowels and are just as harmful. For as the bowel comes to expect stimulation from outside and will not work without it, so the child in this competition-ridden world behaves likewise (Pedley, 1969, p133).

An alternative to the 'parts of the body' approach is the transmutation of young people into animals. This too is linked to the issue of competitiveness. If for Bantock the 'common curriculum' runs counter to the observation that 'geese just aren't swans' (*Black Paper 1977*, p82), Dennison speaks approvingly of exams which 'temper the wind to shorn lambs' (1984, p59), while the position of a bright child in many state schools is 'more akin to that of the ugly duckling' (p82). And for Stal and Thom, writing on France in a book called *Schools for Barbarians* (1988), the bowels of young people, who learn by doing rather than by being taught, actually do need outside stimulation: 'Unlike chimpanzees, which are subjected to the same sort of training, they are not even given a banana to reward their efforts' (p50).

  Bombs, bowels, barbarians.... none of these colourations adds to our understanding of education. As far as I know, bombs are still, 20 years after Cox' prediction, an unknown phenomenon in the education service. Indeed, it has to be said that Cox himself, after an unhappy experience as chair of the government's committee on English in the national curriculum, has since recanted that extreme position.

> Now that the government has taken over the school curriculum in English, they are planning to rewrite the history curriculum. Where this will stop? Will the freedom to learn, which is every individual's right, be curtailed in the universities and in adult education? (*Times*, 1.3.93)

The similarity between this and his comments in the 1972 issue of *Critical Quarterly* is remarkable, except that now the enemy within is different. Later on, another traditionalist, who had written that an effective teacher 'will not have scorned the old-fashioned exercise of "learning by heart"' (Marenbon, 1987, pp34-36), chaired the English Committee of the School Examinations and Assessment Council (SEAC), only to resign, because 'the TGAT model is not compatible with short, simple, written tests' (*Independent*, 10.5.93), and in Marenbon's view only the latter will work. Marenbon had also earlier expressed doubts about the national curriculum because there is every danger that 'it will succeed only in reinforcing principles and practices which its political proponents would be the first to repudiate' (1987, p40). Perhaps the answer is to leave well alone. However, it is not only the far Right that expresses new methods of control. In proposing that, in effect if not in law, the school-leaving age become 18, with 16-17 year-olds being encouraged to stay on through making completion of a new A-level equivalent called the Advanced Diploma a requirement for subsequent government-subsidised training (Finegold *et al*, 1990), new left-wing policy proposals continue to force young people to do what their betters think is good for them. The sense of crisis remains, and with it the demand for control.

  In most cases the source of crisis is one of myth, and further myths accompany the solutions. In the case of the Education *Reform* Act of 1988 this is also self-justifying,

2

automatically charging what went before with inadequacy. The 'Education Act' might do as much as the 'Education Reform Act', but not say as much. Change is seen in terms of some ineluctable trend (seen as starting before the accession of the Conservatives in 1979, eg with Mr Callaghan's Ruskin speech). The signs tend to be contradictory, but include concern over declining standards, cultural-political conflicts (for instance, the preservation of English culture), a perception of an inadequate skill-base, the ability of education to adapt to modernisation, and the growth of consumerism. The argument of this book is that these trends are illusory and cannot serve to produce a realistic basis for educational reform.

One general illusion is that education is inevitably better elsewhere, a result of which is that Britain appears magpie-like in its willingness to raid other systems - though in all the faster-growing countries that Britain looks to there have been, and still are, sources of extreme dissatisfaction with education. In Japan, efforts began in the 1970s to liberalise education.

> Increasingly even certain conservatives had started to recognise that the 'qualification-based social structure' (*gakureki shakai*) so useful in the 'catch-up' phase of Japan's economic advance might prove to be a barrier in its next phase. They argued that.... the economy of the future required creative scientists, fluent foreign-language speakers, specialists in extremely complex technology and workers who could express their views rather than just follow orders. The examination-based system.... was seen to be less suited to meeting these new economic needs (Schoppa, 1991, p50).

It could be argued that both Japan and the UK are moving towards a more flexible, postFordist educational structure. Yet Japan's system remains inflexible and highly centralised. Equally it could be argued, therefore, that the UK is beginning to follow Japan's traditional system of rigid curricula, tests and status hierarchies. But at the same time as an informed critic of the British system can laud Japanese education as a system which 'knows itself, knows what it is about, and what it is trying to achieve' (Howarth, 1991, p85), an equally informed Japanese critic seeks the influence of the West.

> the conditions in which our children are growing up have reached the crisis stage, and there can be no doubt that our educational system is in a terrible mess.... the problems of delinquency, truancy, cruel physical punishment by teachers, bullying of weak students and teachers by other students, and diminished academic performance are continually becoming more serious (Horio, 1988, p362).

In Horio's view recent attempts to liberalise education in Japan, eg through seeking a much greater variety of school types, simply indicate how 'many of the totalitarian aspects of prewar educational thought were revived and reworked within the context of the modern welfare state' (Horio, 1988, pp4/5).

In Germany, meanwhile, there has been public discussion of the value of 'Japanisierung': copying whatever the Japanese do. In the middle of the period when British crisis-mongers were lauding German education, a German sociologist of education, Ulrich Teichler, described Japan's system of education as close to ideal, calling it in 1982 '*the* modern "educative society"'. For him its promise was its ability to combine major expansion with full competition. 'Economic and social success follow in considerable measure from educational success' (quoted in Sommer and Waldburg-Zeil, 1984). Earlier, in 1971, at the height of the German boom, a major dialogue over German education had begun with a series of articles by Georg Picht called 'The German educational catastrophe'. In these he declared that education in Germany had reached a state of emergency. The demand was for growth, without which there would be 'the third large-scale breakdown of German history within this century' (quoted in Fuhr, 1989, p15). Envious comparisons were made, this time with France.

But in France, some time later, in the book mentioned above called *Schools for Barbarians* (Stal and Thom, 1988), the bitterness of the attack on standards could easily have been taken from the British *Black Papers* in the complaint of

> the inability of our pupils to express themselves, their crass ignorance of history, geography and literature, their inability to follow a simple chain of reasoning, their confusion over the most elementary logical distinctions - not to mention their considerable spelling mistakes (p84).

France has had its own equivalents to Illich's *Deschooling*, for instance a book entitled *L'enseignement ne sert à rien* (education serves no purpose) which argued that 'the time is close when societies will consist mostly of people who are self-taught' (Marquet, 1978). More prosaically, there is much concern in France over rising levels of violence in schools. In a newspaper interview, the president of PEEP (*parents d'élèves de l'enseignement public*: parents of students in public-sector education), which claims a membership of 430,000, said that PEEP 'favours the restoration and renovation of discipline'. Two adjacent articles gave the professional view. A head of a school in one of France's most violent areas said the key to success was to use the school 'to create an island of tranquillity which allows the student to forget for the moment the problems of the streets', while a psychiatrist located the problem firmly outside the school in poor socio-economic conditions. 'One can easily see how an unemployed father, constrained to remain at home, may hardly appear credible when of a morning he pushes his children to go to school' (*Le Figaro*, 20.5.93).

However, at the level of policy-making education is still expected to carry a heavy burden. There have been many reforms in French education, from comprehensivisation, through the opening up of post-16 education, to attempts to make institutions more autonomous of the state. These have often contradicted each other. This fact, supplemented by protests from students, parents and teachers, encouraged Chirac to declare, in the wake of the 1986 Conservative victory, a pause in all reform in education. For Weiler (1988) this is merely a temporary end to the 'politics of reform and nonreform'. Commenting on more steady change in Germany he argues that the range of competing demands in education forces governments to do something to restore their legitimacy, in particular through curricular reform and centralisation, one part of which is a 'symbolism of change and innovation' (1990, p16). This notion of symbolic change receives support from elsewhere. For instance, as unemployment rises it becomes increasingly difficult to pretend that education is a universal benefit. One central response is centralisation of finance combined with decentralisation of much decision-making. The centre 'is tired of taking the blame. Gradually it is shifting the onus of problem solution to the edges of the system' (Ewen, in Marsland, 1987, p202). In Japan, the conflicting pressures for reform, sometimes wholly divergent (eg requiring both liberalisation and centralisation) have resulted in significant failure to effect real change (Schoppa, 1991).

Some Germans want to copy Japan, some Japanese want to copy Germany. France has looked to Germany in respect of vocational training, perhaps even to Britain in respect of decentralisation. Britain wants to copy everyone. Obviously discontents exist in all education systems, but which system should provide a model for Britain? Even if a model is adopted, it is not necessarily the case that the 'loan' country is itself moving in the same direction. The opposite often appears to be the case. France has introduced more community and parental power in recent years, but from a highly centralised system, the opposite of the British starting point for decentralisation. Perhaps the two countries are converging, becoming in the process more coherent. But an alternative view is that Britain has a bit of centralisation with a bit of parent power, and is, unlike France, becoming not more but less systematic. Britain is also trying to mimic the USA's concept of magnet schools and performance-related pay for teachers, while moving radically away from the USA's decentralised and democratic system. Indeed, this is generally at odds with the more elitist and segregated nature of education in Western Europe. Yet the problem with copying bits of systems is that all education is historically driven. It cannot be said that German technology teaching is good without putting it in its context, and it is precisely this context which is missing in much policy making (and in much commentary).

Even the most universally accepted and overtly rationalising element of recent change, the national curriculum, is ridden with contradictions. If the ex-head of the National Curriculum Council, Duncan Graham can base the justification for change on declining standards, seen to result partly from 'child-centred education and learning by doing, basing all teaching on arousing a child's interest', while at 'the same time, Her Majesty's inspectors of schools were saying that people were still doing too much of the three Rs and that children were being given too narrow an education, which led to frustration and boredom' (Graham and Tytler, 1993, pp1/2), it is not surprising that contradiction rather than consistency is central to the curriculum.

One of the core tensions concerns the very issue of breadth which the national curriculum is supposed to instill into British education. What is breadth? Mrs Thatcher's goal was a core curriculum of English, maths and science (to be the basis of simple tests), which Graham and Tytler describe as 'nihilistic and negative' (p6). Narrow maybe, but the rest of the curriculum would be free. Mr Baker wanted a range of 10 foundation subjects. Very broad maybe, but these put enormous pressure on any alternative subject matter. At the same time, science and technology have been greatly extended. This may well be in the national interest, but the considerable expansion of technical subjects is perhaps a reslanting rather than a broadening of the curriculum. The National Curriculum Council sought to establish the concept of a 'whole curriculum' (ie including cross-curricular areas of study such as citizenship) at the national level, again in the interests of breadth, but is pre-establishing everything a school may do a broadening or narrowing of teaching? As a further example of internal inconsistency, the fee-paying sector of education, free of the national curriculum, helped prevent the establishment of the national curriculum at keystage 4 (14-16) in order to protect a broad interpretation of its own narrow interests (eg to ensure study of classics at GCSE is not squeezed out). Finally, when Clarke took over the Education Department a process of gross simplification resulted. This appears to some a repressive narrowing down, to others a liberation from prescription. Graham and Tytler are defensive about the latter.

There was panic in the first year at any suggestion that the grand design might be fundamentally flawed. It was left to their successors to complain about over-complexity and over-prescription. This was a bit rich as the council has said from early on that the curriculum as originally planned could not work. I and the few professional staff who were there at that time were clearly beginning to see that the whole thing could grow into a monster, but at that stage there was very little we could do (1993, p37).

The paradox is that it appears that teachers may resent the impositions of a broad national curriculum at the same time as fearing any narrowing as the basis for simplified testing (the real effect of which is to test teachers rather than students). The chaos of the national curriculum still manages to be a neat Catch 22 for teachers. For students the national curriculum is a series of trade-offs. 'Perhaps because of pressure from other aspects of National Curriculum English, there was some evidence that the amount of writing done by pupils was declining' (OFSTED, 1993, p13). Whatever benefits the national curriculum conveys could have been achieved far more cheaply and simply with other methods.

Of course, nationalisation of the curriculum is also a socialist policy. While O'Hear and White (1991) recognise that the current version is too prescriptive and too closely tied to the goal of comparative assessment, they propose a reconstruction around general themes such as social, scientific and personal knowledge, and within these such targets as 'reflectiveness about priorities among one's values' (p123). The problem, however, is that such woolliness cannot mean anything without detailed control, whether through exams, tests, programmes of study, or prescribed reading lists. Without such controls a national curriculum will only be on paper. A national curriculum, as opposed to a national policy on the content of education, brings the civil servant into the classroom.

In general, the arguments in this book contradict some of the paradigms that have been generated in recent years: that educational standards are inadequate, that the UK suffers from endemic skill shortages, that the impetus behind change in education is dictated by a need for greater modernisation, that education can be improved through rationalisation of the role of the teacher, that the local government of education is incoherent, that education generally can be improved by supporting 'good' schools. This is not an arbitrary list. Underlying all these themes is some sense of a primary determinant of change. On the Right this may be economic decline or a loss of moral and cultural standards. Breaking education into fragments makes it replicate the firm or the family, forcing it to relate better to both of these: society is crystallised into its basic building blocks. On the Left, theoretical notions such as postFordism (even postmodernism) - the belief that the dissolution of mass production and consumption entails massive social and political change - seems to require or expect a similar fragmentation.

Both versions of fragmentation seem to accept that the state may have to exert more control as a consequence. Modernisation therefore seems to require a growth in centralisation and rationalisation, but also some sort of streamlining. Often this is asserted in terms of reducing the demands that education makes on society: tight central control is forced by burgeoning demand in a credentialist society. Cuts must follow (Coombs, 1985). Evidence of actual cuts is then produced to substantiate the notion of crisis in education, but in this case is the problem inherent to education or one of policy-making? It is also unclear why a single item of expenditure should consistently take an increasing share of GNP or of government spending. It is obvious that high spending in the past was required by post-war reconstruction, the general expansion of education, and the funding of an increase in the status of teachers. Reduced effort was bound to follow in later years. Equally, practical factors such as falling rolls have since played a part in retrenchment. Neither change, therefore, suggests an inevitable crisis. Indeed, there are many recent cases of major increases in expenditure: in France, after 1988 the government saw education in its own crisis terms and pumped in large amounts of emergency cash. In the UK the costs of the national curriculum, of CTCs, of TVEI, of keeping open schools which opt out to avoid closure, must all be set against cuts being made through LMS. In Japan, proposed cuts have been replaced by increased expenditure, partly to buy off bureaucratic resistance to liberalisation.

One of the main argument of this book is that developments in education should be seen in terms of cycles rather than trends. These are both political and economic. Where these combine as in the UK (a right-wing government intent on imposing new constraints during a recessionary period) the impact can be powerful, though there is no particular reason to consider the changes long-lasting. One of the main cyclical effects is caused by high unemployment. Set against an earlier period of continuous growth, this triggers a panic over the value of education, a panic generally transmuted into concern over standards. One result is that the government has been under intense pressure to maintain educational differentials. Its policies may therefore be demand more than supply-led. This means that the apparent rationalisation of recent change - formula-funding, nationalisation of the curriculum etc - simply has another purpose.

This increase in central control may appear necessary to rationalisation and modernisation, though in reality these elements may work against each other. Allmendinger (1989) proposes two criteria when discussing such structural relationships: we need to know whether an educational system is both 'stratified' and 'standardised'. These may or may not go together. European systems are more stratified and standardised than that of the USA, but stratification in the UK has diminished and the system has always been relatively unstandardised. The significant point is that standardisation is now being used to restratify (eg through facilitating inter-school comparison). Similarly, Horio labels attempts to increase segregation in Japan through a common Scholastic Achievement Test 'standardised diversification', because differentiation 'on the basis of ability is premised on a one-dimensional value system' (1988, p301). Eckstein and Noah (1989) review school-leaving examination systems along several dimensions such as control, uniformity and status. In Japan, which has a highly centralised curriculum, an attempt to simplify university entrance exams through central imposition of a single test (the Unified Screening Test) has increased rather than reduced the hurdles young people have to go through. The result is extra protection for elite institutions (Horio, 1988). Movement on one dimension brings the reverse on another.

It is often claimed that education in other countries is more rationally provided than in the UK's traditionally laissez-faire system. However, the range of institutions in some of the main comparators is quite staggering. Germany, for instance has a several narrowly competing vocational colleges (*Berufsschule, Berufsfachschule, Berufsaufbauschule, Fachoberschule*), as well as a vocational grammar school (the *Berufliches Gymnasium*), apart from grammar schools which tend to specialise between broad subject areas (eg classics) and the other two mainstream school types (the *Hauptschule* and *Realschule*). Italy has a profusion of narrowly segregated secondary school types, while France has added to both the range of institutional variety and the certification available.

It may be that this proliferation is necessary in the face of a growing economic or industrial demand for flexibility and variety, but it runs counter to any notion of modernisation as rationalisation. In the past, of course, this was represented by comprehensive (in some people's view, monolithic) structures or systems. However, this seriously mistakes the level of analysis. Variety and flexibility might be more easily achieved within comprehensive than highly segregated structures. The latter may develop not as a supply-side imperative but in response to demands for higher status routes through education in the face of mass access.

Current educational change in Britain strongly suggests an ongoing rationalisation of institutions (eg the siphoning off of post-16 education into a single tier of increasingly nationally orientated institutions, the gradual loss of middle schools, the incorporation of polytechnics into the university system); and of credentials (national tests, national criteria for assessment, closer co-operation between examination boards, the development of NVQs to enforce consistency among 6000 pre-vocational and vocational qualifications). But at the same time, and on the same criteria, it is possible to discern a powerful process of 'irrationalisation': institutional types are increasing (various forms of post-16 provision, grant-maintained schools, CTCs), while credentials are witnessing an astonishing proliferation (eg test results themselves, records of achievement, the CEE, the CPVE, new vocational equivalents of A-levels, the huge variety of NVQ outcomes). The rationalisation represented by the national curriculum is already breaking down into a massive welter of fragmented tasks and targets. Even if some of this overall fragmentation is designed to introduce both choice and flexibility, especially in response to the implicit uniformity of comprehensivisation, various changes nevertheless work against each other. While the Right complained bitterly in the 1960s and 1970s about experimentation and the pace of other change, the rate has become exponential in the 1990s, with one change impelling manifold reactive changes. As the centre gets more involved it gets deeper and deeper into difficulty, inviting further control - but also resistance: teachers have refused to comply with the nationally prescribed tests, and heads have refused to supply truancy figures, in both cases undermining the government's key policy of publishing school league tables.

A further source of irrationalisation stems directly from the 'rationalisation' of LEA activities. This has taken place partly through the removal of a large proportion of their post-16 responsibilities, as well of some schools (those that opt out), into a national pool, and partly through decentralisation (LMS and open enrolment). The combined result is virtually an end of LEAs as planning authorities. This is deliberate, of course, as the market is seen to be more efficient. Yet this effect is very doubtful. For instance, when Leeds decided to remove excess capacity, largely through the elimination of the entire middle school sector, it imposed extra costs as the number of unsuitable sites increased. At the same time, new schools had also to be built in areas perceived to have insufficient supply. But with open enrolment, cost-effective planning becomes impossible. If parents choose to send their children to institutions they already know, there can be no way of guaranteeing the viability of any new school. One new primary school in Leeds, which was expected to cost nearly £1m to build, is said to have acquired about 40 children in its first year. Choice may help eliminate capacity but it can't build schools. As Graham and Tytler put it, taxpayers 'have some reasons for doubt when they have to fork out for under-used plant in one school while at the same time paying for a new building down the road' (1993, p140).

Much of this irrationalisation derives from contradictions between political and social demands, but it also has its own momentum. Society is changing so fast that education must develop new institutions and processes - a new exam for a new range of skills and a new institutional hybrid to make this feasible. Often the new is grafted onto the old, producing yet more variants. Some irrationalisation is also probably beneficial, and government attempts to control it may simply introduce further contradictions. For instance, it has encouraged a range of new curricular initiatives which seem to promote flexibility and variety - the TVEI, CPVE, LAPP, new assessment procedures through the GCSE. But it then introduced a national curriculum which virtually turns this on its head. Fragmentation may not only be desirable but unavoidable - not because the economy is becoming postFordist but because education is able to a large extent to evolve its own solutions to problems. 'The rise of unemployment and the increase in youth training and education post-16 have added fuel to the arguments for abolition of examinations at 16.... The rise of profiling, records of achievement, graded assessment, and modular assessment have each in their way provided alternative models' (Murphy, in Hargreaves and Reynolds, 1989, p69). If governments supported rather than controlled such processes, educational change would at least be less self-destructive.

The underlying theme of this book is that flexibility is inherently necessary to education, and flexibility can only exist through comprehensive structures that maintain channels of progress for as long as possible. In general, young people themselves should map their own educational careers, and this is only possible where closed doors are opened. An implicit argument in much of what follows is that what is right for young people is generally right for society as a whole. It completely rejects any notion of crisis, wherever generated and whatever its focus - skill shortages, standards, cultural decline. It rejects many policies and proposals for reform, largely because they all extend control for its own sake, whether through a national curriculum, nationally based testing, extension of certification, reduction in institutional choice (eg granting parents more choice *between* institutions in a way that reduces choice for young people *within* institutions), control over daily attendance, or enforced participation in education or training in the early adult years. The main counter-theme is the need for greater flexibility so that, at all points, young people have a reasonable choice of alternatives and reasonable information on which to base this choice. This becomes increasingly important in the later school years, when if anything, current change is reducing and hardening choice - and with it the ability of young people to control their own lives.

The opposition of much of what follows to recent change must appear negative, even conservative. The themes of low standards, endemic skill shortages, or inadequate parental choice, are achieving almost taken-for-granted status. In Part One it is argued that there has been no problem with educational standards that can justify radical change to the whole system. Nor is there reliable evidence of endemic skill shortages. The claim for both is obviously connected, as it can be argued that it is the least educated who are the least skilled and therefore the least employable. But this begs far too many questions. For instance, is high unemployment the result of failure *by* or *on behalf of* the 'bottom' 30% or so? The Left rightly claim the latter but also need the myth of skill shortages for a programme of expansion and integration (eg of the academic and vocational components). However, neither policy need be based on the concept of skill shortages. Integration in particular is necessary for efficiency and flexibility. The divide between the academic and vocational must be reduced simply because the traditional demarcation on which it is based is out of touch with modern needs, just as last century the divide between the classics and technical education was obstructive. This was resolved through the incorporation of technical instruction into high-status education. The same must happen to vocationalism.

This is important in its own right and does not require any belief that Britain has a massive deficit in skill production. Such a belief can generate a numbers game in which governments determine when sufficient skills exist and then switch off the tap, or alternatively that skills can best be developed through a highly segregated system of academic and vocational institutions with, as always, obvious implications for class differentials. One reasonable left-wing strategy for integration is the development of high-status academic-vocational qualifications within schools. For instance, it has been suggested that all 16-18 year-olds should be strongly encouraged to remain in school for this purpose (Finegold *et al*, 1991). A-levels would expand and GCSEs would be allowed to wither. While this might work, it might also create a much bigger divide than currently exists between those who continue in education and those who simply will not. It might be just as reasonable to allow A-levels to wither and to boost the GCSE, perhaps building on this in modular form (as, indeed, Finegold *et al* suggest). The main point is that a sufficiently flexible structure is required to enable young people to acquire skills wherever and however they see fit.

When the 1993 A-level results came out, showing yet further improvement, Rhodes Boyson chose to maintain the crisis in education *by definition* in suspecting 'a devaluing of standards'. (The same has consistently occurred with the GCSE.) Reporting this, the *Independent on Sunday* (22.8.93) rightly points out that standards have in fact been steadily rising (largely through increased access into post-16 education). It argues that the problem is rather one of skill production. The government has been seeking to push students into science and technology through limiting finding for arts and social science. This modernisation is in reality a means of maintaining traditional status distinctions by controlling access. That is, standards are being raised in order to suppress entry into higher education. A month before the start of term in 1993 there had been over 26,000 more rejections for entry than at the same stage in the previous year (*Times*, 24.8.93). A similar process has occurred in some continental countries where central controls are levied on entry into particular subjects as part of a general policy of limited access. The *Independent on Sunday* editorial then goes on to propose the abolition of A-levels in favour of a more accessible five-subject curriculum which would prevent students over-specialising. Some such change is probably inevitable and the government's gold standard is surely going to be undermined by the market (as also with attempts to limit money supply or to link EEC currencies). However, this has nothing to do with skill production but is, rather, an issue of access and equality. In addition, the problem is not one of students locking themselves out of science but the extent to which subjects may either avoid knowledge of technology such as data-processing (eg most language knowledge) or may attract it (eg much knowledge of linguistics). In this sense, all subjects can become technical.

The first part of this book extends the argument from education to training. Such supply-side considerations are traditionally the property of the Left, while the Right is generally contemptuous of attempts to manipulate supply, and concentrates instead on creating appropriate market conditions. One (illusory) achievement of the Conservative government, however, is its ability to combine both sides of the argument. Demand will improve standards, and rising standards will improve skills. However, this bit of theory is a Heath Robinson construction, and indeed has no known design credentials at all. In the second part of this book it is argued that the technical goals are in fact superficial. Recent legislation is so scarred by long-term *cultural* panic over education, particularly in the face of working-class growth, of youth culture, and the threat of black cultures to the laager mentality of what it means to be English, that the entire structure of recent change, however much it is supposedly based on the need to modernise or rationalise, must be treated with great scepticism.

The only real legacy of these changes will be increased centralisation and intensified status distinctions. These are the theme of the final section. A return of influence to teachers and local authorities is perhaps the best defence against both. Suppression of their influence has been effected in the name of rising standards, and yet, apart from local variations, which might on average increase rather than reduce performance (ie variation is no proof of itself that average standards are low), there is no evidence that this is necessary. The real reason for the changes is not a crisis of standards or of skill production, but the reverse. Both have been rising steadily over the years. This applies in many countries, but even if some countries might have had a past advantage over the UK, the gap is probably closing (partly because deeper recession in this country may encourage staying on in education). Most industrialised countries have seen a long period of growth culminate in intermittent recession. The result is immense pressure on governments to guarantee greater status differentials in an increasingly competitive environment. In Germany this has had the effect of turning the secondary-modern school into a sink school for the rural poor and for recent migrants. At the same time, the *Abitur* is becoming increasingly necessary for the most prestigious apprenticeships. In France, expansion has been paralleled through erosion of comprehensive provision, with status differentials becoming much sharper in secondary education. In Japan the transition from lower secondary (*chugakko*) to upper secondary (*kotogakko*) is the critical transition. In 1955 only 51% of *chugakko* students stayed on for the *kotogakko*. Now over 95% do so. Only 8% of students went to university in 1955. Within 20 years this had more than trebled.

> Such quantitive growth meant that neither *kotogakko* nor universities could remain elite institutions.... The Japanese system went some way towards addressing this problem of a broad ability range by using examinations to rank students.... Nevertheless, conservatives saw the trends towards higher staying-on rates as constituting even greater cause for pursuing their long-cherished policy of diversification (Schoppa, 1991, p45).

The drive for status probably extends rather than shortens the ladder. The number of colleges and universities in Japan quadrupled between 1945 and 1950. In 1980 there were four hundred and forty-six broadly university-level institutions, with most of the new provision in the private sector. Yet often these institutions 'are insufficiently endowed and possess few sources of income other than the tuition paid by students. These schools form the bottom strata of higher education' (Amano, 1990, p.xix). At one level, reform in both the UK and Japan can be said to be similar even though Japan has a much higher provision of skills. The similarity in fact derives from other sources - political demands for a return to segregation in the face of mass provision. This also means that the explanation of growth should not be sought in supposedly trend factors such as the need to modernise or rationalise, the need to raise standards or increase the output of skills. The source may be far more cyclical: how to cope with growth cut up by intermittent recession.

Part One:
Counting skills

Worldwide economic pressure such as high unemployment has put education and training in the limelight. Between 1968 and 1976 the proportion of under-25s in unemployment went up from 22% to 37% in the EEC, with each country experiencing an increase of over 50%, and most somewhere between this and 100%. The UK's was the highest, Germany's the lowest (Max-Planck-Institute, 1980).

One result of economic stress is the belief that education has failed and that it should therefore be more accountable, more cost-effective, more practical - a set of views which receives support across the political spectrum. An emphasis on greater vocationalism, for instance, is a clear outcome on all sides. The Left may see this in human capital terms - new measures are needed to encourage working-class participation, to release previously under-used capabilities. The Right argues the same, but in reverse: the economy cannot afford to allow this section of society to do little or nothing. It must be forced to work, or learn to work.

Vocationalism involves a wide range of factors: the vocational element at school (eg separate vocational institutions, the entry into the school curriculum of a greater technical or vocational input); the development of new certification systems; the distribution of funding, eg between employers, employees and government; the type of qualification produced (eg general against specific, or theoretical against practical); and institutional provision (access to various forms of post-school training). Creating an effective balance between all these is far from easy. While the government has introduced more vocationalism and training into schools it has not significantly changed the role of training in employment. Indeed, employers now have greater control over state provision. Left-wing alternatives have little patience with the employer contribution, proposing firstly that employers be constrained to provide better, more coherent, and more extensive training, and secondly that education become responsible for the creation of a higher proportion of core skills. The goal is not just the reduction of skill shortages but a bridging of the academic-vocational divide. This is implicit in the notion of *core* skills. The ideological conflict is profound, with one side attempting to free employers of constraint and to extend their control over education, the other seeking to impose constraint *on* employers and reduce their role in education. In the former the state is insignificant; in the alternative, anti-laissez-faire argument, the state is a major actor.

While the programmes may differ they also converge. In a sense the same argument is being forged between two oppositional forces: those that blame employees for failing to keep up with the requirements of a modern economy, and those that blame employers for much the same thing. The language then becomes the same: skill shortages, economic decline, a failure to train the labour force adequately. In fact, much of what the government has been doing in the last 10 years or so appears to accord fairly closely with demands on the Left (high-status vocational credentials within schools, resources for more technology teaching, some government subsidy for training, a transparent system for vocational qualifications). This extends to the language of change. In respect of the provision of skills, while the 1992 Labour manifesto wanted 80% of 16-18 year olds to get 5+ GCSE passes within five years, and 50% to qualify at A-level or a vocational equivalent 'by the end of the decade', the Tory manifesto supported the CBI target of 80% of young people reaching NVQ level 2 'by the end of the parliament' and similarly for the provision of training credits for all 16-17 year olds. It is not obvious that there is a radical difference in these five-year plans, other than that the Tories express targets in vocational and Labour, paradoxically, in primarily academic terms.

The problem as described in the following chapters is somewhat different, if only because the language of skill shortages, used on the Left as a platform to extend training and education to all those who can gain from it, is itself an insufficient (though not unimportant) basis for change. Logically, the close tying of educational provision to labour needs could result not in expansion but in reduction, that is whenever it is considered that shortages have been met. The issue is really more one of how skills are used rather than their overall level. British education and training are now entering a highly planned phase, the purpose of which is to push people into those economic slots that others consider they are suited to. But if there is a need for change, it is for a major increase in flexibility, genuinely demand-led, with those seeking education and training being allowed to assess their own economic advantage. The Right certainly have no interest in such a future, but it is not necessarily the case that young people provoke a different response on the Left. The young remain a planning target.

1 Educational standards

In April 1991, over two years after ERA, a speech by Prince Charles provoked the following front-page headlines.

Prince hits at school 'illiteracy' (*Guardian*)

CHARLES FEAR OVER SCHOOLS (*Daily Express*)

STAND UP TO THE TRENDIES (*Daily Mail*)

As with much criticism of educational standards, the Prince's outburst contained a number of disparate elements, and this was reflected in reactions to it. For Jack Straw, shadow Education Secretary, it 'was a powerful indictment of the Conservatives' neglect of the British state school system'. Trade unionists supported this approach, in particular applauding his targeting of diminished resources. The press added its own slant, while for Kenneth Clarke, Education Secretary, the Prince's speech contained a lot of common sense and said something about 'the way education has been going over the last generation' (though Prince Charles had been especially critical of the way education had been going in the last two years). Assertion of declining standards has for some time been a matter of moral panic rather than of fact.

> Wherever I go I am besieged by people, particularly parents, anxiously questioning the present state of British education. Are standards falling? Is discipline worse? Are children reading less well? What do you think of comprehensive schools? Is a university education worthwhile? On my good days I am patient with my questioners. On my bad days I am abrupt or run for cover..... (Rhodes Boyson, *The Crisis in Education*, 1975, introduction).

15

Never has reform in education been so explicitly tied to standards. Most previous reforms sought either to expand the service as a whole or to distribute it more fairly. Expansion and equality are obviously linked but have now both been replaced by the single notion of quality and standards. Educational reform in other countries tends to lack this single-minded focus. Yes, greater parental rights might have been accorded (eg in France), expansion created (Italy), or liberalisation sought (Japan), but no fundamental claim has been made in these countries that the issue is one of standards as opposed to more education, more efficient education, or more egalitarian education. Apart from the oddity of the reduction of several major educational changes to a single concern - the national curriculum will improve standards through direct improvement of pedagogic content, tests will improve standards through providing a basis for judgement of individual performance, parental choice will improve standards through putting pressure on poor schools, and so on - it has to be asked what 'standards' actually mean. Little in the debate bothers to attempt an answer.

Standards mean different things to different people. The Prince's own measure appeared to be the amount of Shakespeare taught in British schools, though this not widely accepted measure reveals a number of contradictions. The 'general flight from our great literary heritage' was combined by the Prince with other concerns: that many children leave primary school functionally illiterate; that there has been a decline in the basics - handwriting, spelling, punctuation and numeracy; that not enough children remain in education after 16; that sixth-form education is too specialised; that the academic-vocational split is too great; that teachers have been subjected to excessive policy change, that they have inadequate tools to do the job. It is not surprising that the speech was taken up so enthusiastically by so many political opponents.

HMI happened to publish their latest report, on primary education, on the same day as the royal speech, though this was marginalised in most press reporting. HMI reports follow a fairly standard pattern.

> Two-thirds of the work seen was of a satisfactory standard; some of this
> was of high quality (DES, 1988).

> Of 457 lessons seen in Key stage 1 and 752 in Key Stage 2, two-thirds
> were satisfactory (OFSTED, 1993, p6).

While HMI reports seem always to say that two thirds of teaching is satisfactory, newspaper reports of these generally say one third is unsatisfactory.

> Up to a third of the pupils...had unsatisfactory teaching in the
> basics of English last year (*Guardian*, front page).

> **One in three pupils 'is not taught basics'** (*Daily Mail*, p2 headline).

This reversal alone, headlined and repeated, can convert expert assessment that education in Britain is basically sound into a proclamation of crisis, though two thirds/one third sounds a normal distribution of performance. Even then, by the time of the 1991 report 70% of primary education, 73% of 11-16 education and 82% of 16-19 education was considered satisfactory or better (DES, 1992). This does not mean that when HMI find that fewer than one in 10 schools are poor, as in 1988, there is room for complacency, but by the same token 'neither does it support a view of secondary education in general as being in a state of crisis' (DES, 1988, p8).

Whether or not HMI is a liberal and woolly institution (to use the *Daily Mail*'s terminology), its judgements have tended to be implicit and therefore unable to provide a basis for radical policy change. It is not easy in fact to pin down the criteria on which HMI make judgements, as Gray and Hannon (1986) infer from the mix of reference criteria HMI use across reports. HMI's generally inexplicit but educated assessments made an easy target for the Right, who want clear-cut standards enabling direct comparison of output between individuals, schools and LEAs.

Debating standards

HMI's implicit standards might not provide a positive policy basis for change, but they could still be used negatively, for instance by Mr Baker introducing the 1988 Bill in the House of Commons.

> This Bill will create a new framework, which will raise standards, extend choice and produce a better educated Britain. The need for reform is now urgent. All the evidence shows this - international comparisons, the reports of Her Majesty's inspectors and, most recently, the depressing findings on adult illiteracy (*Hansard*, col.771, 1.12.87).

However, this statement also feeds off years of previous moral panic, and it is the deliberate woolliness of this that has provided the real basis for change. Standards have always been used to promote different educational views or philosophies. F.R. Leavis believed that 'it is disastrous to let a country's educational arrangements be determined, or even affected, by the assumption that a high intellectual standard can be attained by more than a small minority' (in Singh, 1982). In the case of the current right-wing low standards are the result of egalitarianism, which suppresses excellence.

> **Equality 'poisoning our State schools'.**
> **Labour gets lashing on poor standard.**
> Mr George Walden, Minister for Higher Education, said standards had been brought so low that the private sector, with only six per cent of all schools, now cleaned up nearly 50 per cent of the places at Britain's top universities (*Daily Express*, 31.1.87).

This requires freeing parents from equality.

> When private school standards are for a time low, parents can escape; they cannot, especially if their incomes are low, escape from low standards in state schools because they are not allowed to take their money with them. That is why low standards persist longer in state than in private schools (Seldon, 1986, p27).

However, the Left too has played along with the notion of declining standards. The Socialist Educational Association, for instance, strongly supports a national curriculum and even echoes the *Black Papers'* call for a return to the basics.

> Commitment to basic standards is the province of the Left, even if that commitment needs to be re-appropriated from the Right by the national Labour Party. As the General Secretary of the SEA, Graham Lane, said in March 1991: 'The Tory attempt to steal Labour's clothes on standards is badly in need of laundering'.... Indeed, the London Charter for Education, launched in 1991 by the ALA, aims to raise standards by ensuring early learning of the basic skills of reading, writing and mathematics (Wilson, SEA, 1992).

Even with a bit of window-dressing in respect of a more egalitarian national curriculum and concern for under-achievement by particular social groups, it is hardly surprising that Labour is no longer seen to have a distinctive education policy. It is therefore also not surprising when right-wing pamphlets quote left-wing concern for inequality as simply another way of re-expressing the need for higher standards. Quoting Frances Morrell, Leader of the Inner London Education Authority, to the effect that we 'have to take the question of quality more seriously', Seldon argues that 'there is increasing recognition on what is called the "left".... that it has grievously neglected working-class concern with numeracy and literacy' (Seldon, 1986, p26).

Of course, the Left has traditionally interpreted standards in terms of inputs (eg lack of resources) rather than outputs. The Right has begun to say that inputs (ie resources) can only be measured by outputs, while leaving the definition of the latter apparently unproblematic. Indeed, in focussing attention on standards the fact that inputs often *are* outputs is itself obscured (eg improved staying-on rates are outputs overwhelmingly dependent on resource decisions such as ROSLA; increasing the numbers of graduates requires extra funding for higher education). The Left must be wary of the abuse of standards. The power of the new paradigm, a generalised and ill-defined concern for standards overall, detracts from assessment of what is happening to particular social groups, from other policy areas of greater practical importance, and from more vital ways of thinking about education.

International comparisons

In international tests among 10 countries using the same questions, the National Curriculum Working Group for Mathematics noted a decline over 20 years in the British performance and a poor record against Japan. The mean score on maths tests for Japan was 64.6. England's was 48.6 and Scotland's 49.7. However, the mean score across all countries was 51.8. If Japan's exceptional score is excluded from the overall mean the British score is at worst average. Japan seems exceptional by most standards: for instance, HMI reported after a visit to Japan that in their judgement 50% of 18 year-olds are up to A-level standard in maths (DES, 1991:b).

Latterly, international comparisons have become more apparent, partly because they are selective (the UK is generally compared to Germany or Japan - not, say, to Italy or Spain), partly because international contrast leads naturally to comparison of economic performance. Not only the countries but the criteria are selective. The USA is often chosen as an organisational model by the New Right. Yet, when HMI visited New York in 1988 to examine developments of interest to the government, such as testing for comparative purposes and magnet schools, it was careful not to compare standards. Indeed, it implied that comparison would have been meaningless.

> more than 6,000 school-age students live in temporary housing... two in every five children live in poverty... Crossing certain neighbourhoods to get to school can be a dangerous undertaking... murder is the fourth leading cause of death for children aged 1 to 14 and the leading cause of death for New Yorkers aged 15 to 24... in 1985 34,000 teenage women became pregnant; 13,000 gave birth... the AIDS epidemic has begun to affect school-aged students (DES, 1990, p7).

Japan is also admired, of course. Yet the negative aspects of Japan's meritocracy - cramming, stress, rigidity, rote-learning, child suicides, violence by teachers (for instance, children died when locked in a confined space as a punishment for smoking, another when a teacher slammed a gate on a child arriving late), as well as major court cases as teachers oppose state censorship of school books - have made many look to the West for a more liberal approach. Textbook screening affects not only cultural products. For instance, a physics text book by a Nobel prize winner was banned because it concentrated too much on material designed to get students to think about physics and not enough on facts (Horio, 1988, p174). And how important *is* ability in Japanese education? 'The Japanese Diet concluded that *it* was, that Japanese industry was, but that Japanese society was not yet ready to accept legislation requiring employment and advancement by merit rather than by sex' (Iben, 1991, p137).

While knowledge of the relationship between educational and economic performance is hazy at best, this has not stopped commentators from assuming, for instance, that because Germany has a higher rate of growth than the UK, and because Germany has a national curriculum, therefore national curricula improve economic growth. There is no evidence for such a link. Even comparison of educational performance is difficult to determine. For instance, if German children get a higher score on a simple arithmetical test at one point in time this says nothing about their retention of this knowledge over time. In addition, German children have to undergo rigorous and regular assessment of the sort that the Education Reform Act has introduced into the UK. They are trained to perform well on a certain range of narrowly based tests. It would therefore be strange if they performed less well on such tests than British children. Similarly, there would be little point in condemning German children for being poor at cricket. The German tests in fact also make much use of teacher assessment. On a study trip to Germany, HMI observed the award of few poor or very poor grades in primary schools visited. While this was a source of complaint from secondary schools, primary schools 'claimed that their pupils should all perform at least adequately given the system's philosophy of encouragement to pupils' (DES, 1986, p18). The HMI report was rather cool in its overall assessment. 'Indeed, to English observers, while the amount and quality of oral work in classes were high, much of the other work seen was unduly theoretical and little concerned with the practical applications of knowledge and skills' (HMI, 1986, p38). This is strange given the linkage commonly made between German educational and economic skills.

It is also very hard to make real comparisons which can distinguish between standards themselves and the impact on standards of structural differentiation. As an obvious example, comparison of average results of a system where perhaps 80% of the population take an exam at a particular age with those from a country where only the elite of the system takes the exam, means little. In this case, at the very minimum, comparison should be made only of a particular proportion of any age range, although even then this does little justice to the broader results achieved by systems with high retention rates. What is really being compared is not outcomes so much as political and ideological factors which shape the educational system.

This basic contrast was brought out early on in Husen's review of test results from a major international survey (1979). The data are old but the principle remains the same. Out of 14 countries England comes ninth in retention of pre-university students, keeping about 20% of the relevant population at about 6th-form level, compared to 75% for the USA. Looking at test results for science, the USA comes bottom by far (because its huge pre-university student population includes a mass of less able students). West Germany, relatively elitist, comes second, and England fourth. However, when looking at the results for the top one per cent only, the picture changes. The USA is no longer bottom, but ninth. West Germany comes tenth. So, the USA's more democratic system may help the most able better than Germany's elitist system. On the other hand, while England comes second equal, Sweden, retaining 45% of pre-university students, performs nearly as well as England at the higher levels while keeping a much larger proportion of the population in education (Husen, 1979, p99).

One of the least useful international comparisons of standards is of the number of school students leaving school with some sort of qualification - not because this is unimportant, but because the numbers getting through are the result of political decisions rather than of the quality of the education system. In Germany most people now stay on in full or part-time education until at least 18, and about 90% of that age group get a vocational or academic qualification. This statistic has often been used as an indicator of a general failure of standards in the UK, though the failure, if any, is obviously at the political level. Education can be made to retain or reject any proportion of students, and at whatever stage, that those in political control consider appropriate - however inadequate or ideological the basis of their decisions. 'Where the American educational structure encourages continuing in education, the English structure encourages departure' (Morgan, 1990, p41), and that is because the political system wants them to depart. This decision feeds directly into standards. For instance, the wastage rate in universities of people failing to obtain degrees has generally been about 10% (DES, 1985, p53). This has not changed much over the years but hides major variation between departments, so in some subjects it is much larger. In its evidence to the Robbins Committee the Committee of Vice-Chancellors justified the same 10% rate as reasonable when compared to that of the USA's 40-50%, itself the price of a far more open entry system.

> It is our view that wastage rates could not reasonably be expected to be less
> than 10 per cent. A figure below this could be capable of the interpretation
> that selectors were playing for academic safety, which we should regret
> (quoted by Malleson, in Butcher and Rudd, 1972).

The paradox is that as universities become more desperate to maximise both entry and pass rates, the government is using cost to suppress numbers, thereby implicitly maintaining high standards. Though the government has indicated that it wants an expansion of higher education, this is to be funded not by central government but by students, whose finances can be supplemented by loans. Entry criteria remain the same. The *Black Papers'* opposition to the expansion of education, the opposition of Mrs Thatcher to a more flexible system of A-levels, the labelling of improvement in GCSE passes as a decline in standards, and the general thrust of ERA's curriculum and testing structure - all these pressures have been geared to ensure 'high', not more widespread, standards.

Educational standards are filters controlling flows through the system, which means that comparison of standards, at least at exam level, is a comparison of flows considered requisite at the political level. All such decisions involve trade-offs. In Noah and Eckstein's terms (1989) these reflect various dilemmas, for instance between an examination system historically designed to preclude the many, and burgeoning demand; or between the need for professional autonomy and the demand for accountability. Each country has its own system and its own costs and benefits. The USA maximises entry into higher education using machine-scored test results of general ability, but at a cost to written skills and the encouragement of short-term recall. Japan is similar but has attempted to make its exam system more flexible with institutions of higher education adding their own exams to the general state exams. One result has been a huge increase in credentialism, with families investing substantial resources into coaching, supplementary schooling (*juku*) and the temporary acquisition of facts. The unchallenging American system brings students into HE without much idea of what to expect, while in Japan students may arrive 'burned-out' (p20). In France, the *baccalauréat* has traditionally been general, like the old matriculation exams, but also elitist. Recognition of the limitations of the model has led to expansion through the creation of a vast range of options and levels. This has been proposed for the UK in the demand by Finegold *et al* (1990) for a 'British *baccalauréat*'. However, it appears that expansion can only occur through differentiation, from which 'a strongly demarcated hierarchy of prestige has emerged, with, in France, the mathematical options at the head, and the vocational options forming the tail' (Noah and Eckstein, 1989, p20). At the same time, expansion of post-16 education rubs up against the expansion of expectations of university education. 'Yet the university system has been held on an exceptionally tight budget rein by successive administrations' (p21). A similar problem has occurred in Germany. Though the *Abitur* has not changed substantially, success in the exam has resulted in suppression of the legal right to a university place. In Noah and Eckstein's words, 'the price paid for expansion has been high'.

The trade-off between access and standards depends to a limited degree on demand and supply in the labour market, but the main determinant is historical, and this history is itself one of struggle over status and opportunity for reward. Standards depend on the political definition of status. Comparison of education systems across countries is really a comparison of their political and social systems.

Chronological comparisons

If international comparisons are of limited use, assessment of change over time within a single country should promise more, as this at least compares like with like. In fact, most of the evidence suggests that educational performance has been gradually improving in the UK. These indicators include both examination results and the results of more narrowly based tests. Even when the cry of failure was first heard, the evidence was thin. The

Newsom Committee (DES, 1963), which reported specifically on the performance of less able children, concluded that 'although this report is about the academically less successful, it is a success story that we have to tell... There are indications of marked improvement in the last fifteen years' (p184). For instance, comparing results of standardised reading tests showed an increase in average scores of 14-year olds from 18 in 1948 to 21.3 in 1961. While the war disrupted education the main gains were made in the late 1950s. From the assessment of past achievements that 'boys and girls are better at their books than their predecessors half a generation ago' the report goes on to predict that 'their successors will be better still' (p185). This turned out to be the case.

The Bullock Report's review of the studies then available also suggested significant improvement. NFER surveys produced the following results: the mean score on one reading test increased in the case of 15-year olds from 21.52 in 1952 to 23.46 in 1971. ll-year olds saw a rise from 12.42 in 1952 to 14.19 in 1970, though this represented a fall from 15.00 in 1964. The second test showed an increase from 28.71 in 1955 to 29.38 in 1970 (DES, 1975, p19). These results, produced at the height of the scare about standards, show a steady increase followed by a small decrease, though this might have been a result of the ceiling effect - an old test not keeping up with rising standards. More recently, rigorous tests have been undertaken by the Assessment of Performance Unit (APU) within the DES. Comparing results of the same tests on samples of 11 and 15 year-olds in 1979 and 1983, there were negligible changes in writing, though there were clear improvements in reading. In England, for 11-year olds, the smallest change on one test showed an improvement of 3.7%. The biggest was 5.4%. For 15-year olds three tests showed no significant change, with one giving an improvement of 3.6% (DES, 1988, pp212-216).

Examination results show the same results as tests. School outcomes have clearly improved. The following covers the period of critique leading up to ERA and shows both an absolute increase in the numbers obtaining good 16+ results and an increase in the proportion of school-leavers getting such results.

Table 1.1: **School-leavers with 2+ A-levels or 3+ SCE H-grades, United Kingdom (000s)**

	1965/6	1970/1	1975/6	1986/7
Boys	48	55	61	66
Girls	32	44	49	62
Total as % all school-leavers	11	13.8	13.4	14.8

Source: DES Education Statistics (1988), p38

The number getting 5+ A-C grades at O-level (or CSE grade 1) rose from 81,000 in 1980/1 to 92,000 in 1985/6 (p38). The proportion of school-leavers without any qualification has been falling steadily for two decades from 44% in 1971 to 8.3% in 1990 (DES, 1991).

Local comparisons

Comparison has often been made between exam results in comprehensive and tripartite systems, if generally for political and campaigning purposes. One study referred to in the *Black Papers*, Bennett's comparison of progressive and traditional teaching methods, stood the test of time - for a time. Yet Bennett (1976) himself was cautious in interpretation of his findings, as well as scorning 'rhetoric which would have us believe that informal methods are pernicious and permissive, and that the most accurate description of formal methods is that found in Dickens' *Hard Times*', (in Finch and Scrimshaw, 1980, p192). HMI also at that time gave a mixed review of mixed ability teaching (DES, 1978).

Such comparisons also tend to be of different areas and this adds to their politicisation as they critique the educational strategies of local planners. ILEA, of course, has been the main target. Mr Baker, introducing the 1988 Bill into the House of Commons, spoke of ILEA as 'uniquely extravagant.... when the performance of its schools is often dismal' (*Hansard*, 1.12.87, col.780). Yet ILEA had helped pioneer authority-wide standardised tests well in advance of the government's drafting of similar nation-wide proposals in ERA. Its Research and Statistics section developed the London Reading Test, in 1977, to provide secondary schools receiving their primary intakes with a systematic indication of the achievement level of incoming pupils. In 1986, after a decade of testing, standards appeared very stable (ILEA, 1987). There is, of course, no reason to think that performance on standardised tests will vary except over a long period. Change is more likely to occur in exam results. ILEA Research and Statistics combined O-level and CSE grades scores showed an average increase from 14.4 in 1978 to 15.6 in 1983 (ILEA 1984).

When a Minister of State for Education released a league table of LEA examination performance (percentage of students gaining five or more O-levels/CSE grade 1 passes), this showed ILEA as 91st out of 96 - sixth from bottom. However, Gray and Jesson's comparisons (1987) produced very different results, taking into account not only social deprivation in each area but the proportion of children in private education. In their study ILEA moves up from position 91 to 56, only 0.5% below what would be predicted from its social composition, whereas the bottom authority is 6.3% below. (Some well-off, Conservative authorities did badly while some Labour authorities in poorer areas did well.) The following shows some of the more extreme fluctuations across six studies reviewed (the last column being Gray and Jesson's own figures).

Table 1.2:   Ranking of LEAs in six league tables

	Number of Study					
	1	*2*	*3*	*4*	*5*	*6*
Bromley	9	15	75	79	96	96
Cleveland	49	61	6	4	2	9
ILEA	91	9	68	55	44	56
Liverpool	78	20	30	23	23	4
Manchester	89	5	25	14	11	10

Source: Gray and Jesson (1987), p39

The argument of the rest of this chapter is that virtually the entire structure of the debate over standards has little foundation in reality. Indeed, it tends to distort this reality, firstly by making a false equation between standards and accountability, secondly through marginalising underachievement by particular social groups, and lastly through reducing the measurement of standards to the point where technical, moral and political definitions are inextricably mixed.

Standards and accountability

The debate about standards, in moving the terms of reference from equality to quality, has substantial implications for the direction of education. One is the link to accountability. This has several themes: education is expensive and should be more beholden to those that control the purse-strings; the professional providers should be made more accountable to parents; and educational targets should be made more accountable, in a different sense, to the needs of the economy. The sources of these themes have often been adumbrated (eg Raggatt and Weiner, 1985; Broadfoot, 1986), though accountability to children and students is rarely heard. The force-feeding currently favoured is, of course, the reverse of the child-centered tenets of progressive education, and perhaps standards become rulers rather than measures.

The ethos of accountability appears to claim that costs can be cut, parents have more choice, and standards forced to rise all in one fell swoop.

> we now spend six billion pounds a year on education, a huge increase over the 1930s in its share of the gross national product as well as in gross terms. With all this increased expenditure should not standards have obviously and markedly risen? The fact that they have declined proves how disastrously informal teaching has affected our schools (Cox and Boyson, 1977).

Yet ERA's monitoring machine is itself far from cheap. Surveys of samples of children whose performance would be used to standardise tests, large bureaucratic structures to evolve curricular change and assessment procedures, training of staff at LEA and school level for both of these, a huge array of printed material through which the changes are disseminated, and a substantial loss of teaching hours now switched to assessment and recording (often combined with the hiring of extra staff to cover for this) - all these extra costs clearly do nothing to make education cheaper, or more accountable to the taxpayer.

There are ideological as well as apparent cost effects. One element of accountability is an intensification of social construction of the family as an inherently moral and cohesive unit. This has required the attempt to undermine the assumption that teachers act *in loco parentis*. Parents hand their children to the care of teachers unwillingly and under strictly controlled conditions. Teachers are to supply pre-established knowledge, to test their charges on the acquisition of this knowledge, and to report the results to parents. While parents have rights, like anyone else, the according to parenthood of an almost mystical sense of moral infallibility goes much further. Related to this ideological effect is the equation between the family and the market - the idea that parents nosing out the 'best' education is a necessary prelude to improvement of the quality of labour. No evidence has been adduced to support this remarkable contention.

Parents are in such political constructions subjects rather than actors. Testing is forced on their children whether they want this or not. However, there are many alternative ways of making education accountable to consumers without enforced comparative testing. For instance, Hopkins and Leask argue that performance indicators in general only make sense in terms of education development plans and in collaboration with those involved in teaching 'rather than being imposed from outside' (1989, p19). Only increased emphasis on the notion of a contract between teacher and student, where individual capabilities and aspirations are negotiated, can really add to individual accountability.

The government has made clear that standards also include discipline and attendance, though it is obvious to most people that publication of such figures will merely drive good attenders away from schools with low attendance levels, with no obvious benefit to anybody. In 1985 ILEA found attendance figures varying from 67.9% in one school to 96.2% in another (ILEA, 1985, p6). There is clearly little point in reducing attendance in the former for the sake of increasing it in the latter. Moreover, what does poor attendance say about the school, as opposed to its intake? From an individual point of view 'levels of attendance are rarely so low as to represent an important educational handicap' (Smith and Tomlinson, 1989, p162). Again, definition of attendance as a performance indicator is likely to impede improvement. There are massive limits to what an individual school can do about attendance (other than to encourage poor attenders to go elsewhere). Positive measures to raise attendance (eg the use of welfare officers) may even be discouraged by devolution of power to the individual school. Unfortunately, LEAs probably no longer have much reason to care about such things as their hold on schools is increasingly tenuous; anyway, it makes no difference to an authority's overall figures if parents shunt good attenders from one school to another.

All counter-truancy action is expensive. From 1987 Leeds put resources into an anti-truancy programme involving intensive liaison with families. The result was a small increase in attendance (about 1%) in the selected schools. Perhaps more important was that this was achieved without taking any children to court, whereas in 1986 250 youngsters had been subject to interim care orders (City Council Newsletter, *Counsel*, March, 1989). In the new competitive environment there are strong disincentives to such action, and indeed it would be understandable if an authority actually increased the share of costs absorbed by the legal authorities. Finally, use of attendance figures to put the spotlight on 'bad' schools again detracts from more important social issues. While the above ILEA study found an overall drop in attendance from 86.9% to 84.4% over nine years, there was also a decline down year groups, with attendance falling to 73.7% at age 16. The drop in the fifth year alone is nearly 10%. Clearly, motivation of young people prior to examinations is critically important; lowering the school average through encouraging good attenders to go elsewhere is at best a fatuous response. Nor is it possible to relate improved attendance to some vague notion of ethos - the critical factor in the study by Rutter *et al* of the model school (1979). David Hargreaves, commenting on an Education Welfare Officer with special abilities in reducing poor attendance, asks: 'Where was this woman in Michael Rutter's study?" she wasn't. Her pseudonym in the Rutter study was "ethos"' (ILEA, 1986).

Recent legislation is attempting to make parents accept a form of accountability which they may be resistant to. Accountability is in effect to government, not to parents. There is little evidence that parents wish to judge schools on the basis of rigid test results. Parents do not feel the government's moral quest - 'Test me, God, and try me, examine my bowels and my heart' (Psalm 26) - to expose themselves and their children. More prosaically, a survey by the *Independent* (10.5.93) suggests significant public antagonism to comparative tests, even after the government had spent £750,000 of public money trying to persuade the public: 'the sooner you spot where she's falling down, the sooner you can lend a hand' because the tests enable you 'to measure your child's progress against consistent, national standards'. Only 35% of the sample of parents believed children should be tested at age 7, even though the tests had been running for three years. While there was strong support for testing at older ages, half said they would prefer the tests to be through continuous teacher assessment, while only 3% wished progress to be measured entirely by government-set tests. Both the national body of the PTAs and the Education Department ran their own polls at the same time, producing very different findings. Even John Patten's own poll, by phone and containing a fairly leading question, found only 57% of parents in favour of testing in the current year. The poll of NCPTA membership found massive votes against (*TES*, 4.6.93).

Accountability is in part a myth, created as much by central and media definition of the terms of reference as by any real (in the sense of truly measurable) upsurge in demand for detailed accounts of performance. There is in fact widespread opposition to this, and this is not new. When IQ tests came out, there was also considerable public concern.

> They seem to me to be ideally suited for selecting first and foremost those children who will make good form-fillers, which is perhaps what the authorities want.... But I doubt if my son Garry will encounter any 'trick questions' at his new school. It's one that apparently concentrates on the old idea of developing a sound character and picking up some useful knowledge in the process (*John Bull*, 11.1.50).

Here, teaching is old-fashioned and tests are new-fangled. Now tests are being used to re-establish old-fashioned teaching. The ironies are extreme.

Standards and underachievement

Cast almost without exception in terms of *general* standards, the debate about standards has diverted attention from underachievement by particular social groups. Even special-needs children have an entitlement to the national curriculum and to be judged against their peers. But is that a help to them? Why do schools have to opt out their special-needs students from the attainment targets? Equality here does not extend to an equality of suffering, which is in fact intensified for those with special needs. This has ideological overtones but its practical impact is also acute. The '"itch" does not distinguish between core subjects and foundation subjects or appreciate that attainment targets have to be met....' (from a National Eczema Society advice pamphlet, 1991). The tests themselves may bring on stressful attacks in children with eczema.

The distinction between general and particular standards is crucial if equality between different social groups is to be taken seriously. For instance, while Swann found that racism was probably a significant factor in the relatively poor performance of children of African and Carribean origin, it was also the case that at least 50% of Afro-Caribbean underachievement could be attributed to social class. Restricted educational opportunity therefore derives in part from restricted job opportunities, which they then serve to maintain. It is at least possible that this is slowly changing. ILEA's Research and Statistics

Department, scoring fifth-year exam results onto a single scale in 1976 and 1985, found that in both years children of Caribbean origin were well below average, but this group showed the largest rate of improvement. Indeed the improvement in *general* standards was in part because in 1985 'the fifth year contained a much higher proportion of pupils from ethnic minority groups' (p8).

Table 1.3: **Fifth-year exam scores in ILEA schools, by ethnic group**

	1976	1985
Asian	18.4	18.9
Other	14.5	18.4
UK etc*	14.0	15.2
Caribbean	10.3	13.6
ALL	13.7	15.6

Note: * English, Scottish, Welsh, Irish
Source: ILEA, 1987, p8

However, racism remained important. The ILEA research organisation went on to examine the relationship between the verbal reasoning score (VR) and banding, revealing substantial differences between actual and predicted exam scores. Caribbean pupils were more likely to be assigned to a band lower than warranted by their VR score while the reverse was true for children coded as British or Irish in origin. The effect may also be indirect. Smith and Tomlinson (1989) found 'a fairly strong tendency for children of UK origin to be put on higher-level courses than those of South Asian or West Indian origin', though this is again because they 'belong to lower social classes: it is not because ethnic group is itself being used as a criterion in the allocation to course levels' (p216).

Of course it can be argued that social differences are just what the national curriculum and associated tests are designed to do something about. For the first time standardised nationwide information will be available on performance levels. But there is nothing in the legislation to suggest that the results will be used by government to try to reverse differential underachievement. Indeed, this would conflict with the principle of parental choice. Moreover, although the data from national tests will enable comparison of different social groups, this does not require the testing of the whole school population, which is an astonishingly expensive method compared to sample tests.

The absolute basis of the tests encourage individual and institutional, not social, comparison. Underachievement is at the individual level converted into *low* achievement, encouraging self-blame. Socialisation plays an important part in this. For instance, a study of attitudes to maths amongst 13-14 year-olds in Australia, Japan, and the USA (Iben, 1991) suggests that performance depends in part on confidence and motivation, and this is gender-related. There is also a strong negative relationship amongst girls between performance and belief that maths is a male subject. The greater the emphasis on tests rather than on understanding the more powerful this is likely to be. 'Experiences relating mathematics to activities important in the daily life of the pre-school, elementary, and early-adolescent child enhance the sense of mathematics' usefulness; drill activities in mathematics without this association do not' (p148). When Galton and Willcocks (1983) found that the transfer from primary to secondary schools could seriously depress motivation and performance - the absolute performance of nearly a third of children declined on standardised tests - they also pointed to the need not for blanket testing or blanket judgements of schools, but detailed and sensitive assessments of particular problems. It is not surprising that many parents do not want their children to be tested: they are defending standards.

The technical and the political

> For so it is, O Lord my God, I measure it; But what it is that I measure I do not know (St. Augustine, quoted by Rowntree, in Finch and Scrimshaw, 1980, p211).

> a test which is highly valid and at the same time highly useful is not possible in the very nature of the case (Schwab, 1989, p1).

A further way in which the debate over standards has introduced major distortions is through the misuse of technical issues. In large measure this results from political pressure to force education into a summative, comparative mode. Current educational change has as its sole purpose the reintroduction of major status distinctions between schools, this being the main reason for the persistent refusal to take background factors into account in test results. Alternative measures of value-added have been offered to the government: for instance, both the Audit Commission and the NAHT proposed a system some teachers use - taking GCSE performance into account in assessing A-level performance in order to show the value added during sixth-form studies. The NAHT have suggested extending this to chronological comparison of performance across testing points. This would at least assess *progress* at school rather than merely the quality of the intake. ILEA Research and Statistics also developed a value-added technique (ILEA, 1987:a).

  The political objective of comparison was not apparent in the early years of the post-1979 government when professional advice such as Cockcroft was accepted if not always liked.

> Mathematics teaching for pupils of all ages should include exposition, discussion, appropriate practical work, problem solving, investigation, consolidation and practice, as well as mental and oral work. Assessment should be both diagnostic and supportive, and teaching should be based on a scheme of work which is appraised and revised regularly. All of this and more is necessary if mathematics teaching is to be effective; all of this is in the hands of teachers (Cockcroft, 1982, p243).

Within a few years of this statement the pressure to return to forced feeding has put the professionals in education very much on the defensive. But control requires elimination of the influence of professional expertise, in particular that of teachers. The only way this can be managed, apart from through the sneering 'common-sense' of the *Black Papers*, is

28

through an alternative expertise, that of the test creators. The test is now the dominant factor in the curriculum.

There is in fact fairly widespread support for increased assessment. Committees such as Bullock have encouraged it. ILEA used tests to determine school allocation (in opposition to rather than in support of segregation). Testing has always been a major part of the educational experience, though often applied unsystematically. HMI reported that tests in the secondary schools they visited were often unrelated to subjects in the curriculum, that little standardisation of information had been undertaken, and that 'insufficient or inappropriate evidence was used to place children in streams in most of these schools' (DES, 1988, p52). So, there is a case for a rationalisation of testing.

The body responsible for overseeing the development of assessment procedures, TGAT, adopted criterion rather than norm-referenced testing. This decision built on a wide body of opinion. For instance, norm-referenced public exams, which ensure that roughly the same proportion of children will succeed or fail each year, in the words of ILEA's Hargreaves report on secondary education, are 'seen to be having profound repercussions on what was valued about pupils; to be making many pupils feel rejected; and therefore to be a major contributing factor to the underachievement of many pupils' (ILEA, 1984, p134). Criterion-referenced assessments (but not tests) on the other hand are held to 'have a powerful motivating effect on pupils' (p73). TGAT argued that it was wrong for children to be able to move forward in knowledge and understanding while at the same time always achieving the same relative position, thus being 'given no sense of having made the progress which must in fact have been made' (DES, 1987, para.98).

This relates to another reason for criterion-referencing. It directly measures what has been learned by each pupil, not how much they have learned in relation to others. This seems fairer and more obviously productive. Criterion-referencing is socially neutral. Or is it?

> Criteria-referencing too can provide more positive, motivating and meaningful certification. Equally, it could lead to greatly increased scope for central curriculum control and the deskilling of teachers to the extent that pedagogy is replaced by a utilitarian drilling reminiscent of the English nineteenth century Revised Code (Broadfoot, 1986, p211).

Criterion-referencing replaces measures of what people actually achieve, albeit scaled in relation to some expectation of the potential of the majority, with what other people think they ought to achieve in absolute detail. 'Aggregation must reflect what is *achievement* for the novice and not be weighted and thus valued on the basis of abstracted "expert" constructions of what is valuable knowledge' (P.Murphy, in Horton, 1990, p45). Murphy, critiquing the TGAT report, argues that the system may turn out to be far from fair. The point had often been made that ERA was for political reasons making the formative and diagnostic functions of assessment (both related to judging an individual's problems and potential) subordinate to the summative and evaluative functions (geared to comparison between children, between schools, and between LEAs). The school especially, like a medieval leper, will be forced to publicise what it cannot help and be shunned by the community. TGAT argued that the two main functions of diagnosis and comparison could be combined. Assessments can be formative - designed to assist individuals - and then aggregated to be summative - designed to compare schools and LEAs. In Murphy's view the different functions are not just socially but technically incompatible. For instance, summative assessment requires a simple division of knowledge into the known and not known (ticks and crosses), whereas formative assessment seeks to understand how these might be linked. It is 'not that formative assessment collects *additional* information to that needed for summative purposes but rather *different* information' (P.Murphy, in Horton, 1990, p40). In the case of summative assessment the pressure is very much to report attainment in general terms; the 'foci appropriate to diagnostic assessment are, however, much smaller in scale' (Black, in Nuttall, 1986, p16).

It is in an attempt to overcome these problems that the tests being developed under ERA are so extensive, detailed, and subject to proliferation. Only through adding tasks and breaking up general attainment targets into a multiplicity of further tasks can sufficient detail be gained to make assessment at all useful as diagnosis. Despite considerable concessions, the attainment targets have overwhelmed teachers.

> The problem about all criterion-referencing is the level of detail at which criteria have to be specified in order to offer an adequate description of what constitutes a satisfactory performance. This produces unwieldy lists of descriptors.... Because criteria are all different and are in no way equivalent to one another they cannot be added together, or summarised, without losing their meaning completely (Barrs, 1990, p15/45).

The need 'to equate sets of component one-dimensional subtests' (Goldstein, in Nuttall, 1986, p173) must result in the publication of either a mass of detailed outcomes, which neither parents nor general public can make use of, or a set of simplified tables which abuse the data, producing at the best 'a score that one can have confidence in but no understanding of' (P.Murphy, in Horton, 1990, p44). The alternative of enforced and consistent teacher assessment then becomes very attractive. 'Test scores, in and of themselves, are not meaningful. They must be *rendered* meaningful using knowledge and information derived from sources outside the test itself' (Stierer, in Horton, 1990, p154). Goldstein, for instance, while supporting improved teacher assessment across a wide range of activities, including social and athletic work, proposes that the referencing should be neither absolute nor relative, but local. 'By locally referenced we mean that these achievement targets are those actually attainable by the students in a particular school' (1991, p7). Norms are then given explicit criteria. It is of note, in passing, that advice to parents in the private school sector recognises that simple comparison of test or exam results is of limited meaningfulness. 'Your child might not be as bright as you think. A school that is prepared to take trouble over the less bright may enable your child to get more qualifications than another school with an impressive list of entrants to Oxford and Cambridge' (ISIS, 1989, p18) - though the fees charged, also clearly listed in the ISIS guide, presumably provide an alternative standard for most parents.

Because criterion-referencing is suited more to formative than to summative assessment, it seems to many that progress is being made. The real problem, however, derives from the attempts to compromise between acutely divergent educational (formative) and political (summative) objectives. The political purpose behind criterion-referencing ends up utterly undermining its stated character. LEAs and schools will be compared in league tables, and children will be compared, not just to each other but to classroom norms, school norms, LEA norms and the national norm. If the marking system itself is not norm-referenced its use and evaluation most certainly will be, bringing with it not a reduction but a huge increase in invidious distinctions. The referencing by norms has merely been transposed from technical to public evaluation. It is not for nothing that Barrs argues that children who do not do well on conventional tests (for a variety of reasons) are unlikely to be helped 'by the constant pressure to assess on essentially normative criteria that the TGAT model leads to' (1990, p47). It is not so much norm against criterion referencing which is at issue as the purpose of the tests themselves, and this is clearly to ensure that 'a population can be labelled as good, average and below average' (p45) - as with norm-referenced exams.

This is inevitable. Tests cannot simply be referenced to expert notions of what children ought to know at a particular age. Norms underlie all tests. Moreover, given continued use of exams as hurdles to restrict entry into post-16 education, norm-referencing is still a major determinant of each person's educational career. Keith Joseph sought with great difficulty to make criterion-referencing fundamental to assessment in the GCSE and Finegold *et al* (1990), seeking the fading away of the GCSE, propose it for a new-look A-level. Nevertheless, the whole of education is built upon the notion of hurdles. It is therefore ultimately norm-referenced, and the norms include cost constraints which, for instance, determine how many proceed to higher education. By contrast, the use of criterion-referenced tests in the USA as an aptitude test that opens doors to higher education is a complete reversal of the British situation, where the 'many are sacrificed for the few who go on, and the curriculum is geared to this sacrificial service' (Rhoades, 1989, p19). It is the system that controls these flows which need changing, not the technicalities of measuring the flow.

The result of the inadequacies of the testing programme is a massive burden on both teachers and students. This is partly a result of the need to make both subservient to political need, but also derives from attempts to make the whole process serve several different functions simultaneously. For instance, although the process of assessment is split into levels rather than tied to age, and TGAT confidently asserted that children who manage one level easily should be able to move onto a higher level, there is literally no indication how teachers are supposed to manage this. The burdens also, of course, derive from criterion-referencing: each bit of absolute knowledge has to be imparted and its receipt precisely measured. Finally, and paradoxically, the complexity is also partly the result of successful resistance by professional educationalists to the ticks-and-crosses approach. Indeed, teachers now find right-wingers calling for a simpler approach to make things more manageable for teachers! When Marenbon resigned from his SEAC position as chair of the English committee, he blamed the government for not going far enough in moving towards the basics: 'Sir Ron [the new chair of SEAC, now combined with the National Curriculum Council] has two main choices. Either he can keep the TGAT model and drop the tests; or he can keep the tests and give up the TGAT model'. Marenbon favours 'a drastically reduced national curriculum, limited to basic English, basic mathematics, basic science' and one or two languages, all to be assessed by simple tests. The result is an absurd paradox, with teachers and educationalists accepting huge additional burdens, at their own cost, in order to undermine the government's political programme, and to protect both children and themselves from this programme, while the government and others on the Right seek to protect teachers by simplifying tests as far as possible into summative measures, and in so doing to tighten control more cheaply. The TGAT model is creaking, probably breaking under the strain, and teachers in the meantime can humiliate a government intent on total control by simply refusing to undertake the tests. The teachers' successful avoiding action in 1993, when many schools failed to deliver test results, begins to show that the government may not, after all, be able to make teachers their own executioners.

Rarely in education has so much technical argument and controversy been generated by political decisions, while the political arguments stand or fall on these technical issues. In one analysis of school results, taking into account social background, even taking the square root of examination results produces 'some marked changes in the rank ordering of the schools' (Goldstein, 1987, p27). Many experts, often derided by the Right for working outside the sphere of common sense, are now working very hard to make a common sense decision technically feasible. The end result may be neither common sense nor technical perfection but the usual botch job.

Conclusion

On most criteria, standards in British education have been rising. The long-running claim of decline and crisis is simply myth. Educational knowledge and understanding will continue to rise, within limits, partly through the ability of the system to absorb more people for longer periods of time (unless constrained from doing so), partly through improvements in the system, partly through social change, which raises the demand for education. Raising standards has little to do with ramming knowledge down young people's throats but much to do with making education a worthwhile option. Indeed, government ministers are increasingly sounding like past Soviet politicians, but with educational targets replacing wheat output in their unwritten five-year plans. Even worse, it is as if the mere establishment of the national curriculum means that education has automatically improved, and the development of human capital has in part been superseded by its measurement, though it is hard to imagine how beer can be improved by strict adherence to pint measures.

The definition of standards is becoming politicised. Does improving standards mean higher quality GCSEs, more GCSEs, getting more people to stay longer in education, widening the range of knowledge, raising the hurdles, getting more people into higher education, or what? All these have significantly different social outcomes. The demand for higher standards is often, for instance, merely a plea for *narrower* standards.

> Let me say at once - I believe in elites. The best in my experience is usually better than the not so good. Elites are the guardians and transmitters of the best. Our various examinations are a means of distinguishing the good from the not so good... We are bedeviled with undisciplined freedom on every side, with the glorification of mediocrity and the preference for quantity over quality (Pollard, *Black Paper Two*, p72).

When Pollard speaks of grammar schools as the glory of British education and sixth forms as the brightest jewel in the crown, or claims that 'our future depends increasingly on our best brains' (p79) he is not arguing about standards in general. Not much has changed since the above was written. The 'bottom 30%' are a source of concern, but as long as they can absorb enough information briefly enough to get through various tests and assessments they can be forgotten, as before. Nothing has been done to better their position. ERA will produce both underachievers and low achievers. The general concept of 'standards' has become an ideologically and politically tainted tool which has deflected attention from more pressing concerns such as providing the sort of education that particular types of young people need.

2 Education and the production of skills

A central element in moral panic over education is inadequate production of skills. This itself is seen as an important source of economic failure. However, the argument of this chapter is that the evidence for this is limited, and moreover that skill shortages are not a useful index of *educational* failure. The distribution of skills is more important and this is determined in the first instance by employment practices. Educational inadequacies must surely limit growth, but as long as the government does not over-constrain expenditure, or excessively limit throughput (eg for the sake of status differentials), it is in the interests of education to provide the right skills. The evidence that it fails to do so is very limited. As a corollary, if there is a problem it is in the *demand* for skills, not their supply. To increase the supply artificially, given demand constraints, may simply result in reduced returns to qualifications rather than the upgrading of status and pay which such a strategy presumably seeks. This does not quite mean that it is 'clearly absurd to maintain economic pressures for more training, more job-related skills, more vocationally oriented education, in a context of diminishing demand for such products' (Ewen, in Marsland, 1987, p205), but it does mean that care must be taken that ever vociferous claims about skill shortages do not encourage government - any government - to determine that there is a sufficient supply of skills and, as a consequence, to pull back on both training and education.

The argument of this chapter is that there are no fundamental skill shortages *given* the nature of employment. Indeed, to use skill shortages as a symbol of economic decline involves a certain circularity of thought. A shortage of skill shortages may be an indicator of a failure to grow (as growth permanently raises the demand for new skills). And even if modernisation suggests that education itself has to be continuously retooled, views may differ as to what that means.

> Of course, *entrepreneurs* are born, not created by education; but a host of less creative but necessary generators of wealth reach their full effectiveness

only after higher training of the mind, whether it is in classics, English or engineering (Minford, 1991, p192).

Classics? Set in an article arguing for excellence in higher education through market principles (eg students paying their own fees), in which money replaces standards (or 'artificially high A-level grades') as the necessary entrance ticket, this reads oddly, but serves to show how even modernisation is subject to ideological appropriation. Retooling often appears to be of aptitudes and attitudes. In 1976 James Callaghan, in his well-known Ruskin speech, expressed concern that 'students who have completed the higher levels of education at university or polytechnic have no desire or intention of joining industry'. However, Callaghan's critique also contained criticism of traditional demarcations, seen, for instance, to prevent women from advancing in the science and business fields. It was as if the 'white heat' of technology should penetrate every corner of a creaking, traditionalist system. The overall tenor was continued in the 1977 Green Paper, *Education in Schools*, where one major complaint was that teachers lack experience, knowledge and understanding of trade and industry, and that curricula are not related to the realities of most young people's work after leaving school.

The task of modernising the economy was passed shortly after to a new Conservative government. In its Green Paper, *The Development of Higher Education into the 1990s*, the government warned higher education to beware of anti-business snobbery: 'The entrepreneurial spirit is essential for the maintenance and improvement of employment, prosperity and public services' (DES, 1985, p4). But there remained a more general, left-wing recognition that change in the economy must have a major impact on education. 'Skills, knowledge and attitudes are tightly enmeshed here in the formation of the post-Fordist worker... co-operative, problem-solving, project-based methods which stress capability - knowing how rather than knowing what - offer the best fit between school and the new work' (Ball, 1990, p126). Whether one likes it or not the 'post-Fordist school' establishes a new correspondence between economic and educational imperatives, bringing together, echoing Bowles and Gintis, both flexibility and control. Thus, *if* industrial processes and structures are becoming fragmented, it appears inevitable that education must follow suit. In this thinking, the break-up of education as we know it seems inevitable. Nothing in this book gives credence to such a notion, whether from Right or Left.

Education, technology and the economy

Assessing the impact of education on the economy is extremely difficult. That educational inputs rise with national income tells us nothing about causality, as a richer country can afford more education, and merely increasing educational inputs, whether in the name of productivity or of equality, cannot raise productivity unless matched to real demand for skills. Otherwise, inefficiency such as more arbitrary rates of return to qualifications results, as Bird, Schwarze and Wagner (1992) show for East Germany.

Given the problems in relating education to the economy at the macro level, this is usually in fact undertaken through micro-analysis of returns to qualifications, though this may tell us nothing more than that employers use qualifications as a basis for selection (their 'screening' function). One estimate of the annual marginal rate of return to undertaking a degree has been calculated (for men only) as 9.5% in the case of science, for engineering 10%, for social science 12%, and for arts 12.5% (Morris, 1973, discussed in Hough, 1987, p73). This does not, in passing, suggest that technical skills have a high market value. Social rates of return take into account the cost to the state of producing the qualification (higher in technical subjects), though at the same time assessment of various 'externalities' which can reveal the full benefits (or costs) of education can be very difficult. One of these is 'the inability to measure the tendency for the education of individual A to increase B's productivity' (Barr, 1993, p719), even where B is less educated. But it is also possible that 'the calculated social rate of return may rise if education allows educated people to gain partly at the expense of the uneducated' (Weale, 1993, p731). In other words, a great deal of unproductive substitution occurs through education. Overall, taking into account various negative and positive biases, in Weale's view social rates of return to education are probably less than 10%. In general, there 'does not seem to be strong empirical support for a powerful external effect of education on economic activity' (Weale, 1993, p736).

The relationship between education and economic performance contains many unknowns, but one of the most important, frequently emphasised in this book, is the impact of economic cycles. For instance, in recessions employers can pick and choose more easily. This might help pave the way for climbing out of recession: not just capital but labour is restructured. This could in turn make qualifications more important, as each individual tries harder to get an edge in the job market. Equally, if no jobs appear, then a few years spent becoming better educated might offer a convenient stop-gap. On the other hand, recessions might also devalue credentials; in such periods it could pay young people to leave school early and get a job quickly - before others waiting for qualifications. College courses might also be abandoned for similar reasons. To the individual, is the extra expenditure (cost of fees, maintenance, opportunity cost of not getting immediate employment) worth a highly uncertain outcome? Given such complexities, the picture of a parallel increase in educational inputs and economic outputs is certainly far too simple.

Education has to compete with many other factors in determining productivity, eg capital investment, birth rates, hours worked, changes in female labour participation, migration from rural areas or from abroad. During the long post-war boom the latter two factors were extremely important in facilitating growth, regardless of education. Even then the rate of supply of labour did not always keep up with demand. This problem was exacerbated by the fact that hours worked were declining. The result was pressure to improve the labour productivity of capital.

> GDP grew fast in the postwar period despite a rate of growth of labor input that was, primarily for demographic reasons, not only unprecedentedly low but declining; and the labor input per head of population was declining more rapidly than in earlier periods, with the exception of the period 1913-24. Labour shortage, due to this cause and to full employment, might have in theory either stimulated investment or discouraged it. In the event it stimulated it. Such a response carried with it an inherent threat of diminishing returns to investment. The rate of capital accumulation did in fact begin to tail off in the course of the 1960's - in manufacturing earlier than in most other sectors - and the capital-output ratio began to show a marked tendency to rise after 1968. The indications of an end or at least a slowing down of the postwar boom were apparent well before the world recession that began in the course of 1973 (Matthews, Feinstein and Odling-Smee, 1982, p547).

While this could imply a demand for more qualified people to operate and control this investment, and indeed such claims are the source of concern over skill shortages, Matthews *et al* do not suggest this. Instead, over-capitalisation may actually limit the proper use of skills. Increased investment does not necessarily produce high profit rates in an era of intense international competition. High capital costs, combined with low labour productivity (when adequate returns to scale are not reached), reduce profits. This must in turn limit spare cash available for training provision, perhaps even encouraging deskilling rather than reskilling. After all, deskilling reduces labour costs directly through lowering wages. So, British firms might well 'prefer recruitment to training. Skills are bought off the shelf wherever possible' (Campbell, Currie and Warner, in Hirst and Zeitlin, 1989, p148). Meanwhile, peaks in capital investment are associated less with a shortage of skilled labour than with a shortage of labour in general, although any subsequent investment programme inevitably restructures the demand for different skills.

It should also be apparent that technological development does not necessarily engender a greater demand for skills. It can make skills redundant: 'in some circumstances, the introduction of new technology, for example, can reduce the need for skilled workers, while increasing that for unskilled ones, whose training needs are minimal' (Rees *et al*, 1988, p1). For instance, the skills may be locked up in data processing machinery, the operation of which might require fairly limited skills. Is a counter clerk in a bank more or less skilled than twenty years ago? Some research suggests the latter, this of course being an addendum to the now well-worn sociological assertion of the proletarianisation of the clerical labour force. If modernisation demands new skills, it also destroys skills.

Skill shortages

it is particularly disturbing that there is a substantial shortfall - an investment gap as I think of it - between ourselves and our principle competitors in almost every area of economic activity: scientific and technical education, skill training, infrastructure (Banham, 1989, p6).

There is now widespread agreement that inadequate schooling attainments - particularly by average and below-average pupils - in comparison with their European counterparts, combined with subsequent inadequate vocational training, are crucial factors contributing to Britain's less than satisfactory economic performance (Prais and Beadle, 1991, p1).

Education for capability alone can keep Britain an advanced advanced technological society and save her from becoming a Portugal, perhaps even an Egypt, of tomorrow (Barnett, in Finch and Scrimshaw, 1980, p74).

Even if the government should be concerned about production of skills, it is by no means clear that it can effectively match demand with supply. Hough (1987) lists a number of the pitfalls. First, time-lags in the educational response to technological demands may make them obsolete. Second, many trained people do not use the skills they acquire. Chemists might go into research, teaching, retailing, distribution, personnel, management or journalism. According to the Labour Party, in 1986 38% of 14,500 newly qualified teachers failed to enter the profession, at a cost to the Treasury of £27 million (*Guardian*,

20.9.88). Third, planning or even estimating labour availability might be based on faulty signals. For instance rising wages might indicate less a shortage of labour in that sector than a response to credentialism - a drift towards the same work requiring higher qualifications. Finally, projections of labour demand find it difficult to take into account the impact of productivity. Technology constantly changes planning parameters. It may also be asked how much the concept of skill shortage is subject to ideological definition, as for instance in Barnett's attempt to relate lack of skills to poor performance in war. The prime criticism in Barnett is of an education system which turns out poor managers and leaders - say, the top third of the labour market, while for others it is the bottom third that causes most concern. Barnett's characterisation of this group as 'coolie labour useless in advanced technology' (p73), however much he might wish them to be leaders too, fails to suggest agreement on the meaning of skill shortages.

Too much weight has been given in recent years to notions of skill shortages. Hough, for instance, argues against the claim, although he does give some credence to the notion of a partial decline in skill production. He demonstrates this using figures from Pearson, Hutt and Parsons (1984).

Table 2.1:   Technology and science qualifications

	Year	Number (000)	%	Year	Number (000)	%
School-leavers with 2 science A-levels	**1971**	27.0	33.4	**1978**	29.0	30.1
CNAA degrees in science/engineering	**1970**	2.0	69.8	**1982**	7.8	26.8
University degrees in science/engineering	**1971**	21.5	43.7	**1982**	26.8	37.3
Numbers starting EITB apprenticeships	**1970/1**	26.6	-	**1982/3**	10.5	-
City/Guilds students in engineering	**1971**	170.0	50.8	**1982**	123.0	28.2
University graduates entering industry	**1971**	6.5	39.0	**1982**	8.4	29.0

Source: Hough (1987), p23

Over the above (variable) period the total number qualified in technology declines by about one fifth. However, this varies by sector. Looking at the top three categories, those most purely in education, the numbers gaining science and technical qualifications rose, though the proportion fell, especially in higher education where massive growth brought in many new departments and subjects. From 1979 to 1983 the numbers of home students graduating from higher education in subjects supposedly broadly useful to industry (science, engineering, and social and business studies) rose from 4.9m to 5.8m (up 17.4%), while the share of total graduations taken by these subjects remained static at around 61% (DES, 1985, p50). Output of graduates in science, engineering, maths, computing, social science (including economics), business and administration was 57% of all graduates in 1988; another 12% were multi-disciplinary (DES, 1990).

Looking at the (bottom three) categories in the above table a different picture emerges, which is largely the well-known decline in apprenticeships. As Eltis *et al* point out, the numbers of young people registered for craft and technician training in the engineering industry more than halved in the 1980s, a fall that was 'more severe than the contraction in total engineering employment' (IEA, 1992, p46). Recession may, of course, explain more thyan this. If an industry is in decline, not only does disinvestment accelerate, but it hardly offers an engaging prospect for aspiring technicians. And once training programmes are cut re-instatement may be far from easy. The decline in training contains its own dynamic.

The decline in apprenticeships certainly has nothing to do with lack of interest in technology. The decline of interest in technology is in the minds of those with comfortable armchairs in gentlemen's clubs. In the real world technology has always provoked fascination. For example, in the 1920s *The Modern Boy* advertised itself as 'the most up-to-date boys' paper in the world!', containing articles explaining how various machines work ('a baseboard view of the Cossor "Melody Maker". Note the easy nature of the wiring'). It also contained guidance on how to find jobs of a 'practical' nature such as hotel cooking: 'The fellow who is determined to get on will not hesitate to attend special classes of training in the work (such as are run by the London County Council), since such training counts as part of the apprenticeship term...' (24.3.28). Partly, of course, such advice obtains its appeal from the competitiveness of a highly limited job market, but this itself suggests that an expanding labour market creates its own demand.

Looking at subjects in higher and advanced further education rather than at qualifications obtained, and coming more upto-date, it is difficult to see how greater adoption of technical subjects could be increased without expansion of further education itself.

Table 2.2:   Percent in further/higher education doing technical subjects (1986/7)

	Full-time HE	Full-time AFE	Part-time AFE
Engineering/			
technology	23.4	32.8	44.4
Science	23.9	15.2	6.0
Other science	7.9	4.6	2.2
Total	55.2	52.6	52.6

Notes: AFE=advanced further education; other science=medical, agricultural, veterinary

Source: DES (1988), p33

Other 'practical' subjects, some of which the government is apparently keen to encourage, also have a significant hold in higher education. 23.1% of students in full-time HE, 24.9% in full-time AFE, and 36.8% in part-time AFE were enrolled on administrative, business or social studies courses in 1986/7. In the same year nearly a million students were in non-advanced FE, well over a third of whom were doing engineering and science courses.

The same trend towards technical learning applies to schools.

Table 2.3:   School-leavers in England and Wales attempting GCE/CSE in technical subjects (%)

	1970/1	1980/1	1985/6
Maths	49.1	79.9	81.0
Science	38.4	62.6	65.1
Technology	22.2	37.3	39.1

Source: DES (1988), p23

If there is a problem it is one of gender. Girls are still less attracted to technical subjects than boys. Only 22.3% of girls attempted technology qualifications at GCE/CSE compared to 52.4% of boys. However, a slightly higher proportion of girls attempted maths (79% against 77.2% for boys) and science (64.9% as against 63.2%). A lot of the problem, of course, is lack of flexibility rather than lack of commitment to science, maths or technology, and concern about this goes back a long way. The Dainton Committee argued for less A-level specialisation as a means of encouraging science. Nearly 40% of intending university applicants were committed to either science or non-science in their O-level attempts and nearly 50% of the upper sixth were similarly limited by this O-level decision. Even then, this did not suggest a lack of interest in science, as 43% of all those in the upper sixth intending to go to university specialised in science subjects (Barnard and McCreath, 1970, pp384/389). The sample of schools was primarily grammar and private, but showed that even at this time, science was recognised as vital for career.

The claim that education is not doing enough for technology is questionable for other reasons. In 1979 13.3% of students failed to complete a course they had started in engineering (either dropping out altogether or moving on to other subjects). In the social sciences non-completion amounted to only 8.6% (DES, 1985, p53). As is well known, subjects such as management science reward more quickly than engineering. This must, of course, encourage transfer from engineering itself to management, both at university and in employment. As the Finniston report revealed, there has been a clear trend on the part of those who begin as engineers to progress to posts 'in which they would not directly be applying their engineering knowledge' (*Engineering Our Future*, 1980). There is nothing new to the complaint. For instance, in an article confidently proposing a five-year plan for science at the end of world war two, an MP argued with some bitterness that 'in the past, the scientist and technician has been paid less than the administrator, because the latter holds the purse-strings' (*Picture Post*, 5.12.45). In 1971 less than 40% of graduate engineers worked in manufacturing (Finniston, 1980). Eltis *et al* report figures from a survey of graduate salaries, which shows that a graduate entering a calling and achieving an 'acceptable' level of performance, is likely to be earning 4% higher in sales and marketing than in mechanical engineering. An accountant will be earning nearly 9% less than the engineer. But after five years the sales/marketing person will be earning 17% more and the accountant 35% more (IEA, 1992, p40). Why, if there is such a shortage of technological skills? In 1982/3, while only 5% of accountancy graduates from university were unemployed upon graduation, the figure was 12% for both civil and mechanical engineers (DES, 1985, p56).

The government itself seem to recognise these problems, especially in its complaint that employers often choose recruits for careers in management by reference to general ability or leadership qualities, and thus fail to provide clear signals of the importance they attach to competence in science and technology (eg DES, 1985). This is strange coming from a government assuring the education system that industry knows what it wants, and that education is failing it. Perhaps only the government really knows what industry wants. But perhaps also the entire notion of skills shortages, in engineering as well as elsewhere, is a myth. And thus we should therefore take the market value of engineers at face value.

This does not mean there can never be shortages of skills, only that the evidence for endemic shortage in the UK resulting from structural inadequacies is limited. Cyclical factors are mistaken for trends. Modernisation may create a constant shortage of skills while intermittent recession may make them redundant. In practical terms it is very difficult to talk in terms of skill shortages other than in a particular industry, at a particular time, and probably also other than in a particular region. Skill shortages might just be another term for spatial, temporal or inter-industry differences. Investment rates, capital substitution, migration across regions, fluctuations in demand and output, and a host of related factors, all determine available skills at least as much as education or training programmes (though there may be a regional maldistribution in availability of different *types* of skill). Skill shortages are patchy and short-term. In the longer term they might be made good by technological changes which make them redundant, through restructuring labour, through recession (mostly favoured in the UK), or by imports. The USA, the world's technological leader, has for long been a major importer of skills. The UK has imported medical skills, for instance from the Indian subcontinent at the same time as it has exported skills, for instance to the Middle East or the USA. Indeed, while the 'brain drain' suggested a problem of inadequate rewards, it also suggested oversupply of skills.

There are, of course, variations in demand for skills, but to some extent these reflect variation in demand for labour in general. The theme of much current discussion, subsumed wholesale into government planning in respect of training support, is the notion that technology displaces unskilled workers while simultaneously creating shortages of skilled workers (to operate new technology). There is truth in this, even if the paradigm of a move from Fordist conveyor-belt production to postFordist, small-batch, more highly skilled production (including computer-assisted design etc), covers only a limited part of the production process. But the fact remains that some regions and industries face a general shortage of labour (outside of major recessions), while others have a surplus.

There is no overwhelming trend suggesting that the labour force finds it difficult to keep up with the demand for skills. Indeed, examination of the CBI's quarterly surveys of employer skill shortages reveals a pronounced cyclical pattern. The figure below, covering roughly 30 years, suggests two periods of about equal length, the first showing that cycles in demand for skilled labour and general labour moved in parallel, the second showing a slight decrease in this parallel movement but at the same time an overall reduction in shortages.

Figure 2.1: Shortages of skilled labour and other labour

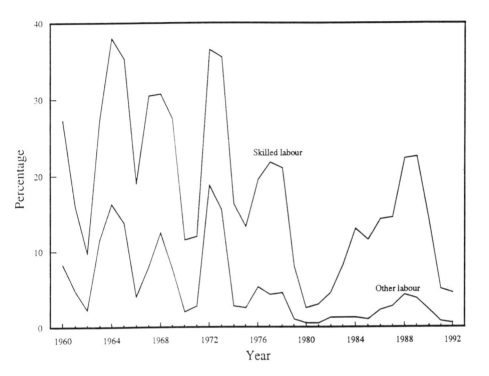

Source: CBI Industrial Trends Survey

The cyclical nature of skill shortages is too pronounced to make sense of any underlying trend. And if in booms the demand for skills rises more in absolute terms than the demand for unskilled labour, what happens in downturns? Do those employers who had skill shortages five years previously jettison the skills they no longer want?

It is very difficult to generalise about such figures. In a recent quarterly report the Employment Department (May 1992), commenting on the latest CBI figures, notes that 'skill shortages are continuing at a comparatively low level', with only 5% of manufacturing firms expecting a lack of skilled labour to limit output in the next four months - a considerable fall from the 27% prevalent in 1988. Despite the fall in skill shortages, 31% were expecting to increase their investment in training while 14% were anticipating a decrease. There are no clear relationships here. The same applies to the supply and use of graduates. In 1982 the unemployment rate for graduates was 20%. By 1988 it had fallen to 8% (DES, 1990). Yet a large-scale survey of demand for graduates (Rigg *et al*, 1990) showed that shortages appear to be limited. 'Although 23 per cent of private sector recruiters identified some difficulties in recruiting, far fewer, 9 per cent, said they failed to recruit all the new graduates they wanted in 1988' (p33). Moreover, there seems to be no clear trend in the use of graduates. 23% expected to substitute graduates with non-graduates and 32% expected to do the reverse. From 1985-88 about 8% had substituted in both directions in recruitment (pp46-48). While the management potential of graduates was highly regarded, a 'surprisingly large proportion of job categories to which new graduates were recruited (about one in five) were considered suitable for A-level holders who could then be trained' (p26).

Hart's examination of the CBI's quarterly data on skill shortages supports the notion that the CBI's figures tend to measure firms short-term expectations during the trade-cycle, rather than measuring fundamental problems arising from the lack of a trained, qualified workforce' (Hart, 1990, p5). In Hart and Shipman's qualitative analysis, reasons for skill shortages were predominantly regional. The south-east attracts firms, perhaps largely for infrastructural reasons, while labour mobility into the area is constrained by high house prices. Meanwhile, there is over-supply of skills in some northern regions. If there is a trend it is towards obsolescence, but this makes skill shortages a criterion of success: in one firm 'half of one's engineering training becomes obsolete after five years' (Hart and Shipman, NIESR Discussion Paper 185, p2).

That skill *shortages* are a poor basis for assessing Briatin's educational inputs does not mean that in a less dynamic sense there is not a chronically inadequate skill base. This would have to mean that there is a tendency to operate with a more labour-intensive technology than other countries. Yet, paradoxically, evidence that British technology is *not* inferior is used to sustain the notion that relatively poor economic performance is the result not of a deficit in technology but of a deficit in skills. But if surveys of stocks of machinery tend to show that 'this is not where the source of Britain's probllmes lies' and that 'the average age of machinery is perhaps even younger here than elsewhere' (Prais and Beadle, 1991, p36), it does not appear that inferior skill supplies are limiting technical investment, as one might expect. Arguments that Britain suffers from a low skills equilibrium (Finegold and Soskice, 1988), in which low level technology, management, labour, and goods all go together, are surely excessively sweeping. The claim that a modern economy demands high-level general skills and understanding rather than job-specific skills, because modern production methods are flexible and non-routine (but also subject to rapid change), will probably describe only a small proportion of labour relations for some time into the future. It underestimates the power of scientific management to adapt and use technology for its own purposes, and it may well be the case that that socialism will not be able to educate itself out of this deepening exploitation.

Comparative skills

Even if the production of technical qualifications is increasing in the UK this could still be at a lower rate than in other countries. For instance, Eltis *et al* (1992, p42) produce figures which show that in 1989 nearly 20% of British firms were constrained by skill shortages compared to less than 3% in both Italy and the Netherlands. But is it really the case that the UK has seven times as many firms constrained by skill shortages as these countries? Such figures are no doubt largely artifactual (heavily dependent on differences in definition) but, in addition, the focus on a single point in time is quite meaningless. As has already been argued, skill shortages are cyclical rather than trend factors. These cycles (as opposed to business cycles) differ in different countries because each has its own infrastructure of skills.

42

This is not just a matter of spending on education, which appears to explain little. The UK's economic growth from 1960 to 1970 is considered to have been relatively poor, yet in 1974 the UK ensured the highest number of years of compulsory schooling out of 16 industrialised nations, came eighth in length of actual schooling, was fourth equal out of nine in number of hours taught per year in primary schools, seventh equal out of nine in the case of secondary schools, had the second highest growth rate in secondary school enrolments from 1970 to 1974, and was tenth in the case of enrolments in education of 20-24 year olds (Husen, 1979, pp47-72). Finally, out of seven countries in the late 1980s, the UK came third in the proportion of college-going population obtaining qualifications in higher education - just behind France but well ahead of Germany (DES, 1990, p10). It would seem from the above that neither good nor poor provision has any predictable impact on growth. As will be discussed below, its distribution may be more important.

Emulation may, anyway, not be a viable option. It was argued some time ago that education in many countries is in crisis (Coombs, 1968). In this case each individual nation's concerns are merely a reflection of a fundamental malaise to do with excess demand, intensifying pressure on the economy, and a growing gap between educational and technological change. The general trend towards accountability, to reduced per capita expenditure, and to greater vocationalism, gives some credence to the 'world educational crisis' thesis. Emphasis on diversity and quality were to replace linear expansion of resources. Returning to these themes nearly 20 years later Coombs locates the same causal problems. All education systems are faced with rising costs and with competition from other demands for government spending. In addition, rapid technological change constantly threatens curricula and institutions. One country copying another can offer limited solace as all educational systems 'will be shooting at a moving target' (Coombs, 1985, p264).

It is very odd that the very same people in Britain who suggest that there are fundamental crisis trends in education, which are supposedly inherent in capitalism, refer to Britain's position relative to other capitalist countries as proof. Yet Coombs' apocalyptic world-vision is not very convincing. The prediction of chaos engendered by Coombs, demanding that all critics 'become more aware of the dynamic societal forces bearing in on educational systems these days, often with crushing power' (1985, p264), is far from helpful, however congenial to a wide variety of political thought.

In this case, perhaps emulation does make sense. It is at least a manageable concept. For instance, it is often pointed out that Germany in particular has more manual and supervisory workers with a higher level of basic intellectual skills than the UK, and that these skills are important to productive efficiency. But is Germany's rise to economic pre-eminence founded on the production of skills? There is no doubt that the establishment of the technical schools last century produced sufficient skills to perhaps create an advantage in some areas of industry. Nevertheless, 'if German and American.... entrepreneurs were so superlatively great at being entrepreneurs, why did they need high tariff walls to keep out their creampuff, backward, epicene rivals?' (Rubinstein, in Collins and Robbins, 1990).

At the end of last century Germany had twice as many academic scientists as Britain. These were the products of the university but also of the *Technische Hochschule* (polytechnic), established in the early nineteenth century, before any British equivalent. Germany was especially successful in translating this scientific lead directly into industrial output. Yet this was by no means always the case. After the first world war demand for some skills fell sharply. In the 1920s 13,000 graduate engineers (at different levels of skill) were unemployed (James, in Collins and Robbins, 1990, p113). If German engineers in the 19th century had relatively high status, their pay was somewhat less than that of teachers.

This has been reversed partly through war.

The reason lies in that shortage of skilled engineers arising from the legacy of the Third Reich's education policies, and in the increase in demand for engineers during the economic boom. The resulting high levels of remuneration were then built into the structure of German social expectations (James, Collins and Robbins, 1990, p114).

If there is a problem it is not at the highest level of skill levels. In 1983 the UK produced the second highest proportion of science graduates from universities out of seven industrialised countries, which at 53% of all graduates was only just below Italy's 57% and considerably higher than Japan's 36% or the USA's 33%, though Japan produces twice the number of engineers relative to population size as the UK (NEDO, 1987, p125). The problem of relative skill shortages is now located at the craft and intermediate 'technician' rather than at degree level. For instance, Eltis *et al* produce figures showing 30,000 people in the UK qualified at technician level in the engineering and technology sectors and 36,000 at craft level. For France the figures were 35,000 and 91,000, while for West Germany they were 44,000 and 120,000 (1992, p44). On the other hand, it is unlikely that the UK would produce as many of the above skills when its level of production is much lower. Taking that into account, the remaining major difference applies to craft levels.

Table 2.4: **Numbers obtaining intermediate engineering and technology qualifications (standardised for size of labour force, thousands)**

	UK	France	Germany
Higher intermediate			
Higher technicians	23	22	13
Meister-qualified	--	--	31
Total	**23**	**22**	**44**
Lower intermediate			
Lower technicians	14	19	--
Craftspeople	27	107	107
Total	**41**	**126**	**107**

Source: Steedman, Mason and Wagner (1991, p61)

Note: Higher technicians are equivalent to HNC/HND. The German *Meister* qualification is a credential that someone with a craft qualification (*Berufabschluss*) may progress to. Lower technicians include BTEC and SCOTVEC certificates in Britain and the *Bac Technologique* (an A-level standard vocational qualification) in France. 'Craftsmen' may be City and Guilds in Britain or holders of the *Berufabschluss* in Germany.

However, this says nothing about use made of skills. It is quite possible that some German labour is overqualified for the work it does, or that some formal skills are under-utilised.

> The view of teachers in the German vocational colleges (*Berufschule*), all with previous occupational and/or professional experience, was that the apprentices would need to use only a small part of the mathematical knowledge acquired in college courses directly in the workplace while employed as craftsmen. They would, however, need the whole range of mathematical skills if at a later stage they proceeded, as some were expected to do, to take courses and examinations leading to positions as supervisor (*Meister*) or technician (*Techniker*) (Oulton and Steedman, 1992, p8).

So, only for some - those progressing beyond craft level - is anything more than a small part of the mathematical part of the coursework useful for a subsequent job. Indeed, over 16% of trainees in the dual system enter with the *Abitur* (equivalent to A-level). This itself is because apprenticeships are becoming increasingly tied to school advantage. But then the subsequent training contains a large amount of repeated school-type work. In 1989 the drop-out rate in North Rhine Westphalia was 20%; 'one of the main reasons given by those who left was a dislike of what they termed the "academic" side of their training' (DES, 1991, p28).

Looking at one particular function adds further insight. The NIESR provide figures showing that 7% of West Germany's manual supervisors (referred to as 'manufacturing foremen' in the text) have no vocational qualifications, compared to 55% in the case of the UK. 42% of UK supervisors have 'intermediate' vocational qualifications compared to 93% in Germany (Steedman *et al*, 1991, p64). France, on the other hand, is remarkably similar to the UK with 44% unqualified and 55% with intermediate qualifications. In the case of qualifications of technicians the distribution was again remarkably similar in Britain and France. Perhaps, then, Germany is the odd one out, not Britain. There are certainly oddities in the German relationship between functions and qualifications, with supervisors appearing to possess very high levels of higher intermediate relative to lower intermediate qualifications, indeed even higher than amongst technicians, the next grade up (Steedman *et al* 1991, p64). This use of qualifications is not replicated in France or Britain.

This suggests a possible misuse of skills, which may in part have a traditional rather than functional definition. A study comparing rates of return to qualifications in both West and East Germany sought to assess degree of over-qualification through analysis of responses to a question asking individuals about the training required to perform their job (Bird, Schwarze and Wagner, 1992). On this measure 25% of West German workers were overqualified (compared to 21% in East Germany). Regression of income on being over-qualified suggested, more so in West than East Germany, that, at the craft, *Meister* and degree (but not *Techniker*) level, being over-qualified tends to lower returns relative to potential earnings (pp6-12). There are more people earning too little for their qualifications in the more developed West of the country.

One NIESR study which does not fit into the general trend of consistent British inferiority - in *use* if not in availability of skills - is Shipman's comparison with West

Germany (NIESR discussion paper 192). This looked at twelve companies (six in each country) and found little support for the notion of a higher level of skill shortage in Britain. More important, Shipman at different points proposes several reasons for casting doubt on the meaningfulness of claimed differences. First, German firms experience skill shortages just as strongly as British firms. This is not a national characteristic but occurs 'generally because of high output growth or adoption of new products and processes' (p3). Second, qualifications do not necessarily indicate skills, or at least skills that are needed.

> Where UK employers had sponsored their top apprentices for a degree, it was because they needed the higher skills, and not just because such sponsorship was necessary in order to promote young people. While this is often the case in Germany as well, the insistence on fixed entry qualifications implies a degree of 'credentialism' (Shipman, NIESR discussion paper 192, p7).

Indeed, 'some of the sample findings might be taken to indicate a degree of overtraining in West Germany', with some German managers worried about wages claimed 'on the basis of skills held' but not in fact used (p27). Similarly, qualifications may in some cases limit rather than extend certain skills, particularly where change is rapid. For instance, in IT 'the effectiveness of German training had been held back by slow-changing public regulations on course content' (p27). Steedman *et al* (1991) note that German supervisors are usually drawn from a large pool of people possessing a craft qualification, but also note that achievement of a supervisory grade usually requires 16-18 years of shop-floor experience in all three countries. How useful are the by now old craft qualifications (as opposed to any subsequent *Meister* qualification)?

In addition, Shipman did not find that British firms 'sacrificed growth or innovation to stay within their skill supply limits'; they simply adapted 'through greater flexibility in the assignment of people to tasks, and more extensive use of the "formal" skills actually held' (p7). Why should skill usage be the same in every country? British plants 'seem to concentrate on raising small numbers of craftsmen [and women?] and technicians to high or multi-skilled status, rather than on training larger numbers in more basic skills' (p5). Perhaps this reflects a choice rather than a constraint. Perhaps, more generally, Britain is highly successful, given its relatively weak industrial base, in establishing an adaptable and flexible system of skill provision and use, and perhaps only faster growing countries can afford systems which are more rigorous and systematic (but possibly sometimes over-rigid). All reviews of small numbers of companies must be subject to considerable sample bias. Nevertheless, it seems as reasonable to accept Shipman's apparent scepticism towards the reality of the impact of skill differentials as studies which suggest the reverse. In fact, a number of assessments of skill availability encourage scepticism. For instance, Steedman (1992) notes that in 1981 Britain produced 24% of Germany's number of craft-level passes in selected building occupations. Against France the figure was 65%. By 1991 these figures were 65% and 152% respectively (p6). The substantial fluctuations these figures show may cast doubt on the utility of *any* comparison of ostensible skill shortages.

In sum, wildly fluctuating relative performance, problems in effective matching of skill availability to real skill use, the likelihood of over-production of skills in some countries, the selective nature of industries and countries chosen for comparison, and the sheer difficulty of endowing comparative analysis with adequate context and complexity, all make the findings of international comparisons at least doubtful in part. This does not mean that skill differentials between countries do not exist; but the evidence of their real extent and impact is ambiguous and partial.

Skills in production

It is impossible to assess skills in isolation. One factor that must be taken into account is labour costs. For instance, how are these affected by upskilling processes? One argument in this final section is that it is far from apparent that it is to the advantage of British industry to pay for higher-level skills. This has been recognised on the Left for some time, though the issue is more complex than is usually acknowledged. Put bluntly, at the national level Britain has a comparative advantage in a relatively low-skilled, low-waged labour force, and that makes any systematic attempt to upgrade skills extremely difficult.

It has already been argued that relating education to the economy at the macro-level tends to be unrewarding, while micro analysis of rates of return to individuals provides a very limited notion of the impact of education. An alternative is the direct comparison of industrial processes, as in NIESR's cross-national matched industry studies. These tend to reveal apparently inadequate skill levels in Britain relative to certain other countries. The NIESR's study of biscuit manufacture in Britain and the Netherlands (Mason, Prais, and van Ark, 1990) is typical of NIESR attempts to grapple with this complex issue. The writers note that Dutch productivity is generally higher. They seek to put this down to the structure of vocational qualifications. For Mason *et al*, of great importance is the early separation of vocationally inclined students into Junior Vocational Schools after the age of 12, in a system with three alternative levels of school institution distinguished by different degrees of academic work. The authors then move to comparison of Dutch and British production, noting that at all levels higher skills are available in the Netherlands. The writers relate the lower priority in production processes given to planned or preventative maintenance in Britain to 'the real underlying shortages of the relevant skills' (p25). Indeed, the analysis is ultimately of time lost through downtime created by faults, in turn a major factor in labour productivity.

But it is far from clear that this is the case. Even tasks that 'are relatively simple and repetitive, and require little by way of expertise' are likely in the Dutch firms to be undertaken by people with qualifications from the Junior Technical Schools. No equivalent is required in Britain. The authors argue that even at this level workers 'were capable of "sensing" many faults before they had become serious' (p27). But if that is the case, other explanations are possible. For instance, does British management create the incentives for labour to act on initiative? It is generally acknowledged that intensified production processes encourage, not remedial action, but relief when a spanner appears in the works.

Mason, Prais and van Ark note that the firms are not precisely the same in the two countries. The British firms are bigger and more reliant on mass production of standardised biscuits. The authors argue that one cause of this is the greater availability of skills in the Netherlands. Similarly, Steedman, Mason and Wagner in a related study argue that while the 'typical British firm tends to concentrate on the mass production of standardised products.... its German counterpart produces a highly differentiated product range', which is more effectively competitive (1991, p60). The writers go on to argue that these differences (at least in the industries studied) 'have been held to arise in part from firms adapting to different supplies of shopfloor skills, in particular craft-level skills'. This is a surprising statement. Does skill distribution really determine product ranges? A much likelier explanation for the different production processes is the type of profit margin and market niche that is sought. Mason *et al* take note of these considerations but are unwilling to accept their implications.

A much more extensive and detailed investigation than the present one would be needed to establish the extent of these differences, and then to establish to what extent they were a response to national differences in consumers' demand, or to lower real wages reflecting the greater supply of unskilled labour in Britain. The reader needs however to keep this caution in mind, and not attribute the whole of our observed average difference in productivity to differences in workforce training and skills in relation to identical processes' (p30).

Biscuits determine skills, not vice versa.

Williams' analysis of the British Leyland (now Rover) car group locates Britain's lack of international competitiveness in vehicle production primarily in terms of investment strategies. At the time of the industry's major decline restrictive labour practices were blamed, particularly in a highly influential Central Policy Review Staff report in 1975 - although in fact, strikes and other restrictions helped mask the company's underlying problems 'because they prevented the company's accumulation of stocks of unsaleable cars' (Williams, in Williams *et al*, 1983, p219). From the early 1950s a major investment programme was successful in increasing output substantially, but the investment was in relatively basic technology and continued the policy of reliance on a few low-profit (sometimes no-profit) lines such as the Mini. Subsequent attempts to move into the growing up-market brackets foundered - in part because of poor design and poor understanding of the market.

Failure to assess markets (eg over-reliance on mass small car sales with little profit) exacerbated the inability to invest in appropriate technology. No amount of workforce training could have made up for this inadequacy. But perhaps of greater importance is that investment strategies actually demanded lesser skills. If 'in cost terms, lower British wages partly compensated for the greater man-hour requirement... the output strategy of earlier decades had ensured that by the mid-1970s BLMC's production methods were necessarily labour-intensive' (p255). And when Williams talks of an entire complex of 'poor scheduling, component unavailability and line breakdowns' (p254), it becomes clear that the root cause of disruption is a more fundamental reflection of management organisation than it is of staff readiness to deal with problems.

Remarkably, the British car industry is now held by some to be fairly healthy. Even Eltis, in an admittedly somewhat more cursory examination of the industry, and despite a desire to give most of the credit for revival to the establishment in Britain of Japanese subsidiaries such as Nissan, acknowledges that 'an important factor is the combination of relatively low labour costs and the improved industrial relations climate' (in IEA, 1992, p38). Putting aside the latter part of the statement, which merely describes the inevitable effect of industrial decline on union activity, there seems as little reason to explain earlier problems in car manufacture through skill shortages as there is to explain relative growth through the production of skills. It is entirely reasonable to assume, in line with the above arguments, that Japanese car manufacturers decided to invest in the UK for its relatively low wages, and despite the apparent lack of skills.

The vehicle industry is a major staple industry, but production derived from electronics is deemed to be crucial to any industrialised country's economic future. From 1978 to 1984 the proportion of people in senior white-collar jobs in the industry rose from 29% to 40%; more specifically, the proportion of scientists and technicians rose from 17% to 24% (NEDO, 1987, p129). This led the Information Technology Economic Development Committee of NEDO to predict a shortage of skilled labour. However, apart from the fact that this assertion is not backed up by reliable data on the supply of skills, the EDC failed to point out that total employment in electronics fell over the period from nearly 396,000 to 334,000 (presumably a result of the recession, competition from imports, but also of the growth in productivity created by IT itself). So, while the number of technical staff grew by less than 14,000, the employment of clerks, supervisors and craftspeople remained broadly static, and the number of operatives and 'other employees' fell by 56,000. The government suggests, in a new form of embourgeoisement thesis, that the upskilling of labour means there are opportunities for all - if people are willing to grasp them (eg through retraining). However, the growth in places for all technical and managerial positions in the electronics industry in the above period was just over 18,000.

The international race to be league-leaders in the new technologies in electronics, computers and telecommunications has led governments round the world into a range of very different policies. Some have adopted highly interventionist positions (eg France), some a highly laissez-faire approach (eg the UK). Moreover, some have liberalised and deregulated their industries from a position of strength (particularly the USA), some, like the UK, from a position of relative weakness. The process of deregulation in these sectors started in the USA because major industrial actors in telecommunications wanted to be free to engage in international expansion. Other countries have followed suit, hoping not to lose out in the race as old boundaries are broken. Thus in the UK the expansion of cable television, encouraged at Cabinet level, was meant to provide a boost to telecommunications in general. But because the government has persisted with its ideological commitment to non-intervention, recently confirmed in a statement that the 'government's responsibility is to create the right climate so that markets work better' (DTI, 1989, p1) - presumably the government must mean work better for foreign competition too - the UK has one of the lowest take-ups of cable in the West. While the British government may well have been right in its refusal to sponsor the development of new technology, as it 'is not for the Government to usurp the role of the market' (DTI, 1989, pii), in Negrine's view the government's policies have been characterised by a mixture of 'crisis management, political opportunism and ad hoc decision making' (in Dyson and Humphries, 1988, p224). However, the government has structured the market, of course, for instance through privatisations. The future of growth in electronics depends less on available skills than on effective decisions at the management and politicl levels.

Conclusion

There is little reason to conclude that Britain's economic problems derive from insufficient production of skills. The cause of relatively poor economic performance does not lie within education but within the structure of employment. To focus on shopfloor skill shortages in general can only divert attention from inadequate management and inflexible structures of control, the purpose of which is to cheapen the supply of labour. The problem for any socialist critique of this situation is that it cannot argue only for better or more training as a necessary factor for national economic improvement. Investment in 'human capital' might have other justifications, but making good ostensible skill shortages is not one of them. The danger in the concept of skill shortages is that once proven not to exist, education (and training) can reasonably be cut. Once the role of education becomes simply one of production (of skills) the scope for control becomes enormous. The emphasis should instead be on eliminating demarcations within education that prevent people providing the skills of which they are capable, and on encouraging incentives to obtain and retain these skills. Efficiency certainly requires continued investment in education and training as only through this can sufficient flexibility and slack be built in. In other words, the focus of reform should not be the production of skills (ie of people with skills), but the development of a better infrastructure for the production of skills. These are by no means the same thing. The latter is necessary regardless of assessments of skill shortages, most of which, in particular taken out of context, are highly misleading. Both skills and standards can become passwords for control, cuts, and segregation as well as for expansion and integration. The numbers game means little. Above all it discounts the relative weakness of an economy which has more freqent and deeper recessions than other countries. These are not caused by skills shortages but they do make the development and retention of skills more problematic. The solution probably requires some intervention by the government to create more stability in skill availability and distribution, but under current circumstances this is a long way off. The problem of reliance on firms to spend more on training is not so much their laissez-faire attitude, as they are not in fact ungenerous, but firstly their more fragile economic position, and secondly the fact that the entire labour relation is built upon the use of skill shortages (ie deskilling) to keep down adult wages. This issue will be discussed in the next chapter, but it suggests a much more intractable problem than the notion of a skill deficit, which is a very different matter.

3 Training and employment

This chapter takes up the arguments of the previous chapter and relates them to the issue of equality. The focus is not skill shortages but skill redistribution. It was argued in the last chapter that assertions of skill shortages cannot be taken as a reasonable indicator of an inadequate system of education. To some extent the same applies to training. If there is a failure it is one of demand rather than of supply. Current training structures fit current employment practices. From the worker's point-of-view training possibilities must clearly relate to employment possibilities.

> No amount of change in the availability of training or its content can significantly improve the career opportunities of the bulk of (potential) workers in isolation from the development of new kinds of employment in the local labour markets which continue to define their realistic job horizons (Rees *et al*, 1989, p242).

Employers still require much low-quality labour as this is an important means of keeping down costs. While improving training may help create a more advanced aristocracy of labour, it is not clear whether a demand exists for a labour force that is more expensive across the board (because generally better trained). That does not mean that there should be no attempt to improve general training, only that improved training may not change employer practices.

Such practices are reinforced by the state. One of the big problems is inequality in opportunity, in particular as faced by those caught in the no-person's land between full-time education and employer-led training. For instance, many students seeking to do courses such as City and Guilds may only be eligible for discretionary grants from local authorities. Nearly 152,000 students depend on these, compared to the roughly 700,000 that receive mandatory grants or are entitled to loans for degrees or higher diplomas. Local authority budget cuts, forced by broader central government cut-backs, have taken their toll here. As one example, Lancashire has been reported as giving no new grants to most full-time students over 19, while Islington has halved the amount of individual grants for 16-19 year-olds (*Guardian*, 8.8.92). One concern must therefore be who gets qualifications, not just how many qualifications are obtained in toto.

Indeed, looking at the latter does not give as clear-cut results as is often claimed. In the late 1980s the proportion of 16-18 year-olds in full or part-time education or training (including schemes like YTS) was 69% in the UK, 74% in France and 90% in Germany (DES, 1991, p31). However, the German system contains compulsion. The 'dual system' enforces training on those leaving school before 18 and 14% drop out of this - though sometimes rejoining later (DES, 1991, p12). The system also limits choice. For instance, only 2,000 out of 38,000 companies in the Duisberg area are accredited training firms (p13). The British system is relatively informal, and therefore subject to more fluctuation. In 1991, according to the School-Leavers Destination Survey, 61% people in Britain stayed on in full-time education after the compulsory school-leaving age, another 15% were on YT, while 46% of those in work were doing some sort of training (not necessarily for a qualification). It would appear that around 80% of people of this age were doing some sort of education or training (Employment Department, *Labour Market Quarterly Report*, May 1992). The issue is one of inequality rather than of total provision. Looking at Britain's vocational qualifications, Mason *et al* (1990) note that 63% of the workforce have none, compared to 53% in France and 26% in Germany (p16). The figures for the proportion of school-leavers getting at least one A-level or equivalent are 55%, 88% and 90% respectively (Finegold, 1990, p50). However, on OECD definitions, in the late 1980s the UK ranked third out of seven countries in proportion of college-age population with higher education qualifications, at 33% well above Germany's at 24% (DES, 1990, p10). Less than half of these qualifications are first degrees (p49), with higher vocational and professional qualifications providing much of the remainder. The British system, in both education and work, is geared to producing high-status qualifications at the expense of, and perhaps in order to produce, low-quality labour elsewhere.

If there is a limited demand for increased skills in British industry, and that is the implication of much of this chapter, then increasing supply may not the sole answer. The single-minded focus on skill shortages, even if this is blamed on a laissez-faire economic and political structure which overemphasises the immediate needs of employers at the expense of the nation's long-term needs, underemphasises the historical and structural development of a system which is built on cheap labour. One policy might be an attempt to make labour more expensive (by increasing its formal expertise), but this might backfire and simply reduce the returns people receive for their qualifications. There can be little doubt that government policies such as YT increase the tendency to limit skill opportunities, and these are one obvious candidate for reform. It is not so much that overall skills are too limited but that severe demarcations exist, demarcations which may sometimes be congenial to trade unions. This fits in with the needs of employers as limiting the spread of skills beyond core workers reduces labour costs. It is not obvious what solutions there are to these problems. One might be to try to address the training needs of those marginal to employment better than currently, and this means focusing policy less on higher-level training provision. Another might be to seek to erode the manager-worker divide through eroding the academic-vocational divide. This means boosting the deployment of intermediate level skills in British industry. Both require a change in employment practices.

Redistributing skills

It was argued in chapter two that notions of skill shortage should not drive development of educational policy. Cyclical effects in skill demand and obsolescence are more important than trends. Indeed, recessions are seen by some as helping growth.

> After all, those business failures and repossessions do not mean that physical assets are destroyed; the plants, the factories and the houses are still there and, if worth using, will find new owners more capable or less burdened with debt... That is why recessions are a two-edged instrument, particularly if interest groups are powerful and the people tender-hearted. Instead of being creative, the recessional destruction can too easily become a source of permanent invalidity (Minford, in IEA, 1992, pp95/6).

But recessions do not just empty factories, which might be re-possessed (as shopping malls if not as production units); they also destroy skills. The 'small' individual is not just the little entrepreneur but the individual who has invested heavily in personal skills and now finds nowhere to apply them.

> One of the major symptoms of the current confusion is the much-publicised skill shortage. The problem is one that first began to surface on a large scale with the limited economic recovery from 1983-4 onwards. Previously the question was seen to be one of oversupply, not shortages. From the recession of 1979 onwards companies began accelerating their restructuring programme and eliminating labour in successive 'shakeouts' (which are still continuing). Technological advance and 'restructuring' did in fact provide an effective smokescreen for the disappearance of large sections of British industry. Reductions in the number of technical workers were generally seen to result from technological advance, whereas in fact they were, overall, due to the collapse of manufacturing (Campbell *et al*, in Hirst and Zeitlin, 1989, p134).

So, the 'puzzling coincidence of high unemployment and skill shortages' (p133) is not forced solely by any technological imperative. Training for new skills obscures the fact that a wide range of other skills are lost during recessions. It could be that for skill shortages we should read skill displacement.

Those who suffer most from this are also those who are most affected by the lack of integration between education and training in Britain, as qualifications tend to be a one-off achievement which make or break people at an early age. This derives from age-old status distinctions. For instance, apprenticeships have traditionally taken young people away from college, producing a clear separation between craft and college skills; those doing higher level technical qualifications still choose this route at an early age. In Germany, by contrast, those who acquire craft skills are able to move on to technical qualifications at a later stage. The UK's more elitist system separates these two streams out too early. Paradoxically the way round this problem is 'an ever more elitist recruitment and training policy', including a 'bias towards university graduates' (Campbell *et al*, in Hirst and Zeitlin, 1989, p137).

It is easy to see how the process outlined above leads to greater specialisation in British industry. The scarcer the skills, the more they will be differentiated and specialised. This also leads to a self-reinforcing cycle - greater specialisation leads to a greater demand for specialists, requiring more specialised training, the difficulties associated with which lead to renewed shortages (p137).

So, skill shortages derive not from inadequate training provision so much as from the way skills are distributed. They are partly an artifact of an employment structure which creates an exceptionally wide gap between management and worker. The gap appears to be a skill shortage but is in fact a structural part of the system. As has been noted in more than one NIESR report, well qualified staff are used for excessively low-level work (eg when a machine breaks down); and because they are not on tap, inefficiency results. But this may be less a matter of inefficiency than of inequality. A detailed within-task division of labour, with control exercised by management and management assistants outside the shopfloor, means that pay for routine and repetitive skills is highly reduced (Braverman, 1975). Skills cost money not just to produce but to reward (though some savings are lost as a result of the extra pay required to recruit office-based staff to substitute for shopfloor skills). From the point-of-view of the employer the British system might well be cost-effective as it lowers average wage costs, if at the cost of some inefficiency.

Even Eltis *et al* are prepared to admit that the 'long-term persistence of some shortages of skilled labour and graduates with particular areas of expertise suggests that the appropriate pay signals are not always generated' (in IEA, 1992, p42). Industry knows what it wants and gives pay signals appropriate to its profit structure. Campbell *et al* note research which indicates that in the UK 'the differentiation and professionalisation of non-line management was inversely related to the degree of professionalisation of workers, technicians and line managers' (in Hirst and Zeitlin, 1989, p140). West Germany's system is the reverse of this: shopfloor workers tend to be more 'professionalised'. This is associated with a milder division of labour. The UK perhaps suffers less from skill shortages than from excessive specialisation, which then exacerbates reported skill shortages. In other words, employers pay a price for control. Campbell *et al* cite a case study of management in a company which resisted purchase of equipment for training in computer-aided design 'since their understanding of the technology was geared to cutting back manpower and skill requirements' (p145).

Current government policy appears to be widening the gap between education and training. This is apparent from the NIESR study of the maths content of building qualifications (Steedman, 1992). The new National Vocational Qualifications (NVQs), which apply consistent credentials may portend improvement, but these will be tied to the immediate needs of individual employers who help devise them. Not surprisingly Steedman suggests short-term interests must prevail. 'Instruction in raking back a brick wall will have to take precedence over learning how to calculate the number of bricks required to build it' (p16). In Britain the employer pays for most training while in 'France and Germany, the trainee and the state bear the cost of vocational education and colleges are insulated from the pressure to provide specific job training' (p18). Steedman predicts not a rise but a fall in standards, as the NVQ merely consolidates current practice, while reducing the academic component of qualifications such as City and Guilds. This will not *appear* to be the case because NVQs are a new qualification, thus 'raising at a stroke the number of young people on Youth Training obtaining a recognised vocational qualification to numbers greater than those found in continental Europe': p10). Standards in training are being lowered while in education the government is demanding tighter standards. Are we dealing with standards or double standards?

This possibly growing differential also has implications for deskilling. Despite long-term benefits through increased productivity, training contains a double disincentive for employers: it is expensive to run and raises wage costs. So it is not surprising that there 'is currently a conflict between the wage moderation required to retain competitiveness with a fixed exchange rate, and the relative wage increases needed to encourage training effort in the shortage skills and sectors' (Shipman, NIESR discussion paper 192, p1). In general it would appear that the structure of British training reinforces less a low-skills equilibrium than a low-wage equilibrium. The two may well go together but the latter is primary, and it is by no means certain that breaking the low-skills barrier will help break the low-wage barrier.

The issue is not simply one of 'short-termism'. It might be to the long-term advantage of employers to keep skill availability to the bare minimum, confined in particular to a class of staff who retain control at the expense of shopfloor staff. British employers are, in fact, not lacking in generosity, as they bear most training costs (training wages and course fees, though the government offers some subsidy through Youth Training), while in France the latter are provided by the public authorities. British employers are also generous to their trainees, paying them up to 75% of a skilled worker's pay, compared to 30-40% in Germany (DES, 1991, p13). Forcing employers in Britain to extend their training would certainly be at the cost of employees' wages, and so it is ultimately the employee who would pay. What makes this workable is the cheapness of unskilled labour. In Germany, while employers bear the cost of tuition fees for apprenticeships (with the State providing the colleges), employees pay for their own training for the *Meister* qualification (financially and through evening study). However, British employers do almost the reverse, investing in formal, high-level skills at the expense of lower-level craft skills. The corollary is that British employers are compensated for their generosity through a bigger wage differential between skilled and unskilled grades. The differential is 26% in Britain and 21% in Germany (Steedman, Mason and Wagner, 1991, p71). British employers pay more for training the few, but save by paying less to the many. They have much to gain from 'skill shortages'. Complaints of skill shortages therefore serve to mask the central role played by the distribution (as opposed to the absolute level) of skills.

> Although absence of productivity data prevents a unit-cost comparison, some UK employers in the sample appeared to be gaining a cost advantage by not adjusting wages with measured skill to the extent common in Germany, and obtaining their skilled craftsmen, technicians and graduates relatively cheaply. Training was a means of raising supply directly, without resorting to market mechanisms (Shipman, NIESR discussion paper 192, p26).

Indeed, there is in the UK generally great reluctance to use wages as an incentive to attract needed skills. Some of this resistance derives from union opposition to the creation of new differentials. Rigg *et al* (1990, p50) note an increase in willingness to pay more to attract graduates, though substitution and other strategies such as importing graduates are also very important. CBI data also indicate a slight increase in the use of the wage incentive. 'Even so, over industry as a whole only 46 per cent of firms improved wages in order to ease skill shortages; they preferred to use other methods such as increasing overtime, subcontracting, retraining and deskilling' (Hart and Shipman, NIESR Discussion Paper 185, p5); deskilling here means designing out complex processes.

As a corollary, the apparent generosity of British employers in respect of higher-level training makes sense in relation to the nature of the British academic system.

> employers compete with universities and polytechnics for the scarce resource of 16 year-olds with 'good' GCSE (grades A-C) maths and science (approximately 25 per cent of the age cohort). British employers, unlike their French counterparts, cannot rely on a high status technical route to attract able young people in sixth forms to technical careers (Steedman, Mason and Wagner, 1991, p69).

Such conflicts in recruitment policies, with profound implications for the relationship between education and training, reflect the way British employers have boxed themselves into a particular recruitment strategy, from which it may not be easy to change. It is difficult to see how mere increase in the availability of skills can break the constraints imposed by presumably profitable labour relations. The only result can be the downgrading of returns to employees. There could be a role here for government intervention, though its precise role would be unclear. There is certainly a case, however, for undoing the effect of much recent central policy-making.

Government intervention

> *The transition from school to work is not what it used to be* (Raffe, in Wallace and Cross, 1990, p52)

If there is a problem with British training it is less with the nature of the training itself than its uncomfortably sandwiched position between two established structures: education and the labour market. Perhaps only government can ensure that training's place in the sandwich is widened, but unfortunately much of its policy, even if it does not reduce the role of training, gives it an ambivalent status.

Apart from the development of NVQs, the core change in British training in recent years derives from government support for particular schemes, with Youth Training (YT) in the forefront. While these schemes have been heavily criticised for their association with the political need to soak up youth unemployment, YTS (later YT) tried to kill several birds with one stone. British firms pay the full cost of employee attendance at colleges. YT, in providing a fixed payment for an employee in training, subsidises employer training costs (with the implication that training can then spread more widely). Second, in requiring some college training it reinforces the demand for greater input into general or portable skills. Finally, it takes a step towards completing the German model where most 16-18 year-olds are in either education or training. By 1985 about 45% of 16-year old school leavers and 30% of 17-year olds were on YTS schemes (Lee *et al*, 1990, p4). In 1990 23% of *all* 16-year-olds and 21% of 17-year-olds were on YT.

However, from the start, government training schemes sought to do the impossible. The contradiction between massive youth unemployment and assertions of skill shortages was always too great to be bridged other than in advertisements: ET (Employment Training for adults) will 'train the workers without jobs, to do the jobs without workers'. The simple logic of this MSC advertisement contained a clear political message - high unemployment is not the result of economic decline but of a mismatch of skills. It had an additional connotation: unemployment appears a characteristic of individuals themselves, falling behind economic development through their own inadequacy. However, if social or personal factors are important it is employers themselves who make this so. In times of high unemployment when too many suitable people are seeking work, employers may depend 'as often on the *social attributes* of potential employees (age, sex, ethic background and so forth), as on their technical competencies' (Rees *et al*, 1988, p10). Rees *et al* (1989) argue against 'a highly functional model which posits direct and unproblematic links' between improved technical competencies, employer requirements, and increased competitiveness (p229). It is important not to exaggerate the role of new high-tech skills: 'for the bulk of employees, it appears that the technical requirements of their work tasks are minimal' (p230), making social attributes a rational basis for choice.

To repeat, if employers do not consistently demand more skills, it is possible they have no compelling need to upgrade their staff. Thus, pressure on industry is now applied solely through exhortation. In 1985 the MSC and NEDC went so far as to commission a report called *Challenge to Complacency*. This was a response to a letter from the MSC to 1,000 leading British firms which asked them to produce a statement on training needs and provision. In 1986 the Employment Secretary complained that barely 200 firms had responded to the letter. Publication of the report and its criticisms of employers 'did more to raise their tempers than to increase their commitment' (Anderson, 1987, p68). The criticism, though, is odd for a government which believes in the power of the market, and that industry knows what it wants.

However, it is increasingly apparent that the government itself is relaxed about the provision of skills on to the market - no doubt also a result of awareness that upgrading means higher costs. While a central focus of government training schemes has been the absorption of youth unemployment, a second goal may be an attempt to bring down the pay of the young, which is in part why the schemes have been conceived as a wage subsidy. They may then help establish a pay norm rather than pay for specified training outcomes. The schemes have been part of a major restructuring of the position of young people in the economy, indeed in society. The critical position of young people at the crossroads between education and work (but also housing demand) makes central control a tempting prospect.

One aspect of this process is what has been called 'segmentation', related to dual labour market theory, which sees the market as split into two basically non-competing sectors, one with well-paid workers with a career structure internal to the employer or industry, the other with more dispensable workers who form a more fluid substratum of low-paid workers. While the dual labour market thesis is somewhat simplistic, Rubery, for instance, rightly arguing the existence of 'a whole continuum of shades of segmentation' (in Giddens and Held, 1982, p346), the principle itself seems correct. A variety of social groups are prone to be more marginal to the labour process than others. This 'lowest' segment may include women with family commitments and black people. Education may be similarly demarcated. In the case of young people this could be reinforced by training. In Jordan's view (1986) effective training involving genuine reskilling is likely to benefit core workers most. Cheap, off-the-peg training such as YT involves mostly non-core workers and may result in deskilling.

Raffe (in Brown and Ashton, 1987) argues that the youth and adult markets are not distinct, even if young people receive lower pay for the same work and are more likely to be dismissed in hard times (when firms seek to protect their core workers). In addition, the high incidence of youth unemployment does not have structural causes such as technological change (creating demand for more skilled and experienced workers). Raffe puts high youth unemployment down to recession, arguing that recessions hit the young harder because the young are more vulnerable. Ashton, Maguire and Spilsbury (in Brown and Ashton, 1987), by contrast, argue that young people do form a distinct part of the labour market. The labour market is segmented in such a way as to exclude youth employment in sectors where training might actually be of help; for instance, skilled manual work, which once offered sheltered recruitment to young people expecting to start off low down, is becoming increasingly closed - because apprenticeships are declining, because technological change (such as robotics) makes many skills obsolete, and because management strategies aimed at creating flexibility are destroying traditional internal market mechanisms. While much semi-skilled work offers partial openings, employers in capital-intensive industries such as chemicals, characterised by expensive equipment, dangerous material and a frequent need for 24-hour operation (thus requiring shift work) tend to consider young people unsuitable. Large labour-intensive industries such as textiles do recruit young people but the need for training is often limited here, as manual dexterity, the main requirement, is quickly picked up on the job. Finally, in the case of semi or unskilled work (eg retailing), much full-time labour has been replaced by part-timers, making training less relevant. This leaves much training located in largely unskilled sectors such as the hotel trade, where it is even less relevant. All in all, YT(S) has limited impact on the youth labour market. It is 'essentially on the margins, and is more likely to modify its operation, than to transform it' (p168).

YT has at best a limited impact on job chances. Of those who left YT in 1990/91, only 57% actually left for a job; for ET leavers the figure was a mere 30% (Department of Employment, May 1992, p8). Looking at a single cohort from the Scottish Young People's survey, in 1984 about 57% of those with some YTS experience were employed 18 months later, compared to 36% of those without such experience. However, Main and Shelley also argue that one cause was the ability of those on YTS to get employment with their current sponsor. Removing this effect reduces the difference from 21% to about 12% (in Raffe, 1988, pp150-1). Analysis of outcomes before the two-year scheme (using Youth Cohort data), showed that 55% of those in YTS (outside inner-city areas) in 1986 were in full-time work in 1987. Getting work through training sponsors, which suggests that this may not be a result of the training so much as the convenience of recruiting through YTS, was an important part of this process, with 32% expecting or having got work in this way (Gray et al, 1989, pp15/16). YT(S) may therefore be a form of selection rather than of training. Lee et al use the term 'surrogate labour market' to describe the impact of YTS in producing its own structure of employment outcomes. Raffe, using ex-trainees' own views on the effect of their training, found that about 34% claimed to have got work through internal recruitment established by a YTS scheme; only 11% got work with another employer (in Wallace and Cross, 1990, p61). 'Its apparent failure to sell in the external labour market would seem to be a poor endorsement of the training and in particular of its general and transferable elements' (p70). While 87% of another sample of young people who were YTS trainees felt that YTS did help the unemployed find work (Lee et al, 1990, p90), YT(S) is also often considered the best option in the circumstances rather than as a good career move in its own right. Trainees appear to view YT(S) in highly practical terms.

Andrew, with no CSEs, was put on warehousing against his will. However, the training included forklift truck driving and 'A fork-lift truck driver's just left, and I've passed the test so I've got a chance'. In contrast, another trainee found the same training irrelevant in a smaller warehouse: 'Look at it, you couldn't get a forklift truck in here if you tried' (Lee *et al*, 1990, 108-9).

While about 95% of a very small sample (Baxter, 1988, p35) believed that YTS 'gives useful skills', only 15% gave YTS as an option when asked what they hoped to be doing the following year (p30/31). 20% of a much larger sample (the Youth Cohort) were on YTS in spring 1986. 5% of the sample expected to be on YTS a year later, but the actual figure was 11% (Gray *et al*, 1989, p18). In the Scottish survey mentioned above, over 60% of trainees said they joined YTS because they could not get a job, not for the training/work experience itself. Between the time of establishing the sample and undertaking the survey about 30% had left the scheme, nearly all prematurely. About half of these left for a job. 'Implicit in their responses was the view that the youth training scheme is a temporary refuge for the unemployed, to be left as soon as a permanent job becomes available' (Raffe, 1987, p48). YT is not popular. The 1991 School-Leavers Destination survey showed a decrease in full-time employment from 17% in 1990 to 10%; despite this, entry into YT fell from 17% to 15%. Staying on in education (up from 53% to 61%) appeared to be the most favoured alternative (Department of Employment, May, 1992, p19); and a mere 38% of YT entrants completed their courses in 1990/91 (p8).

There have been many critiques of the poor quality of the actual training provided (Benn and Fairley, 1986; Bevan and Varlaam, 1987; Lee *et al*, 1990). Of particular note, however, is the way YT(S) has been used as a form of control. Even if it is not 'an extremely ambitious attempt to remake the British working class' (Finn, in Benn and Fairley, 1986, p54), it is part of an attempt to fix more securely the place of working-class youth in a unique position that is neither work, nor education, nor training. Shortly after YTS became a two-year scheme, the government removed the right to income support from 16-17 year-olds not in work, in education, or on a training scheme. YTS in effect became compulsory for the unemployed, thus establishing the American 'workfare' system in Britain for the first time. It is of great significance that this actually makes it harder for many to improve their education, as income support is an important means of funding continued part-time education for many school-leavers. Forcing young people into YT forces them out of education. The cutting of LEA discretionary grants is a further curtailment of the right to part-time education. The problems of YT force the government to impose ever more stringent conditions to make the scheme a success. In the process it further segments the employment market, and allocates young people a more highly controlled space within this.

YT and wages

If young people form part of a segmented labour market, youth pay would be likely to be low relative to adult pay. In the past this has not been the case, though in recent years the gap has been rising. However, that basic distinction is over-simple. More important are distinctions between young people themselves, in particular between those that remain in education, those that go on to employment, and those that move into unemployment. The latter have been particularly important to government attempts to lower youth wages, as it sees the historically relatively high ratio of youth to adult wages (that is, relative to some other countries) as an impediment to reduction in youth unemployment. It is possible that YT was intended to widen the gap. The Scottish School-Leavers Survey, for instance, revealed that those who had full-time employment had an average pay of £51.60 per week, compared to the then YTS allowance of £26.25, and that this YTS allowance was considerably less than the average minimum wage of £32.15 that unemployed young people would accept (Raffe, 1987, p47). This does not mean that government action is necessary, as youth unemployment is likely to widen the pay gap unaided.

Neither does this mean that relatively high youth wages were a problem before high unemployment encouraged the government to try to 'price' young people back into work. A study of experience of work in over 300 establishments in three parts of the country by Roberts, Dench and Richardson (in Brown and Ashton, 1987) found that employers tended not to take advantage of the potential to drive down wages in areas of high unemployment, which they could be expected to do if youth labour were overpaid. This was partly because firms which were branches of national companies had to pay national rates in order, for instance, to avoid leap-frogging - but also because managers 'emphasized that youth pay was only a minute fraction of their total wage-bills and an even smaller proportion of total costs' (p208).

One way of looking at this is through the effect of YT on human capital. Does it increase human capital (raising skills) or reduce it (lowering wages)? Insofar as it may increase the chance of getting a job, it certainly raises income. However, it may not raise wages once in work. For instance, the hourly earnings of people sampled in the Scottish Young People's Survey in 1986 were higher for people never on YTS (£1.55) than for those who had ever been on YTS (£1.44). In addition, the gap within the latter between those who had found employment with their YTS scheme provider and those who had found an alternative employer was even wider, possibly suggesting that getting out of YT(S) is beneficial (Main and Shelley, in Raffe, 1988, p152). Indeed, it 'can be argued that the most successful trainees will in fact be those who manage to get a job during the course and that those acquiring the certificates will be the less successful' (Hough, 1987, p115).

The cause of these disparities does not appear to be that YT people are inherently less employable. 55% of YT participants examined in the Scottish Young People's Survey had no Scottish O-Grades at A-C level, compared to 47% in a job, while the figure for the unemployed was 72% (Raffe, 1987, p45). In an analysis of the Youth Cohort Study, Dolton, Makepeace and Treble (1992), compared the earnings of individuals differentiated by criteria such as education and work experience within different training regimes. A person with the typical characteristics of someone whose only training experience is YTS is likely to have average earnings, suggesting that YTS does not attract a type of individual who is inevitably likely to end up a low earner. Gray et al's own analysis of Youth Cohort data shows that YTS entrants tend to be 'those with "middle" exam attainment' (1989, p21). The system (or structural constraints), not the individual characteristics of those within it, determine wage outcomes.

This assessment of the starting position of trainees enables the effect of training itself to be set in context. Dolton et al confirm that YTS may well be linked to reduced pay. The analysis takes into account the impact of continuing in training after YTS (which is likely to continue to depress earnings in the short-term) by treating such people as a distinct category. For individuals likely to end up with only YTS experience, earnings would be £2.18 per hour. Those in apprenticeships and with no YTS experience could expect to get

£2.41. As the authors comment, 'this makes depressing reading for advocates of YTS' (1992, p7) - although it has to be pointed out that these results refer to immediate earnings, not to any longer-term benefits from training. But should such an effect be interpreted, if true, as a success for right-wing attempts to lower wages, or as a failure to improve human capital? Given the limited impact of YT wages on general wages (unemployment having a much larger impact), the latter interpretation seems inevitable. In other words, YT segments through deskilling. Low pay is the result of being labelled YT.

YT is at best a stop-gap for the unemployed, who undoubtedly prefer work. Education may also be a hidey-hole in times of trouble, though probably less so. Australian data suggest that during the boom in apprenticeships the demand to remain in education was limited (DEYA, 1983), but this was reversed by recession and the collapse of paid training for the young. Similarly in Britain, staying-on in full-time education rose from 53% in 1990 to 61% a year later, while full-time employment amongst school-leavers fell from 17% to 10% (Department of Employment, May 1992). However, this tendency may not apply in areas of relatively high unemployment, when searching for work may become more critical (Elias and Blanchflower, 1986). Examination of FES data on the whole household (Micklewright, Pearson and Smith, 1989) found that regional unemployment rates again did not encourage staying on. One reason might be household unemployment: as local unemployment rises, parental job loss might encourage children to leave school to find work for the family's sake. On the other hand, it has been argued that good market conditions act as a disincentive to enter higher education, while high unemployment, as in Liverpool, encourages entry to HE (Finegold et al, 1990, p17).

Education, work and training are, from the point-of-view of their users, potential alternatives dependent in complex ways on the business cycle. Attempts to encourage staying on in education or to enter into training may have to give assurance of both short and long-term benefit. Young people are not easily manipulated and will no doubt choose the best alternative - education, work, training, or 'doing nothing' - in spite of government attempts to push them in one particular direction. In addition, suppressing wages through training is bound to fail. There are too many factors to control. This will become even more so with youth labour shortages through and beyond the 1990s. Only a secure long-term benefit is going to make a career dependent on training worthwhile.

A coherent training structure?

The critique of YT makes quite clear that this form of government intervention is concerned with the short term, with a reduction in official unemployment and with a (vain) attempt to lower the cost of *general* youth employment. The issue then becomes one of inequality rather than of training inputs *per se*. Many critics of current schemes have also engaged with this issue, in particular Green (1992) and several contributors to NIESR publications. But the solution is far from clear. Both lay the blame for British training failure on a laissez-faire system which fails to require employers to act in the national interest. However, employers can hardly be blamed for seeing training as one input like any other, and costing it accordingly. Do British consumers buy British for the good of the nation? More generally, it seems hardly more helpful to blame employers for doing too little to produce skills than to blame workers for doing too little to acquire skills. While the state must act to ensure that the short-term interests of employers do not detract from the nation's long-term interests, the distinction is far from clear-cut. The most important trainers are large companies which must plan their labour needs in the long term, and this includes the provision of skills which are portable over time if not across employers. It is unlikely that employers act in their short-term interests in the long term.

Nevertheless, it is likely that the government could do much to place training in Britain on a better footing. The suggestion of several NIESR publications is to get the system of funding right, while Green emphasises the importance of a strong corporatist approach. Both give considerable emphasis to a clearer, more coherent system of certification, as do Finegold *et al* (1990) in their demand for a 'British *baccalauréat*'. A final important element is institutional provision. A number of countries rely heavily on schooling to provide core vocational and technical skills (eg in separate vocational schools). Germany has a 'dual' system of education and employer-led training. Britain has more of a mixed model where routes multiply but are less clearly defined.

> The fragmentation at the heart of Britain's mixed model makes it very difficult to introduce common curricula, to devise coherent certification systems (because certification needs to perform different functions in different contexts), to plan flexibility and progression, and to design the later stages of compulsory schooling. In part, this fragmentation reflects the divergent pressures of the labour market upon the different sectors of the education and training systems (Finegold *et al*, 1990, pp18/9).

The authors propose the replacement of A-levels and a range of vocational qualifications with a new diploma containing both academic and vocational elements. They also propose a highly expanded tertiary college system as a new locus for its provision.

The latter institutional element is critically important (and will be taken up again in the final chapter), largely because it is surely institutional provision (organisation and funding) which determines staying-on, not the certification available. This is one reason why the latter may be somewhat of a red herring. Obviously a comprehensive form of certification, which for many has been a long-term goal, is the logical final step in the quest for a fully comprehensive education. However, if this is the case, the issue is not really one of greater consistency or coherence, but desegregation. It is by no means clear that this will be aided by mere uniformity. Even if take-up is encouraged as with the French *bac*, the British *bac* is still likely to be a relatively elite qualification. Virtually enforced on all young people at age 18 (with an intended reduction in the significance of age-16 exams), the new qualification will for many become a sentence, not an opportunity. While the modular nature of the exam would be a great benefit, and should be a goal in its own right, in part this can only disguise the nature of the hurdle to be jumped.

The issues of coherence, transparency and portability are closely inter-related. Steedman (1992) has complained that while NVQs create greater coherence, the emphasis on the practical reduces the generalisability and therefore long-term value of the skills they represent. Prais and Beadle (1991) have argued that academic tests are both cheaper and clearer than tests of practical competence. Green (1992) is concerned that the multiplicity of skill components in NVQs reduces both their equivalence value and status. In general, the more academic the content of the test, the more portable the skill which is assumed to have been acquired. If this is so, it is a paradox that Germany and Japan, countries which do so well in producing crystal-clear qualifications, need portable skills the least. Continuity with an employer is highly regarded in both countries and turn-over is considerably lower than in much of British industry. In other words, the stable employment environment that effective training requires is much less prevalent in Britain.

Perhaps the emphasis should be on stability rather than on portability. After commenting on findings by Haskel and Martin (1990) that there is 'an insignificant effect of training activity in reducing skill shortages, apparently because of the effect of poaching', Hart and Shipman (1991, p78) give credence from their own research to the greater stability of firms in Germany. The firms in their sample 'expected most trainees to stay with them and even to return to them, if they left their apprenticeships to study full-time for a degree'. Within six months of completing their training, 33% of German trainees leave for military service, further education or training, or for unemployment. Another 19% change occupations or their specialism. 41% remain with their employer and only 7% change employers within their specialist field (DES, 1991:a, p10).

It is also by no means certain that flexibility requires general training, or training criteria, imposed by government. The French system, which does the latter, is commonly acknowledged to be cumbersome and poorly adaptive. The German system has many fans despite the fact that it may both overtrain and delay the updating of skills. In addition, it does in fact produce training which tends to be fairly job-specific. Moreover, its range of vocational schools and colleges, while impressive, are monotechnic and nothing like as broad and flexible as British FE colleges. In general it can be doubted how far transparency in qualifications itself can raise productivity. It is also possible that 'core' skills themselves become redundant in time and what is really needed is a continuous updating of skills over time.

The abandonment of concern for coherence and portability returns the issue where it belongs, to one of increased access, and this is a matter of funding and organisational through-routes. This must have strong trade union support. Green's argument that training policy can only be effective if trade unions are fully involved is undoubtedly right, implying a need for a return to corporatism. Union resistance to any realignment of differentials resulting from improved training is a problem for the mode of implementation, not for the fact of training itself. If union influence is to be disregarded then employers must at least be able to guarantee fairly secure employment, as in Germany or Japan; otherwise potential trainees really have very little basis on which to plan their futures. Campbell *et al* (in Hirst and Zeitlin, 1989) put Germany's superiority in training down to the retention through early capitalism of an essentially guild-based system, which used state regulation to protect the production of skills. It is very difficult for government to invent such structures, though they can be reinforced if they exist. The German *Berufbildungsgesetz* (vocational training law) of 1969, for instance, makes concrete the corporatist nature of trade union and employer relations in the provision of training. The more fragile structures present in Britain before 1979 have been damaged too easily.

In any new training structure, certification may help, and union support certainly would, but the system of funding and its impact on access must be the cornerstone of any new policy. The issue contains many complex questions: institutional costs, the cost to employers of reduced productivity during training (including time spent on college courses), the employee's willingness to defer full pay, and the question of who funds training for those not currently in work. As has already been pointed out, British employers are fairly generous, paying for the full cost of training (course fees plus maintenance) as well as higher training wages than, for instance, in Germany. The problem is achieving a better balance so that more people benefit. Britain's training structure is an interesting parallel to its restricted but well subsidised system of higher education: major expansion may well require more financial input from individual beneficiaries (Barr, 1993). The alternative of restriction in pursuit of quality, on the other hand, may help generate new aristocracies of labour. When trade unions in Leeds proposed to the City Council that it withdraw from ET, designed to take 1,200 people, and replace it with its own 'high quality scheme of 400 places' at a cost of £3m (*Leeds Action Against Workfare*), who precisely would benefit? This parallels the relatively elitist, school-based British *baccalauréat*.

On the other hand, state schemes aside, if training expenditure were spread over many more people, but funded by employers' contributions, the employee's incentive to train would be reduced, as the cost and quality would go down. This might necessitate an increase in post-training wages in order to compensate. The more employees that receive training, the more people will expect higher wages in the long term. How feasible is this? From the employer's point-of-view, there is no guarantee at all that this higher long-term cost will be compensated by consistently higher productivity. It has already been argued that the low-pay equilibrium probably works well enough for most employers. Perhaps a leap of faith is needed that a major investment in training and in skilled wages will mean a leap not only to a high-wage equilibrium but to a high-skill equilibrium. But faith is not a sound basis for action. Other factors outside many employers' control must explain Britain's productivity record, even if training is one that can be controlled.

It could well be that employers should be required to spend more on training, but this is always likely to be fairly marginal to current training input. It would not necessarily help to spread the benefits to more workers, and to non-workers. This, it would seem, is the task of government. While it is not the government's job to subsidise employers, it can take over much of the institutional costs of training, thus leaving it to employers to sort out their own wage structures for trainees (as well, of course, as their own internal programmes). This means that training must be considered an aspect of education, but without constraining outcomes as in the British *bac* proposal. The latter is clearly highly directive, making it difficult for people to leave education before 18 - through enforcing costly day-release on employees and, apparently, as with the current government, removing rights to benefits under age 18. All 16-17s would be expected to be in education or work (Finegold *et al*, 1990, p37). However, it is not obvious why these adults should lose their rights merely because of their age.

If Finegold *et al* wish to encourage young people to stay on for a new academic-vocational A-level, for Hart and Shipman young people have simply to be persuaded to be less concerned about the academic route. 'The firms we interviewed are well aware that they have to persuade teachers and their pupils that it is in the interest of many pupils at 16+ to take apprenticeships, and study for a technical qualification, rather than to proceed to A-levels (Hart and Shipman, NIESR Discussion Paper 185, p12). But is it in the interest of these young people to do so? The government, in the meantime, has its own very different target of 25% of 16-year olds to be studying for NVQs by 1996.

An excellent review of funding alternatives by Hart and Shipman (1991), which assumes some sort of government subsidy in each case, breaks these down into three main types according to who ultimately pays (though these are not mutually exclusive): employers (through a levy), employees (loans), and government (subsidies to employees, eg though vouchers; or to employers, eg through tax concessions or through expansion of training in education). The levy system, which failed in Britain but operates in France (though there it is a pseudo-levy because of its similarity to corporate taxation), appears to be relatively unproblematic, apart from high administrative costs. It is also favoured by various critics as a means of forcing employers to live up to their obligations to society, as well as minimising the state's contribution (though tax concessions could be established to offset this). It is certainly better than the current system in which the private sector is responsible for managing public funds. However, levies can create powerful disincentives for employers and may relate very poorly to their individual needs.

An alternative is for the employee to bear much of the cost through reduced trainee wages. In Germany the state pays for the institutions, while employees meet much of the cost to employers through reduced wages. Employers pay a training wage but perhaps get off rather lightly. Green, favouring the German system with some qualification, acknowledges this: 'Relatively high wage rates for young people and poor differentials for those with skills and qualifications thus provide a disincentive that perpetuates low levels of training in the UK' (1992, p10). The constraints that Finegold *et al* propose be placed on employment of young people would also lower pay (to compensate the employers). Others are more blunt about the supposed need to reduce youth wages. 'Are youth wages in the UK now sufficiently low relative to adult rates to make possible a high level of training?' (Oulton and Steedman, 1992, p18). With men under 18 getting 68% of the wage for 18-20 year-olds, while for women the ratio is even higher at 74%, the 'temptation for a young person to drop out of a traineeship in favour of a "real job" is therefore strong' (p19). The authors seem to lament that YT may not bring down wages sufficiently, partly because 'the actual amounts paid by firms are often higher' (p18). But why, if British firms are so mean with training money for the young, are they so relatively generous with pay for the young? And how will those who seek reduced youth wages argue their case as employers compete during the 1990s for a diminishing supply of youth labour? It does not seem a viable response to make the young cheapen their labour for the privilege of raising national productivity. Human capital may well convert into national capital, but a direct equation between the two is not straightforward. In the meantime, passing the cost of this dual investment onto the individual worker helps the state avoid the fundamental need to make training as much a right as education, and thus extends inequalities, as post-16 education is free for those who can take advantage of it.

Nevertheless, the employee's contribution could be subsidised, for instance through training vouchers, guaranteeing the right to training at any appropriate institution. This is favoured by the CBI but also by some on the Right (the parallel with the failed attempt to introduce education vouchers is obvious). The scheme has the advantage of directing effort away from a wage subsidy (YT and ET) and towards payment of fees, thus not affecting wage structures and their use to attract trainees or labour. Hart and Shipman point out that vouchers would nevertheless pay for some training that employers would otherwise willingly pay themselves, but in addition their similarity to gift vouchers would do nothing to structure or control training. Vouchers would deny both stability and status to the institutional basis that effective training needs.

A final approach would emphasise the role of institutions, in particular through a much closer integration between training and education. A start has been made through TVEI, CTCs, and GNVQs, though this patchwork set of policies appears to have no coherent goals. Finegold *et al* (1990) rightly make this integration a central part of their proposal for change. However, virtual compulsion could be damaging and either limit the supply of jobs or lead to a fall in wages to compensate for lost time. It would also be expensive. Shipman suggests an extension of vocational qualifications in schools through allowing part-time school attendance for those in work. This would at least help deal with reduced numbers of young people in the 1990s (and would approach the German dual system). Prais and Beadle (1991), favour separate technical institutions of the sort that exist in many other countries; investment would then be matched to ability or aptitude, if not formally.

But there is a profound danger here of rigid tracking, as in the Netherlands, where those deemed to be unacademic are weaned out of general schooling at an early age. The lack of success that often attends such divisions, as earlier in Britain with technical schools must make their effectiveness doubtful. In general, the pressure to get into or return to the academic stream has been a major impediment to the success of this simple approach.

This argument will be returned to in the final chapter, but for the meantime it can be noted that if education were to take on a more vocational burden it must be with the benefit of substantial integration between the academic and vocational elements. The sort of institutional reform required is perhaps something like the complete removal of post-16 education to institutions like tertiary colleges (primarily for 16-19 year-olds but with some adult courses). Teaching would be academic, technical and vocational. Everyone would have the right to enter these and to take any course. Government would bear the tuition costs (possibly partly supported by a general employment levy), but maintenance could depend on entrants' own resources (including loans), on employers paying for their own workers, or on government grants to the unemployed. (The Labour party proposal to pay a student grant for staying on at school, by contrast, would, as Finegold *et al*, point out, be highly inefficient.) The end result would be full comprehensivisation outside of higher education up to the age of 19, not twin or multiple tracking.

Of course such general blueprints have little, if any, value. The main point to be made here though is that education and training needs to be better integrated, and that government must bear some of the cost of this improved institutionalisation. None of this prevents employers providing their own highly specific training.

Conclusion

If there is a tendency in Britain to produce too few people with technical skills the cause does not lie in the performance of the education system, nor in the content of British education; nor can it be equated merely with the number of engineers or people with craft qualifications that the system produces. The fault lies in the failure of the UK to integrate the educational system in such a way that does not 'lose' young people as a result of blocked avenues, biases between different social groups, or lack of real opportunities after school. These are major problems in the UK. The acute divisions in post-16 education and training in conjunction with high unemployment have made not only post-16 provision but also schooling pointless for many. It is difficult to avoid the conclusion that the combination of high unemployment and strict post-16 segregation is designed to prepare some not for the world of work, but for its margins. One essential element in any new approach is that training should be 'trainee-centred rather than firm-centred' (Lee, Marsden *et al*, 1990, p194). Imposition of new controls and credentials, other than the extension and modularisation of A-levels, should not be part of this ultimate goal

Greater access is needed, but without the setting of new targets and hurdles. Greater state intervention is not the same as greater state control. The latter tends to be geared to investment in 'programmes' rather than in 'a strong full-time technical sector' (Raffe, in Wallace and Cross, 1990, p71), and the value of such programmes (such as YT) is limited. The difference between intervention and control is also one reason why critics of current government training schemes do not necessarily agree on the solutions. On the one hand, training such as YT is seen as being of low-quality, and designed to constrain the pay of the young. The solution is to resist this and to attract people into training through adequate rewards. On the other hand, those who take a more international and comparative approach point to the ability of German employers to pay highly reduced youth wages and, partly through this, to fund substantial training activity. These two basic approaches are fundamentally contradictory. Those concerned with issues of direct equality want greater pay for those in training, and for the young generally. Those concerned with raising skill levels usually see this as requiring a short or even medium-term sacrifice of pay on the part of trainees. Both may make sense, but an alternative solution is to leave pay to the market and to concentrate on radically improved institutional provision - the job primarily of the state.

Finally, if training in employment is to be improved it is unlikely that this can occur without improved job security. Though this is also likely to set core against other workers, it has to be recognised that relative unwillingness on the part of British employers to expand training is closely connected not only to less stable profit margins, but to an employment policy geared to expendability. Perhaps Japanese training is better not because Japanese training is better but because Japanese employment is better. For instance, one big electronics company gives all its employees between five and nine months' induction training, has its own colleges, and altogether spends 0.5% of its turnover on training.

> This large investment in training is worthwhile for the company because, like many Japanese companies and especially the larger ones, it has a lifelong employment policy (DES/HMI, 1991:b, p24).

On the other hand, some business interests in Japan itself now seem to be suggesting that there is a 'need to reform business hiring practices and university admission policies to favour diverse talents rather than just success on the standard examination' (Schoppa, 1991, p124). This does not mean an end to job security but it does suggest that Japan has done very well in the past on a system that differentiates rather little on entry and protects employment quite considerably once a contract has been made.

Part One: Conclusion

In any assessment of constraints on economic growth, seeking the source in the system of education is rarely helpful; there is no connection between low standards and skill shortages, neither of which serves as a useful indicator in its own right. Concern over standards, which inexorably rise, merely detracts attention from more fundamental problems of economic and political management. As for skill shortages, in their foundation on employers' perceptions (which we are told rarely extend beyond the short term), they may be little better than taking current share prices as an indicator of long-run economic prospects. With labour force projections predicting a fall of over 22% in the 1990s in availability of people aged 20-24, and an absolute loss of under-35s by 2001 of 1.2 million (Department of Employment, May 1992, p9), it is not so much skill shortages but labour shortages that will be the problem in the medium term - unless, of course, the government solves the problem through extending and deepening the recession of the early 1990s. Critics of current policy should also avoid the numbers game that talk of low standards or skill shortages invites. The game detracts from the fundamental issue of rights and opportunity. Both are lacking for the bulk of young people in particular. There is no need to plan what these people should do. They have enough knowledge and understanding of the market (pay-offs between different job strategies over time) to choose the mix of education and training that is both good for them and good for the economy.

Neither does it help to look to particular countries doing much better than Britain for a panacea. One obvious problem with such comparisons is a proper assessment of cause and effect. It is assumed that the German system, for instance, has resulted in improved economic performance. Is it not more reasonable to assume the reverse? German firms can simply afford more training. British firms, less successful, can afford less. If the latter also resist government pressure to raise their spending on training, this does not mean that the UK government should bow to such pressure; but it does mean that referral to systems in other countries should look critically at the complex web of factors which influence educational and training outcomes. Following on from this, it is fairly clear that the British system probably falls somewhere between that of Germany and the Italian model (if model it is). Much of Italy's education and training structure, though typically continental in many respects, is highly incoherent and underfunded. Comparison with the weaker economies in Europe might be distasteful for some, but would be a healthy corrective to policy demands to mimic the rich. The German system is successful because the small scale of unemployment (and the more stable profits of its employers), enables long-term and consistent training to be provided. Britain has to develop a system applicable to its more fragmented and uncertain employment situation. Copying the German system may help, but may also be putting the cart before the horse.

The government can certainly do something to offer the unemployed a better form of training, to improve vocational education in schools, to force employers to work with trade unions on training policies, and to extend the spread of vocational certification. But the most critical task is to provide incentives to young people to continue to improve their skills, and to establish the institutional basis through which these will be provided. The result will not eliminate skill shortages - it may even, in making the economy more effective, generate deeper shortages; but it will, through eliminating archaic demarcations, increase the flexibility of Britain's system of education and training.

It is not apparent, however, that opportunities for young people figure highly on the agenda of the Right. Control mechanisms - extensive tests, comprehensive certification, limited rights to post-16 education, and compulsory youth training without any quality control - these are the means that have been chosen to deal with economic problems. While the alternative of simply loading the burden of improved training on employers may be heavy-handed, there is certainly scope for the government itself to seek to extend opportunity. However, the control mechanisms that are increasingly being put in place appeal to fundamental right-wing leanings which persistently put cultural fears at the head of the agenda for educational reform. The Left has its own versions of such fears, and the combined effect is a considerable distortion of the functions of education. These are the theme of Part Two. However, these are not the result simply of an antagonism to youth culture or any other threat to traditional standards. They are fundamentally related to concerns over the distribution of education. These concerns arise out of a long-term period of growth which threatens traditional demarcations within education (eg based on class), but culminating in a further long period of intermittent recession, when qualifications become a less secure guarantee of a job. This means that change in education may be far more closely related to a crisis in the demand for rather than in the supply of education, which was the theme of Part One.

Part Two:
Education and culture

Education is a peculiar process...
(Roger Scruton, *The Meaning of Conservatism*)

Peculiar or not, education probably seems from the point-of-view of its participants a relatively invariant morass of routines and procedures. For students it is a bit of a grind and always will be. And over the last 20 years or so at least, despite variably low pay and demoralisation, and consequent strikes, teachers have just got on with the job. Crisis there may be, but it is increasingly apparent that this is being generated by reforms designed to restructure education along highly ideological lines. The crisis is not, of course, generated solely on the Right, as the notion has for long been part of left-wing mythology too. Traditionally, the causes have differed (inequality rather than inefficiency) as have the readiest solutions (expansion rather than segmentation), but the language is now increasingly similar. The Right's market decentralisation becomes the Left's postFordism. New policies for vocational expansion stem from all sources, and there is widespread support for a national curriculum. Standards, choice, skill shortages - few seem to question what are now general shibboleths.

Merger has even been possible at the theoretical level, with crisis universally posited as a result of expansion of the social at the cost of the economic. For the Right, led by critiques of erosion of the 'wealth-making' sector of society (eg Bacon and Eltis, 1978), the State has indulged in massive over-provision, especially through the welfare state. If traditional Marxism focussed on under-provision (slumps leading to violent reaction), later Marxism adapted to the relative stability of capitalism and reversed this. Crisis had been bought off through massive expansion of the welfare state. But this merely postponed the crisis as declining profit margins cannot support this level of social over-provision (Gough, 1979). A further crisis of legitimation developed (Habermas, 1976). The end of consensus has also affected education, for instance raising questions about its value when its impact cannot be measured. Education has become a major site of social conflict (CCCS, 1981).

But it is by no means certain that the crisis is real. In the case of education there is a clear cyclical pattern in political and social attitudes to growth and distribution. While trend pressures exist, many of their supposed impacts are illusory. It took very little time for belief in the 1944 Act to give way to widespread concern over the impact of the tripartite system, and within two decades or so education was riven by bitter struggle over comprehensivisation. It is better to see the 'crisis' as a recrudescence of ideological conflict over the distribution, not the extent or cost, of educational provision. Since the end of the last century there has been steady underlying growth in this provision, perhaps partly because of the 'sharp elbows' of the middle classes (Le Grand, 1982). There is no crisis, but there is conflict, and this is connected with the distribution of economic benefits: who gets what, and when. This sort of public fear is most pronounced in the case of welfare benefits and their derivation from tax contributions. Hence, frequent political and media attacks on welfare 'scroungers' (Golding and Middleton, 1982). Redistributional benefits are treated with greater suspicion than those which are more universal (Taylor-Gooby, 1985). On the other hand, in the case of the universalism of health spending, and especially its specific crystallisation in the NHS, there is universal acceptance of the need for increased spending, and the government has found it hard going persuading people that health should also be treated on a competitive basis.

Education is somewhere between the two extremes of the welfare state, being both a redistributional and a universal benefit. Educational spending might benefit the public as a whole but it also benefits some more than others. This contradiction provides a platform for political action, but also explains the central role of standards, which are indissolubly tied to cultural and moral assessments of social worth. The claim that we live in a state of educational crisis is economically unfounded, but is rooted, rather, in a sense of cultural crisis, and this has extended to fear that there should be a failure even to recognise its nature. 'For nearly twenty years now I have been arguing that the crisis in our secondary education is cultural...' (Bantock, *Black Paper 1977*, p78).

A balancing act

While the *Black Papers* campaigned for the privatisation of choice in education they also, and far more significantly, campaigned for limitation and reduction of access: there is simply too much education. It therefore needs to be more closely geared not to the needs of the economy - far from it - but to the (measured) capabilities of people going through the system. The objective of a more segregated system is not the production of particular skills but the selection of particular aptitudes: inputs rather than outputs. There is a world of difference between the two. The assessment of skills is a technical, the assessment of worth a cultural matter. ERA is fundamentally informed by this campaigning background, in many respects reflecting a straightforward translation into legislation of the demands of the *Black Papers*. There is only one exception to this. ERA is more interventionist, more disposed to expansion of a technological input than earlier right-wing campaigners would have liked. ERA's replacement of blackboards with computers is, in fact, a reversal of the *Black Papers'* belief in the basics, in 'chalk and talk'. However, ERA is fundamentally concerned with separation of the wheat from the chaff, of the 'good' from the rest.

The culture of the 'good' school - traditionalist, not modernist, is at the heart of the legislation. Indeed, the clash between culture and technology runs throughout the educational fabric set up by ERA, especially in connection with the national curriculum. On the Right generally, but also more particularly within the Tory Party, there has been significant ambivalence towards the national curriculum. Does the nationalisation of the curriculum represent a furthering of comprehensivisation, or centralisation, or modernisation? The answers are muddled. Although state control of the curriculum (or curricular development) was undoubtedly a *Black Paper* project, this was not tied to any conception of the state as an engine of change or modernisation. Rather, it would ensure rigour, consistency, and standards. This ambiguity is more apparent when it is considered that the national curriculum, albeit a less omnipresent 'core' curriculum, could have been conceived by the Labour Party. It is not surprising that one right-wing view of this is as another unwanted step towards comprehensivisation.

> Mr Dennis Marsden, a lecturer in sociology at the University of Essex, writes that the progressive aim is 'to seek positive unstreaming, a common curriculum and flexible teaching methods to promote a new co-operative atmosphere...' [in D. Rubenstein and C. Stoneman, 1970] What does Mr Marsden mean by 'a common curriculum'? Presumably that all children must study the same subjects... Naturally in the new society all will be equal, and no more respect will be paid to people who do responsible and onerous jobs than to idlers and layabouts (Lynn, in Boyson, 1972, pp2/3).

Boyson himself repeated these doubts in the main Commons debate on the Education Reform Bill, despite the support the *Black Papers* had given to state intervention in the curriculum. 'I do not like the specification that all children, from the most able to the least able, should do the same number of lessons on the same curriculum. That is the ultimate egalitarian comprehensive curriculum which I do not want.' Keith Joseph, no longer Education Secretary, opposed the national curriculum. Ted Heath attacked many aspects of the Bill, including the national curriculum, which he linked to the government's long-term project to undermine the influence of teachers and LEAs. Similarly, Norman Tebbit, concerned about rule by civil servants, warned Mr Baker to 'beware that the concept is not wrecked by the paternalists and bureaucrats in the Department of Education and Science.'

Yet for Mr Baker the national curriculum was 'the bedrock of our reform proposals', fairly obviously because it had to form the basis for a national testing programme. The TGAT plea (DES, 1987) that the 'assessment process... should be the servant, not the master, of the curriculum' was always pie in the sky. The national curriculum's main task is not to standardise but to divide, not to produce new skills but to test aptitude and ability. It is more an instrument of traditionalism than of modernisation. Other right wingers merely wanted a less interventionist means of securing this goal. Paradoxically, in HMI's view, further stultification of the curriculum was not even necessary.

> In a time when there is youth unemployment and when parents can choose between schools as rolls fall, the expectations in terms of examination results which governors, parents and employers have of schools, have also led schools to resist curricular innovation lest it affect examination performance (DES, 1983, p25).

ERA's juggling of very different and often contradictory demands, some traditionalist, some modernist, is a virtuosic balancing act, but is doomed to fail. The balance is in particular between opposed right-wing factions. Gordon and Klug (1986) divide the *New Right* (that is forgetting where the 'Old' Right may fit in) into 'libertarians' and 'social authoritarians'. The former are primarily interested in the economy and in promoting the ideas of Friedman and von Hayek; translated into British conditions this nexus of ideas was realised intellectually in the writings of people like Bacon and Eltis (1978), and politically in the creation of policies designed to reduce the public sector share of GNP. More freedom for the individual (usually from taxation) is necessary for economic regeneration. The social authoritarians, by contrast, see Britain's supposed decline in moral rather than economic terms. Indeed too much freedom - the 'permissive society' for instance - is one of the problems.

The inherent conflict between these two wings of conservatism, and within the party itself, is far from superficial. There is after all no reason to think that a believer in untrammelled freedom and social choice will be especially interested in religion, high culture and moral values. The authoritarians on the other hand have a strong fear of the impact of massness and its putative impact on standards. There is little obvious compromise between the two positions, though Gordon and Klug do suggest some areas of overlap. For instance, the libertarians require the state to be strong enough to establish free market conditions, including tight trade union control, and greater economic inequality may engender social conflicts which then require further state intervention. In addition, both wings have some suspicion of democracy. For the authoritarians it gets in the way of social control, while for the libertarians democracy is acceptable as long as it does not get in the way of the market, for instance through demand for public spending on health or education. Nevertheless, the conflicts needed to be reconciled.

> the main tasks for conservative rhetoric are to establish in the public mind
> the inseparability of market freedom and economic leadership, and to
> integrate the philosophy of the market into the underlying principle of order
> (Scruton, quoted in Gordon and Klug, 1986, p5).

Gordon and Klug argue that Thatcherism brought together the two wings of the party around a set of policies and ideological statements which hinge on the above areas of common ground. For Levitas, too, there 'is no evidence of a consensus supporting either of the New Right's promised lands'. However, in this case 'the forces of coercion are being progressively marshalled to prevent the formation and expression of a consensus against them' (1986, p103). Coercion and compromise are probably a fair description of recent Conservative support for several recent social changes. There is no inevitable trend towards hegemony even within that fairly narrow political ambit, let alone elsewhere. Moreover the common ground that commentators tend to specify - the market place - is a high level concept which by definition differentiates very little. At one level or another most people believe in the market. Within the Right itself there are those like Boyson who still believe in the efforts of the individual tackling life on a do-it-yourself basis, while others promote policies that require the government to clear the decks for international capital. For these the former might appear quaint, if not a little cranky. All that can really be said is that, ideological linkage is possible around concepts such as individualism and competition. '"Privatism", the ideology of "look out for number one", is exactly the attitude behind the new conservative elder's demand for discipline in the schools and more 'back to the basics"' (Kohlberg, in Munsey, 1980, p461).

Many countries are now experiencing these conflicting policy pressures (and outcomes).

In Japan, for instance, there have been powerful demands from business quarters to make education less rigid. This is 'correctly' interpreted at the political level as a reduction in comprehensive structures but not in the hold of the national curriculum or tests - nor, under pressure from conservatives concerned about status differentials, as a more fluid set of routes through alternative institutions. The routes, now even more dependent on test performance, have hardened. Moves to liberalise *through* central direction have inevitably nullified themselves (Schoppa, 1991). And, at the same time as Nakasone sought to internationalise Japanese education, policy has been encouraging a moral revival which stresses traditional virtues such as loyalty and the monarchy: 'internationalization here means nothing other than Japan's ambition to rise to a position of singular importance and power' (Horio, 1988, p378). The call for greater moral training followed closely on the heels of projects such as 'Plans for Doubling the National Income' (1960), one long-term outcome of which were proposals to allocate educational opportunities more clearly in line with labour demand.

On the other hand, the market alone explains very little as it is subject to highly divergent ideological interpretations. For Scruton it is an institution allowing exchange between individuals. It is not a means to any specified end such as economic growth. 'Conservatives place politics, culture and morality before economic order and the distribution of power' (Scruton, 1988, p11). The market is right by nature, not as a result of what it produces. It is not the task of conservatives, therefore, to seek modernisation. 'They see politics not as the pursuit of some ultimate goal - whether national supremacy, social justice, or economic growth - but as the attempt to reconcile conflicting interests and to establish law, order and peace throughout society' (pp11/12). All conservatives do is create a level playing field where highly unequal teams can play out the facade of competition. They certainly do not seek to improve the skills of either side. Modernisation must come naturally, if at all.

This does not mean there are no old-fashioned modernisers on the Right. Jones distinguishes a third tendency, a modernising arm which, although the reverse of socialism in its rejection of modernisation through planning, is just as goal-orientated. This is basically the 'Old' Right, favouring some intervention, and only mildly obsessed about moral or cultural decline.

> The modernizing tendency, however, has a more positive conception of the state's powers. Strong government action is needed - particularly in an area like education - to correct historic weaknesses and set down the clear outlines of a path along which the system should go (Jones, 1989, p80).

So, ERA can be seen as a balancing act between the free marketeers, the modernisers, and an authoritarian school who see education through a rosy but jaded prism of traditional culture. Ball takes a similar approach in his expansion of Raymond Williams' classification of 'industrial trainers', 'old humanists' (suffering from an almost aristocratic disdain for the practical), and 'public educators', with strong beliefs in human capital. Both of the latter oppose specialisation, unlike the industrial trainers (Williams, 1962). Ball, taking up ideas based on Foucault, argues that economic crisis has produced tensions between various highly divergent interests which between them produce a discourse that extends power over education which is power in its own right rather than reform geared to real and explicit goals: 'my emphasis is upon conflict and incoherence within the state and within and across the various sites which make up the state' (1990, p21). One obvious disjunction is between the 'old humanist' demand for a 'pre-Fordist idyll' and the industrial trainers' demand for 'open, contest mobility' (p130). A part of the discourse is the myth generated by notions of individual inability to keep up with change, justifying the new vocationalism, which serves a political rather than an economic need (ie to control high unemployment). At the same time the Right's new vocationalism (aimed at segregation) resonates with left-wing demand for *more* vocationalism (in opposition to elitist academic curricula). One result of both economic and political fragmentation is the 'post-Fordist school', a new and flexible component in skill provision. Inflexible, monolithic structures evaporate, but control is nevertheless extended.

Chitty's characterisation of change, influenced by Lawton, as the result of the workings of a 'tension system' is similar. For instance, modernisers in the DES, in part stimulated by an OECD critique in 1975 of the department's lack of direction over education, sought increased control and rationalisation. However, this bumped up against right-wing belief in decentralisation and flexibility, and any immediate gains by the DES, initially through HMI, amounted to 'a short-lived victory' (1989, p16). All the initiatives from the late 1970s on, including Labour's 'great debate', were responses to different perceptions of economic crisis. Things are still fairly open, however, simply because major political and social disjunctions have been patched over, enabling those 'still committed to the principles of comprehensive schooling... to seize upon and exploit the contradictions and tensions within New Right and therefore government thinking' (p227).

All of the above accounts emphasise the weakness of the current consensus, though insofar as there is an argument in favour of a balance between opposed forces, coming together at some stage as they rather inchoately do, this feat is surely not managed round the concept of the market, Fordist or postFordist. They come together through an act of political will, exemplified in particular through ERA. It seems likely that even if the mixture does not come apart explosively it will leak heavily at the seams. This is already apparent. A critical element in the balancing act is the professional support the government is reliant on to produce the curriculum and the tests. Here the leaks are already threatening to damage the fabric quite critically. One example is the unofficial *National Curriculum for Education*, 'set up in the teeth of ministerial opposition' (*TES*, 12.7.91). This is chaired by Professor Thompson, deputy chair of SEAC (the School Examinations and Assessment Council) and who had also chaired the science working group. The commission was set up in 1990 after a speech by Sir Claus Moser (a committee member), in which he demanded higher standards but linked to higher spending: improved performance in technical and scientific education requires substantially greater resourcing. Scientific advisers to the National Curriculum Council called the science curriculum itself a 'mess'. In the words of a former member of the science working group: 'The terms "mass" and "weight" are confused, Ohm's law of electrical resistance is described incorrectly and examples of mistaken ideas are presented as fact, for example "all metals are magnetic".... The treatment of energy is wrong.' At the more general level, 'the physics is appalling, with statements of attainment which are much too theoretical' (*TES*, 12.7.91). At the same time, much of the national curriculum remains on paper only, with several hundred schools having said that without extra funding they will have great difficulty in providing technology courses (*TES*, 4.6.93).

Meanwhile, the government papers over the cracks. As the cost in time and money required for the assessment process becomes all too clear, government leaders begin to suggest that the fault lies with the professionals who have put the curriculum and tests in place. Many assessments, painfully worked out, have been replaced with a smaller number of much simpler tests. Attainments targets have been greatly reduced, to the extent that one can only doubt their meaning. This was followed by successful teacher union balloting to abandon co-operation with the tests for 14-year olds, and their temporary abandonment. At the same time, two government appointed advisers (Brian Cox and John Marenbon) protest against the nature of government intervention in the assessment process. Duncan Graham, Chief Executive of the National Curriculum Council, left unhappy with growing politicisation of the national curriculum, ending up by calling it a 'magnificent aberration' (Graham and Tytler, 1993, p118).

Again, the UK appears to be emulating Japan. There a national 'scholastic achievement test' was introduced in the 1960s ostensibly as a measure of rationalisation, but in reality to test teachers and schools. On its introduction, teachers refused to distribute the question sheets. Thereafter the issue has been the subject of a number of court cases in which the legality of the tests was questioned. We are entering an era where education will be increasingly riven by political conflict. Each intervention creates a crisis which then requires further intervention. This is the theme of the next three chapters.

4 Culture and technology

With the expansion of technology in the curriculum, TVEI, NVQs, DTI's Micros in Schools funding, DES support for IT teaching, and several other initiatives, it seems reasonable to believe that education is undergoing fundamental modernisation. It appears that education is being streamlined, sharpened, and its content more closely geared to the needs of the economy. Yet, paradoxically, recent legislation, especially ERA, is often accused of backwardness - of attempting to return to the basics, of Victorian values, of 'payment by results'. Both assessments are accurate. ERA attempts to combine the past and the future.

Earlier forms of technicist argument were inextricably linked to notions of human capital; better education would tap a submerged reservoir of ability, though theories of educational value have also been important in modernisation attempts - for instance, the campaign by French mathematicians for more structural analysis as opposed to calculation, and set theory rather than Euclidean geometry (Wojciechowska, 1989). As socialist alternatives in education have been strongly influenced by such liberal-humanist values, a specific working-class and work-related education has remained a largely theoretical entity, submerged within the optimism of general growth and liberalisation. One result is the failure to prepare for a right-wing sponsorship of segregated vocationalism.

> everyone on the left shares some responsibility for the long policy vacuum
> which dates back at least to the Great Debate in 1976 about preparing the
> working class for work. It was a sham that went unchallenged because few
> had really thought about work and its real relationship to education or
> training (Benn, *Interlink*, Summer, 1987).

The main argument of the following chapters is that technology is less a vehicle for modernisation than simply another attainment target. Over a long period of time it is cultural conflicts which have been the most fundamental source of critique in education, and this has often been in opposition to the technicist impulse. If the official line was a maximalist approach, working on the assumption that more educational inputs produce more economic outputs for the nation, the 'culturalists' sought to redefine human capital in minimalist terms: concentration on supposedly the most productive inputs. But opposition to expansion as demeaning of standards also entailed opposition to technical education, as these two elements are inextricably intertwined. Even if technology helps economic expansion, after the critique of public spending promoted by writers such as Bacon and Eltis (1978), it appeared far from clear to some what economic gains there could be from any extra inputs in education, technology-related or otherwise. The culturalist critique of expansion in education, now supported by a broad right-wing attack on the public sector, inevitably became a suppressed critique of the link between education and technology. The concern was standards in and for themselves, not standards in technological education - or indeed any other subject.

This is very clearly the case in much of the propaganda that paved the way for recent legislation. A simple count of the chapter headings in some of the *Black Papers* indicates how the path beaten out for recent change has little to do with technology or the functioning of the economy. In *Black Paper Two* (ignoring editorial and other miscellaneous articles), 11 articles are on comprehensive education and similar matters and five are on progressive methods (in primary education). One of the latter concerns maths, the only technical subject mentioned - and this takes just four out of a total of 160 pages. *Black Paper Three* contains nine articles attacking comprehensive education, three on issues to do with progressive methods and subject matter, and two on the importance of examinations. Of the three articles where subject matter is introduced, one is on reading, one on music, and one on chemistry. Out of a total of 126 pages in this issue a mere three relate to science or related subjects. Nowhere is technology mentioned - nowhere, either, national economic requirements. The much later *Black Paper 1977* is more clearly targeted on all elements of non-traditional education. Concern over maths, science and technology is slightly more apparent than in some of the earlier papers, though all subject interests are fully bound up with propaganda against comprehensive and progressive education. While the editors of *Black Paper 1977* claimed that we cannot 'remain as we are with a monolithic, failing comprehensive system, if we are to preserve scholarship and survive as an economic community' (p61), nowhere appears a specific concern with education related to technology or to economic performance. Two out of 23 articles are in principle about technical subjects, but the themes are still segregation, discipline etc rather than the value of the subject matter itself.

The *Black Papers* represented a wide range of right-wing opinion and their general ethos continued directly into the media publicity accorded education over a number of years, for instance in respect of the decline of standards, left-wing indoctrination, or bureaucratic control. ERA deliberately rode on the waves created by this propaganda, and most of the measures brought into effect by ERA derive quite precisely from the demands of the *Black Papers*. Indeed, some of their contributors, or like minds, continued to wield influence through and beyond the gestation of ERA. Rhodes Boyson had already been Education Minister. Quite late in the day people like Baroness Cox were successful in persuading the government to incorporate the requirement of predominantly Christian worship in collective assemblies. Brian Cox and John Marenbon became influential figures in the English curriculum.

Sometimes the above and related sources expressed downright opposition to technology. Shrugging off computers as part of a 'visual and electronic cult', in which there is the danger that 'computer terminals and teaching machines would turn the teacher into a mechanic-cum-counsellor', Boyson (1975) argues not just for a return to the basics but for a rejection of the modern.

> In school 'chalk and talk' are still the most effective visual and aural aids, and the more equipment that is put into a classroom the more they are downgraded... No, the cult of the visual aid is dead and the most deprived children are often those in schools with most equipment (pp131-33).

Of course, few parents of children being sent to private schools would agree, as spending a large chunk of your income on 'chalk and talk' would appear a pretty raw deal. But for Boyson, education appears to be a matter of discipline and little more. Human capital is merely 'part of the romantic idea which saw all children as naturally good and eager to learn'. Standards are cultural, not technical. 'The worship of the mechanical, which has itself produced some of our problems in the revolt of youth...' (p133), can be resisted only through 'a return to the Arnoldian concept of a tradition of literature, art and ideas, which it is the responsibility of the cultured to maintain' (p139). Science is deemed to be in part an obstacle to the defence of our cultural heritage. Thus Jacques Barzun, a *Black Paper* contributor, blames the decline of what he sees as basic reading skills not only on new methods but on 'the emotion of scientism, which for seventy-five years has preferred numbers to words, doing to thinking, and experiment to tradition' (*Black Paper 3*, p75). The obsession with facts rather than experience is related to this. In the words (from a personal interview) of a contributor to the educational publications of the right-wing 'think tank' the Centre for Policy Studies (set up by Keith Joseph and Margaret Thatcher), an organisation which campaigned hard over education during the development of the 1988 Act: 'We can only get to understand things by knowing them. They will never understand if they don't have the *knowledge* to understand things. We make the mistake that understanding is important'. Computers get in the way of knowledge, because they are (a very expensive) intermediary between fact and action. The supposed superiority of German children on various tests is because 'they are not expected to understand but to do them'. Chalk and talk, not computers, continue to hold favour.

Britain is by no means unique in this traditionalist backlash. In France, through a propagandist book called *Schools for Barbarians*, Stal and Thom (1988) speak of 'technological culture' with contempt, which has helped make France's education system 'an unprecedented disaster' (p84). Talking about the then education minister, they say that;

> For M. Chevènement... the struggle between the forces of light and darkness has never ended. The fight for reason is more important than ever. The minister laments that 'in France the number of fortune-tellers exceeds the number of psychologists!'... M.Chevènement, so indignant about fortune-tellers, should have remembered that Madame Soleil had recourse to computers before anyone thought of putting them into schools (pp 39/42).

Whether this has led to a decline in the quality of fortune-telling is not stated.

Expansion in Germany has also produced a right-wing backlash. In 1978, a forum of conservative educationalists and politicians called 'Courage to Educate', in a rather dry sort of '*Schwarzes Papier*' listed nine theses for reform, the third of which, given the context, sounds slightly chilling. 'We oppose the mistaken idea that the virtues of diligence, discipline and order have become educationally obsolete because they have turned out to be open to misuse. The truth is that these virtues are needed whatever the political system' (Fuhr, 1989, p227).

This does not mean there have not been powerful pressures to make education engage more directly with the world of science. The issue has indeed been alive throughout official reports over many decades. At the time the *Black Papers* were about to campaign against technology and in favour of the basics and 'facts', the Dainton report was investigating an apparent trend away from science and technology with the complaint that when a subject's 'essential qualities are shrouded in heavily factual content' then 'enthusiasm will surely be quenched' (DES, 1968, p78). Official reports have also espoused technology-through-education as a means of releasing a pool of talent. Practical education will utilise the talents of the less academically able and thereby release talent which has hitherto been suppressed. The Newsom Report expressed this very clearly in its 'economic argument for investment in our pupils'.

> Briefly, it is that the future pattern of employment in this country will require a much larger pool of talent than is at present available; and that at least a substantial proportion of the 'average' and 'below average' pupils are sufficiently educable to supply that additional talent (DES, 1963).

The problem with this very reasonable paradigm is that 30 years on, despite continued talk about the less academically able or inclined, belief that modernisation requires a much higher general level of skills than would be apparent in simple practical tasks makes such solutions seem doubtful. The response in this country is acute ambivalence between an attempt to raise the profile of the whole normal curve through the establishment of the national curriculum (a fairly absurd quest), and a sharper specialisation of ability and aptitude which would not merely give the less able something practical to do but would ensure they did it somewhere else.

Better Schools (DES, 1985), produced under Sir Keith Joseph and one of the Conservative government's more significant documents on education, was the first major document to reveal these sorts of tensions. Arguing that 'more emphasis needs to be given to science and technology; to practical application of knowledge and to practical skills' (para. 76), it placed education directly in relation to perceived national requirements. At the same time it also clearly rejected the 'back to the basics' movement.

> The mistaken belief, once widely held, that a concentration on basic skills is by itself enough to improve achievement in literacy and numeracy has left its mark: many children are still given too little opportunity for work in the scientific, practical and aesthetic areas of the curriculum which increases not only their understanding within these areas but also their literacy and numeracy. In a majority of schools over-concentration on the practice of basic skills in literacy and numeracy unrelated to a context in which they are needed means that those skills are insufficiently extended and applied (para 18).

The concern with the technological gap is apparent in one official report after another, whether under Labour or Conservative governments.

Nevertheless, there are important disjunctions that cut across this continuity. For Newsom, as already indicated, technological input could be increased through production of 'a much larger pool of talent'. For Joseph, however, it would be not so much increased as enhanced, and then not through pulling more people through the system but through the encouragement of good schools: quality not quantity, exclusive not inclusive structures. Certainly resources have gone into technology (TVEI), but the main perceived mechanism for improvement is promotion of the good school. 'If the standards achieved in these schools could be achieved at all the schools in similar circumstances, the quality of school education would rise dramatically' (para. 10). It is standards which count, not content, though this view of standards, and of change through education, is strangely alchemic: 'It is the government's longer-term aim to raise pupil performance at all levels of ability so as to bring 80-90 per cent of all 16 year old pupils at least to the level of attainment now expected and achieved by pupils of average ability in individual subjects' (para. 80). The result is a set of objectives as meaningless as Russian five-year plans. Why make only 80-90% of at least average ability? But this pseudo-modernism aside, the means by which the less able will become average, however oddly defined, is the creation of a model 'good' school. The new testing programme will simply reinforce age-old cultural signifiers, and it is this traditionalism which is the central theme of both *Better Schools* and ERA.

But, to repeat, in some respects *Better Schools* is a truly modern document espousing new content and condemning old techniques. In its own way it equates curricular restriction and direction with *limitation* of human capital - on both an individual and a national basis. The national curriculum may from this viewpoint be seen as potentially detrimental to modernisation, restricting rather than extending skills. After his departure from the DES, Sir Keith Joseph became a major opponent of the national curriculum. In the words of Stuart Sexton, who had been Keith Joseph's adviser:

> I am very unhappy with a legislative curriculum. Independent schools follow a uniform curriculum but this is determined by the market. Parents expect English grammar, parents expect maths and science. You've got the influence of the market on the independent schools in effect to create a national curriculum.... What worries me is that by setting up the national curriculum by law it would fossilise the curriculum as of this year. (Personal interview)

There is nothing new to these conflicts between modernist and culturalist trends. Even at the birth of the greatest modernist expansion in education this century, the 1944 Act, when release of human capital through expansion and improvement was universally accepted as necessary not just to economic performance but to equity, culturalist concerns were often at the forefront of discussion. This was literally the case with the main Commons debate on the legislation, dominated by religious controversy. 'To us the whole object of education is to love and serve God in this world so as to live with Him in eternal happiness in the next. So religion must permeate the whole of our curriculum' (MP Evans). A fear of professional neutrality is already apparent, teachers, *in loco parentis,* being seen by some as unable to provide the real essentials of education. This fear has survived through to the 1988 Act, which inexcusably, if quixotically, requires that the religious syllabus must 'reflect the fact that the religious traditions in Great Britain are in the main Christian'.

Of the 28 speeches in the 1944 House of Commons debate (excluding the opening and closing speeches from the government), religion was the only theme in five, the main theme in eight, a subsidiary theme in another eight, while in only seven speeches did it fail to appear at all. The astonishingly intense religious rivalry in the debate derived from the problem of how the religious schools could fund the modernisation programme required by the Act. An agreement had been reached between the government and the Church of England on the proportion of the extra expense that the government would bear, but many schools would be faced with a choice between closure and passing over total control to the state. This bothered spokespeople for the Roman Catholics most of all, as their small number made much harder the critical mass required for survival. As one Catholic MP put it (Colonel Evans), why should Catholics be forced to accept a 'pooled Christianity'? The Catholics felt their best bet was to abolish the dual system of state/religious institutions (ie to get all schools fully state funded) but at the same time to abolish the prohibition on a religious curriculum within state schools.

> What we must not forget in this country at any time is that we must have a spiritual background for every objective of our national life. If the whole Christian principle for which we have fought in the tempestuous story of the past is to be disregarded, I say 'God help the future of this country, both from the social and economic point of view' (Sir Patrick Hannon).

The Church of England accepted a compromise but could not always draw back from wider cultural concerns. Excellence is a moral not a technical value. The claim that 'by far the most important work of the schools is done on the spiritual side' could be consonant with the need to expand technical education as part of 'an enormous struggle to get back our export trade'. But even this set of ideas might be linked to a fear that our education system is a 'kind of mass production' (Captain Cobb). Moral control was at the forefront of much of the debate: 'without the training of habits and the attempt to apply some of the shining principles of the New Testament to everyday life it is quite impossible to answer the yearning of the awakening child' (Lindsay). More simply, there were too many children who 'had never been taught to pray' (Professor Savory).

Several times this cultural and religious fear was expressed as direct opposition to scientific understanding. In the words of an advocate of the Church of England, 'the Free Churches know as well as we know that a materialistic outlook is widespread nowadays, and that there are many in the teaching profession, as elsewhere, who look to science as the new religion' (Brooke). Moreover, the fear of modernity was not always religious in origin. Thus one MP who, pre-echoing Mrs Thatcher's derisive comments on the meaning of 'anti-racist' maths, questioned the meaning of 'Roman Catholic biology', 'Plymouth Brethren physics' and 'Presbyterian chemistry', but could still doubt the benefits of scientific education.

> It was not until you got the popularisation of science on an enormous scale during the last years of the last century and the opening years of this century that you met with what I will call the new mentality, the dogmatic scientific materialism, which on a great many of us produced a very unpleasant impression (Colegate).

The above quotations suggest a pronounced paradox: consensus over the need to modernise the system of education combined with widespread fear of its impact. Of course, those who failed to speak might have had little interest in the religious controversy, but it is the latter, not any assessment or projection of the impact of the new developments on technical or economic change, which was the parliamentary midwife of the reform. The debate was not the first step in a new future but the last of an inglorious past, the capping of centuries of religious argument and struggle.

Jumping 40-odd years to the birth of the Education Reform Act, there is again a conspicuous lack of concern in parliamentary debate for issues to do with technology or economic performance (though religion and morality also have little say). The central part was given to the ideological issue of choice. In the 1944 debate choice was linked to religious schooling, while by 1988 it had become secularised. However, both versions are connected to notions of moral excellence and to distinctions between selective and mass provision. The following is a count of selected representative words made of all the speeches on school education in the 1988 debate, classified under certain themes.

Table 4.1:   Themes in the Commons debate on ERA (word count)

	Favouring ERA	Opposing ERA	Total
Parental/Local Choice	72	45	117
Governmental Power	16	97	113
Equality/Unity	9	95	104
General Standards	60	38	98
Rationalisation	37	37	72
Extra Resources	5	47	52
Supporting LEAs/Teachers	11	29	40
Technical Subjects/Needs	25	8	33
National/Economic Needs	26	6	32
Criticising LEAs/Teachers	25	5	30
Religion/Morality/Discipline	24	1	25
Low Achievers	5	-	6

Note: The analysis is not an account of individual speeches, the word-counts cutting across these. Where words and themes have more than one meaning, the one that seems dominant has been accepted, and correlates of words are grouped together, eg closures=rationalisation. Word counts can give a biassed weighting, as one word representing a theme might be mentioned several times in one sentence. But it seems reasonable to assume that repetition bears some relationship to motivation.

The major difference between supporters and opponents is apparent in the first four rows of the table. For the Tories the issues were choice and standards. For most opponents they were power and the distribution of educational opportunities. As can be seen in the final column, technical subjects got a mere 30 or so mentions, as did generalised statements concerning the UK's economic needs (including a number of comparisons with other countries). In only one speech out of 23 did technical subjects or skill shortages figure significantly (though they were also mentioned in connection with higher and further education). Both this issue, and Britain's comparative standing, were no more than superficial bit players. One speaker even went so far as to complain that the 'international perspective... has hardly been mentioned in today's debate'.

It could be argued, as in the case of the 1944 debate, that technology did not feature simply because it was uncontroversial, taken for granted. It then has to be asked if the same could be said about low achievement or special needs, which barely figured at all. And there are, of course, plenty of controversies about technical education: is the government doing enough, should there be separate technology schools, is vocationalism the way forward? Time and time again this was simply not the issue for MPs. The agenda was set by the government, and this was responded to in like terms by the opposition. The core of the debate was not progress through technology or some conception of modernisation but a bland and undefined notion of standards, treated totemically in the first instance, of course, by Mr Baker himself.

> we must give consumers of education a central part in decision making. That means freeing schools and colleges to deliver the standards that parents and employers want. It means encouraging the consumer to expect and demand that all educational bodies do the best job possible. In a word, it means choice.

There was still a flickering echo from the 1944 debate, predictably given vent by Rhodes Boyson.

> I believe that man's knowledge of his place in the universe and the purpose of his life is more important even than English and maths. These days we have more moral than political problems, and many political problems would go away if we could solve the moral problems.

Thus one of the most active proponents of recent 'modernisation' in education, an ex-Head and ex-Education Minister, appears to believe that 'in most cases a school will be better if it has religious unity and feeling'.

5 Culture and crisis

Education is often accused of two simultaneous, barely compatible, failings. It has failed to keep pace with technology, but has also lost track of its cultural moorings. Current educational developments, inspired mostly on the Right, seek to provide a solution to this contradiction. The Left has also felt this tension: consistent demands for increased spending is matched by cynicism towards education as a whole, especially its potential to ameliorate the class structure. Technology may in this approach be repressive (offering through vocationalism an inferior educational career for working-class children), while education in general may be culturally repressive (through the imposition of elite modes of learning). Such fears begin to make the Left seem old-fashioned. The Right, by contrast, begin to sound modern: the basics become the nuts and bolts of education; to progress in a technological world, education should can be simplified, streamlined, shorn of humanist burdens. The goal of equality is discarded and the goal of quality is set in its place. Where fear of modernity is expressed it is often not of its technological but of its social implications, various aspects of youth culture being good examples. Across a variety of political and social thought, therefore, modernisation poses a threat rather than salvation. This chapter is about such perceptions, and argues that much recent change in education, whatever its modernistic content, is based on a long-term and fundamental culturalist programme, the only clear result of which is highly extended control over all those who participate in education.

Culture and economy

On the Right, moral panic over education has been triggered not by economic decline, nor by crisis, but by growth. Working-class aspirations, associated with growth, have often been treated as a threat, for instance in Evelyn Waugh's 'keenest fear: that together affluence and universal education will fulfil the promise or rather the threat of democracy by removing the fact of difference which alone confers value' (quoted by Hebdidge, in Waites *et al*, 1982, p197) - a comment made in 1957, a good decade before widespread credence was given to the claim that education, far from promoting standards, erodes them. The problem with education is that it undermines leadership, or, more specifically, the ability to control the labour process.

Leadership is both an economic and a cultural concept. For instance, the thesis of Wiener's *English Culture and the Decline of the Industrial Spirit* (1985), that Britain's economic decline is the result of cultural decline, identifies a loss of 'industrial spirit', epitomised by the nanny state, as the source of current problems. The critique of Wiener and similar minds suggested something very wrong with education. Those reared to think themselves a superior class by nature have resisted change, avoided getting their hands dirty, and failed to bring the country forward in the race to modernise. Paradoxically, it is 'good' education that has done the damage.

> The public schools gradually relaxed their entrance barriers. Boys from commercial and industrial families, however, were admitted only if they disavowed their backgrounds and their class. However many businessmen's sons entered, few future businessmen emerged from these schools, and those who did were 'civilized'; that is, detached from the single-minded pursuit of production and profit (Wiener, 1986, p20).

This concern for the production of an industrial leadership is obviously different from the claim that the country as a whole is lacking in technical skills, and might indeed conform with a belief that the working class is over-educated, or at least 'too well trained (as opposed to too well educated), too disciplined and skilled to encourage their employers to abandon handicraft techniques' (Payne, in Collins and Robbins, 1990, p45). So the middle class has been squeezed between the aristocratic organisation of elite education and working-class organisation. This tension continues in attempts to meet 'skill shortages' at the same time as protecting the elite nature of education.

While the writings of Wiener (1985) and Barnett (1986) have been influential, their intellectual weaknesses are apparent, in particular as the precise mechanism of the cultural-economic link cannot be established. Even on its own terms Wiener's thesis is weak. Public-school education has not been backward in modernising its curriculum or in producing future managers of industry. Indeed, as Rubinstein (in Collins and Robbins) points out, sociologists have for some time pointed to an elite within the upper class which is increasingly united across industry, finance, and the civil service, and which derives in significant measure from the public school system and Oxbridge (Urry and Wakeford, 1973; Stanworth and Giddens, 1974).

The culture of modernity

The right-wing concern for leadership is one aspect of an intended cultural revision which seeks to establish a new form of modernity, and this conservative modernism invokes a deep, basically humanist antipathy. It is indeed unhelpful to view the reactionary forces behind change in education as merely old-fashioned. It is true that Dickens' famous

87

opening lines to *Hard Times* have often been quoted as a critique of the backward-looking dependence in ERA on facts rather than on understanding.

> Now, what I want is, Facts. Teach these boys and girls nothing but Facts. Facts alone are wanted in life. Plant nothing else, and root out everything else. You can only form the minds of reasoning animals upon Facts: nothing else will ever be of any service to them.

Quoted as a parody of the *Black Papers*, of the call to return to the basics, of attainment targets, the suggestion is a return to the past - to a past just starting in Dickens' time. Yet his satire was a romantic defence against industrialisation, against modernisation, against quantification. For Dickens, 'Facts' (beautifully reified with the capital letter) stand for Coketown - a symbol of greed, of the hypocrisy of the self-made man, but also of modernisation. Coketown is

> where the piston of the steam-engine worked monotonously up and down, like the head of an elephant in a state of melancholy madness. It contained several large streets all very like one another, and many small streets still more like one another, inhabited by people equally like one another, who all went in and out at the same hours, with the same sound upon the same pavements, to do the same work, and to whom every day was the same as yesterday and tomorrow, and every year the counterpart of the last and the next.

The regimented streets and people are an image of modernity, of a culture now quantifiable. The *Critical Quarterly*, sober parent journal of the *Black Papers*, could echo Dickens' dislike of quantification and, in so doing, claim to be following a long line of socialist humanism.

> In the second half of the twentieth century we face new challenges. There are the dangers of political enslavement, as forecast by Huxley and Orwell, and the danger of enslavement by machines. Steiner rightly emphasizes the growing influence of mathematics, and who knows what effect the development of computers may have on the future of human language? (*Critical Quarterly*, 10, 1/2, 1968, p7)

Nevertheless, the journal could sound more modern than some of its left-wing antecedents. Even if the facts of Coketown are also the basics of the *Black Papers*, when the *Critical Quarterly* started in 1958, one stated purpose was 'to *oppose* cultural pessimism.' It is important for good culture to become popular, even if popular culture can never become good. '*The Critical Quarterly* has attempted to assist such processes of education.... and prevent it from stagnating among groups of mutually unintelligible elites' (Cox and Dyson, 1968, pp5/6). Thus, at the same time as the *Black Papers* (established in 1969) were demanding a return to the past, the parent journal was arguing that: 'Advocates of the myth of decline have wanted to retain old habits and values, and have therefore reacted blindly and emotionally to modern developments' (Cox and Dyson, 1968, p3).

Modernity, meantime, may look to the past. There have been few more modernist credos than that of the famous architect, Le Corbusier. On the face of it, this modernity embraces all.

> We must create the mass production spirit.
> The spirit of constructing mass production houses.
> The spirit of living in mass-production houses.
> The spirit of conceiving mass production houses.

Le Corbusier's credo (1970, pp12/3) is archetypal. Yet his modernism contains an inherent conservatism: the very process of streamlining demands selection. Through continuous streamlining, refinement, weeding out - the very principles that supposedly define an elite - a perfect mass product is created. Le Corbusier, prophet of massness and modernity, becomes a traditionalist.

> Civilizations advance. They pass through the age of the peasant, the soldier and the priest and attain what is rightly called culture. Culture is the flowering of the effort to select. Selection means rejection, pruning, cleansing; the clear and naked emergence of the Essential (p128).

Whether talking about society or its artifacts Le Corbusier expresses a severe social rigidity. 'A standard is established on sure bases, not capriciously... The social contract which has evolved through the ages fixes standardized classes, functions and needs producing standardizing products' (Le Corbusier, 1970, p126). Adulating the selective, cleansing, basic, uncluttered - many aspects of this thinking resonate with current educational change. This is how Boyson spells out his programme of education reform.

> The necessary sanction is either a nationally enforced curriculum or parental choice or a combination of both.... It is not difficult to draw up a basic curriculum occupying some 60-80 per cent of teaching time in the infant, primary and secondary schools. All that would be necessary is the stipulation of standards in numeracy and basic literacy, geographical, historical and scientific knowledge to be attained at various ages by the average child. Achievement could then be monitored by nationally set and marked examinations.... (Boyson, 1975, p141).

Modernism streamlines, separates the chaff from the wheat. It therefore continues age-old lines of division. If the message of the *Black Papers* and similar campaigning pamphlets was primarily social and cultural rather than educational, the resultant demand to retrench, to delimit the objectives and scope of education, happened to resonate with a modernist imperative to reconstruct and streamline. The *Black Papers'* steely anti-humanism is peculiarly modern sounding, while humanism, and the progressive education this gave rise to, seems in this new world somewhat quaint and 'olde worlde'. Modernism - a harsh and stark simplicity, crushing those that get in its way - is very much in the forefront. As a corollary, while the Left may be concerned about class, colour, or gender - all these to the modern-thinking Right smack of a sort of tribalism. Reaction dressed in modern garb makes an extremely difficult target for the Left.

Streamlining and selection

Le Corbusier's vision may be seen as one of archetypal socialisation: public housing, health, schooling. Yet the aesthetic of standardisation, like any normative rule, establishes standards, which involve moral judgement. Standardisation and standards, while at one level meaning the same thing, are at another clear opposites. The same applies to equality and quality - concepts that can be made to sound the same (eg where they mean 'entitlement'). Attempts to reconcile these oppositions has helped to generate the myth of crisis, as, while conflation requires extending success to all, there are no means of achieving this. The crisis was, of course, of society, not merely of education. A brief look at some of the chapter headings in Boyson's book *The Crisis in Education* (1975) - *The Decline in General Culture and Personal Participation.... Retreat from Authority.... The Fashion for Change* - indicates clearly enough that education is only one aspect of a much broader cultural malaise. Such writing holds out little future for a society and culture in decline. Only a massive streamlining can ensure the quality required for regeneration. There is 'no moral justification for compulsory education without the state guaranteeing and enforcing minimum standards' (the editors, *Black Paper 1977*, p8). Boyson argued against increasing the compulsory school-leaving age to 16 '*whatever* the wishes of the pupil, the teacher, the parent and the neglected taxpayer' (1972, p.vii, my emphasis). So much for choice! So much also for skill shortages: 'there seems little sign that the great increase in graduate numbers has led to an increase in clear thinking, let alone an improvement in the quality of our national life' (Boyson, 1972, pps.vi-viii). If the *Black Paper* editors are prepared to educate 'the underprivileged clever child, avid to learn, able to learn' (p56), the less able are, in effect, to be disabled.

> To put it in its broadest terms, I suggest that we place a greater emphasis on action than on reflection and that such powers of reflection as these low academic achievers are capable of should spring out of such activity.... Work with subnormal children has already shown the benefits to be gained from this sort of emphasis; and the world of the mongol can be regarded as an intensified form of the world of intellectual dullness to which many of the reluctant learners of our schools belong (Bantock, in *Black Paper 1977*, p80).

The goal of restricting educational access has brought women within its remit, the apple of knowledge apparently remaining a gendered threat. 'Parenting is a sacrificial profession, time-taking and uneconomic... Alas, education is turning out young women unable to bear or even carry their children once they are out of the womb' (Eickhoff, in Boyson, 1972, p41). Daddy, by contrast, 'extends the horizons of his child, not only by carrying him shoulder high, but by being less in the picture than mother, being therefore the special bit of the parent complex, the thrill of emphasis, the treat, who can do things impossible for the mother to perform' (pp36/7). For such writers the aim is not so much an educational as a social reconstruction. If only young women would not work, if only fathers always had jobs (in order to come home as a 'treat'), if only parents did not physically abuse their children, if only people would not become single parents, if only children never had step-parents to contend with, and so on. How plangent but depressing is Eikhoff's appeal for 'homes that run like clockwork.... providing regulated monotony' (pp38/9). Coketown enters the nursery, where efficiency may demand that women play their naturally allotted roles. Such writing echoes the Victorian Brave New World with some precision. In the words of a nineteenth-century doctor, competition with men in education could only sap the 'vital forces and energy' of women to such an extent 'as to leave a remainder quite inadequate for maternity.... That one truism says it all - women are made to be, not men, but mothers of men' (quoted by Purvis, in Purvis and Hales, 1983, pp156-59). Boyson himself expressed these themes more overtly. Nursery schools 'are not only expensive, but downgrade the mother for the professional teacher and will be largely if not totally ineffective like most attempts at reverse discrimination' (Boyson, 1975, p105). The objective is not to cut costs, for Boyson also demands 'that mothers should be paid to stay at home with their children' (p105). As it turns out, efficiency demands the reverse, and the government is anxious to encourage work-place nurseries so that women can stem an anticipated labour shortage caused by the end of the baby boom - though it may not be unreasonable to suggest that if an earlier generation of women had stayed at home having more babies this problem would not have occurred in the first place.

In the USA during the 'permissive' era groups such as MOMS (Mothers for Moral Stability) were established to oppose sex education, despite widespread parental approval of the concept. The John Birch Society's *Bulletin* asserted in January 1969 that 'this whole scheme is, from beginning to end, in execution and in purpose, simply a part of the overall Communist design' to 'destroy one whole generation of American youth'. Yet in reality much sex education was probably family education in disguise. 'It's all part of my Family Life Program. In the senior grades, there's always been a Marriage Preparation course. Before I arrived, they used to talk about weddings and such' (a teacher in one of the most controversial districts, quoted in *Look*, 9.9.69).

Scruton, writing in more refined circles, after an attempt to prove that education is an 'autonomous' institution (ie people seek education for its own sake; so that the state, for instance, does not have to concern itself with production or with economic efficiency), goes on to argue that this means education is wasted on some.

> For what opportunity does an intelligent child have to partake of the
> advantages conferred by an institution which demands intelligence? His case
> is no different from that of a plain girl competing with a pretty girl for a
> position as a model (1980, p157).

It may be of note that Scruton chooses to compare education to the ephemeral tides of fashion. Is it worth no more? But even on the grounds of fashion Scruton is wrong.

> It is even more difficult if the girl is pretty... So many attractive features
> just melt in front of a lens. And others, who seem downright plain,
> suddenly blossom in the developing tank (Jean Shrimpton's agent, quoted
> in Shrimpton, 1964, p19).

Scruton is also apparently unaware of rapid change in the definition of attractiveness, or plainness, in the world of fashion. 'The flat look is very important, but the face has changed in the last year or two. It is now a little rounder, a little more individual or different, with a slightly fuller mouth. Not the old classical high cheekbone look' (ex-model, quoted in Shrimpton, pp19/20).

Scruton's alternative equation of *real* education with 'language, custom, tradition, fellowship' (p155) has by contrast a decidedly elitist ring to it. Culture is refined and must be distributed parsimoniously. If in different terms from those of Wiener, whose vision is perhaps closer to Boyson's hardy nineteenth-century individualism, education is still about leadership. The threat to this is not modernity or technology but the egalitarianism associated with these. If 'revolutionary Puritanism' seeks to go back to a more equal life, it does so, 'howling from the echo-chamber of a technological society' (Wain, 1972, p15). The critique of the crisis-mongers is not necessarily traditionalist. It resonates strikingly with a modernist credo of refinement, selection, streamlining (though its adoption of modernist tenets is itself selective).

Cultural decline and modernity

The fear of modern technology is by no means inherently conservative. It has strong liberal and humanist origins.

> It really *is* a new civilisation. I have been born at the end of the age of peace and can't expect to feel anything but despair. Science, instead of freeing man - the Greeks nearly freed him by right thinking - is enslaving him to machines.... God what a prospect! (E.M.Forster, diary entry 1908, quoted in introduction by Stallybrass to *Howards End*, 1973).

Significantly, technology is not the sole source of disturbance in the early decades of the century. For others it is a sense of massness, of cheapened access, of threat to cultural standards. Whatever conveniences modernity brings, cultural shallowness comes with it. Education is part and parcel of this. If technology brought the depredations of the penny press, education brought its readership. One decade, the 1890s, 'saw the introduction of compulsory elementary education and the launching of the *Daily Mail*' (Mulhern, 1979, p55).

What is there in modernisation which causes the trouble? Is it technology, rate of change, mass participation, or what? The steam engine considered by Forster as a symbol of all that is bad about modernity, carving up the countryside, is now a symbol of an idyllic rural past - white puffs of smoke embroidering green hills and blue skies. The real source of the problem is mass demand for increased access to the benefits of education. The critical contradiction brought to the fore by mass culture, therefore, is an impasse between access and standards. This was, for instance, the argument of Daniel Bell's influential book, *The Cultural Contradictions of Capitalism* (1976), in which education and culture are different aspects of overproduction, and both lower social standards. Within education the response to the development of mass access was the preservation of standards at largely unobtainable levels. Perhaps the most important publicist of this approach in the early part of the century was F.R. Leavis. It is indeed of note that for Leavis the use of exams to exclude talent was itself an aspect of modernity that had to be rejected. Examination get in the way of understanding and therefore lower real standards. For Leavis, educational thought was 'marked by strong tendencies towards standardisation and abstraction whose origins lay in the economic and political system, and whose effects were culturally destructive' (Mulhern, 1979, p103); and *Scrutiny*, Leavis' journal, promoted the slogan 'standards in criticism, revolution in education'.

Leavis' critique led to two wholly divergent cultural paths, which have for the last few decades been the prime source of cleavage in education. On the Left, his concept of critique and his contempt for authority influenced people like Raymond Williams, who helped develop cultural studies as a source of social and (in later writers) ideological critique. On the Right, however, Leavis' concern for separating the wheat from the chaff influenced journals such as the *Critical Quarterly*. The early response was a top-down cultural imperialism, exemplified by the first Director-General of the BBC.

> **Malcolm Muggeridge:** The interesting point in terms of social history is that this particular accent which the BBC produced somehow identified the BBC with a certain section of society, certain social trends, so that to this day the BBC is thought of as the organ of the, as it were, genteel and respectable elements in society.
> **Lord Reith:** Anything wrong with that?
> (Lord Reith in interview on a BBC programme, *Lord Reith Looks Back*, reproduced in the Campaign for Broadcasting and Press Freedom video *It Ain't Half Racist Mum.*)

Reith's mission as director of the BBC in its formative period was to use broadcasting as an *educational* tool - not in the classroom but in the home. Educational, cultural, and missionary - the BBC could be all three, and indeed the three were hardly separable. Since then, of course, the BBC has had to face up to the onslaught of commercial broadcasting, and Reith's elitist campaign was replaced by the pseudo-populism of the likes of Mrs Whitehouse, speaking up for the vulnerable masses. Here too appears a straight equation between television and education, by now without hope.

> For all television is educational. It may teach self interest rather than philanthropy, violence rather than gentleness, a disregard for human dignity rather than a respect for it. It may not always teach the truth but teach it does (quoted in Tracy and Morrison, 1979, p76).

For Mrs Whitehouse broadcasting is a threat: in infiltrating the home environment it breaches the 'Englishman's castle', the sanctity of the home. The last bastion of morality, the family, is vulnerable to intrusion, whether broadcast from outside or inculcated in the classroom. Education does not differ from mass culture in its degree of threat, but at least you can switch the television off.

The Left: celebration or critique?

The despair over mass culture might have affected the Right, and an old school of humanists such as Leavis, but the Left too has often been ambivalent, even negative, particularly, of course, in the case of writers associated with the Frankfurt School.

> The less the culture industry has to promise, the less it can offer a meaningful explanation of life, and the emptier is the ideology it disseminates... Its very vagueness, its almost scientific aversion from committing itself to anything which cannot be verified, acts as an instrument of domination (Adorno and Horkheimer, in Curran et al, 1977, p369/373).

The fear that pop culture would lead to decline of working-class resistance and culture is well known, in particular in the prediction of 'one-dimensional man' (Marcuse, 1964). In places Marcuse, despairing the 'invasion of the private household by the togetherness of public opinion; opening of the bedroom to the media of mass communication' (1964, p29), sounds like Mrs Whitehouse. Broadly left-liberal writings also promoted the above fears - the theme of Vance Packard's well-known book on the threat of modern advertising, *The Hidden Persuaders*. If 'many of the nation's leading public-relations experts have been indoctrinating themselves in the lore of psychiatry and the social sciences in order to increase their skill at "engineering" our consent to their propositions' (1957/1981, pp11/12), the role of both culture and education in modern society is questionable - though Packard hoped that education would provide a counterfoil to the detrimental influence of the media. People need educating to resist the lowering of political and social standards that derive from mass culture.

The above quotations are obviously selective, at best indicating the survival over time, and across perhaps the entire political spectrum, of a wide range of fears in the face of modernisation. Enlighted, humanist ideals have, no doubt, predominated, perhaps offering a source of defence against the crisis-mongers. If the 'conservative is afflicted with nostalgia for an age when England had an empire and when life - for the few at any rate - was more gracious' and the 'progressive is disillusioned because he has realized that political panaceas seem prosaic if they are practicable enough to be implemented, and throw up yet another set of problems' (Peters, 1970, p319), liberal humanism still has most of the answers. Yet even here doubts recur. Peters proposes a well-known educational programme built on humanist principles - almost training for democracy, but now it is materialism that gets in the way. 'The teacher, in other words, has identified himself with the attitudes of a consumer-orientated society. The techniques of the supermarket have succeeded those of the prison' (p263).

The equation between education and culture occurs also on the opposite side of the social spectrum, and may indeed become conflation.

> 'I love you,' he said a little unsteadily. 'And now tell me, my darling, what you feel for me.' 'I love.....you! I love.....you!' Romara cried.... 'Aren't you going to answer me?' he asked....'I love you,' she whispered.

> If these exchanges seem more suggestive of the classroom than the bedroom, it may serve to remind us not only that in every case the experienced male is instructing the inarticulate female in the grammar of domesticated rapture, but also that Cartland's texts assume, for their readers, an important educational function. The climactic enunciation of the marital sentence is only the culminating lesson - a literal 'matriculation' - in an extensive and purposeful sentimental education whose nodal emphasis is not sex but motherhood and domesticity (CCCS, 1980, p259).

While this is patently overdriven - another example of 'the magical metaphor of cultural reproduction' (Wexler, 1987, pp100/1) - the implicit portrayal of 'the grammar of domesticated rapture' as part of the hidden curriculum makes total the equation between education and culture. The terms of the two fields intermarry. Cartland educates ideologically outside the school, while cultural ideologies are promoted within the school -

not through the use of writing like Cartland's, which education obviously rejects, but through simplifications just as stultifying.

The above suggests strong parallels between right and left-wing critiques of culture. By the 1960s, however, true divergence began. In part, and perhaps paradoxically, this trend also stems from Leavis. Even if the 'disaster that threatens to be final *is* imminent' (Leavis, in Singh, 1982, p185) - because of dependence on quantification rather than on understanding - Leavis was only partially sympathetic to more elitist conservatism, as represented for instance by Eliot's 'profound conviction of the utter abjectness and worthlessness of humanity' (p174). Leavis' humanism is positive. It is this optimism which was later taken up by the Left. Education might be under threat but it has a potentially important social role. 'And "fighting" is encouraging the life that grows, or might grow, in others, who are many - if not by the standards of the *quantitative* civilisation' (Leavis, in Singh, 1982, p185, my emphasis). Education must play a part in resisting cultural decline - including amongst other things the influence of standardisation.

The coterie around the Leavises included many on the Left for whom standardisation reflected not industrialisation (Leavis' target) but capitalism. The critique they developed, and which partly derived from Leavis, had considerable influence on the growth of (primarily) left-wing cultural studies, particularly through Raymond Williams and the CCCS. For Raymond Williams, as for Leavis, there 'are clear and obvious connections between the quality of a culture and the quality of its system of education' (1961, p145); education must reflect the full breadth and depth of social cultures, but must again always be based on critique. Much of Williams' work was an attempt to redefine the concept of quality, to make it more inclusive and expansive than obtainable through rigorous concern with academic standards. Williams' thought has been directly or indirectly central to some of the more important new lines of thought of the 1960s and beyond - the New Left, the 'new sociology of education'. In schools, children are taught to use the mass media and, for instance, to recognise the ideological in advertising. Williams' goal of a common culture was of course radically different from that of Leavis, a concern which was practical as well as cultural. For instance, English teaching should incorporate a range of communications needed in everyday life - not because, as in the past, the unacademic should learn only the practical, but in defence against the impact of an elitist pedagogy. Thus, learning to *write* (as opposed to read) official forms would be necessary 'not only because so many are unnecessarily difficult, but also because their ordinary social tone is as regularly a kind of licensed bullying as that of the commercial letter is a kind of non-committal crawling' (1962/1976, pp142/3).

To teach a common culture, neither high nor low, requires teaching both. It means teaching about all communications. Therefore 'we must be prepared to look at the bad work as well as the good' (1962, p147). Comics, ad's, and magazines should be studied not only so that 'once you know the good you can distinguish the bad', but because 'the world of ordinary communications... has crucial bearings on the whole social process which education is supposed to prepare us for' (p147). We should learn to criticise all aspects of culture, not to dismiss one sort and appreciate another. Celebration joins hands with critique.

Much of Williams' latent curriculum has now become manifest in the routines of everyday teaching: the media are plundered as resources, popular culture is a part of education, English teaching lays great stress on the ordinariness of everyday communication needs. Williams' message was translated into official language, for instance in Newsom. 'Here we should wish to add a strong claim for the study of film and television in their own right, as powerful forces in our culture and significant sources of language and ideas' (p155). For Bullock, 'one of the most powerful sources of vivid experience is the general output programmes of television, particularly documentaries and drama' (DES, 1975, p322.)

Nevertheless, there is a naivety to Williams' socialist humanism. He underestimates the corrosive reality of social divisions, almost wishing them away. A vestigial fear occurs therefore in his analysis of mass culture.

> Even in English, despite the efforts of many fine teachers, most children
> will leave even grammar schools without ever having practised the critical
> reading of newspapers, magazines, propaganda, and advertisements, which
> will form the bulk of their actual adult reading (Williams, 1961, p173).

And thus, too, in Newsom: 'We need to train children to look critically and discriminate between what is good and bad in what they see' (DES, 1963, p156).

There is nothing objectionable about this, and nor in Williams' account of a general, humanist curriculum, but who decides what aspect of common culture are good and bad, or, if you prefer, hegemonic and counter-hegemonic? Where does celebration end and criticism start? Perhaps, in attempting to 'forestall criticism from any flank, aesthetic Right or sociological Left' (Dunn, in Punter, 1986, p80), Williams wanted it both ways, appealing to both Beauty and the Beast - and in the end creating a hybrid.

In evangelising a modern 'common culture' Williams' avoided the trap of creating a mythical past. The work of the CCCS on culture and ideology, by contrast, was much more directly influenced by Hoggart's espousal of a specifically working-class culture - a type of thinking which has also had great impact on education in encouraging rejection of notions of working-class cultural inferiority. Hoggart, however, unlike Williams, was worried about the impact of mass culture on the cultural basis of working-class community. As Hebdidge puts it, he had 'common cause for concern' with people like Eliot and Leavis over cultural decline - 'the bland allure of post War affluence - television, high wages and consumerism' (Hebdidge, in Waites et al, 1982, pp198/9). This nostalgic contempt for mass culture could again make the 'Coketown Right' the prophets of modernism.

> it should certainly be clear today that these themes, where they are more
> than so much sedimented common sense, have lost whatever element of
> radicalism they ever possessed: their most energetic continuators today, at
> the level of public debate, are not the analysts of 'popular culture' and
> teachers of 'media studies' (who have re-worked their 'heritage' to a point
> where it is merely sentimental to speak of origins) or the liberal-humanist
> theorists of education (whose conceptions, long since irreversibly
> hybridized, are now falling into official disfavour) but the *Black Papers*, the
> leading intellectual agency of the meritocratic counter-culture (Mulhern,
> 1979, p330).

So, the Left begins to echo the exclusiveness of the Right. Williams might have sought a common basis for culture, but even this implied exclusiveness of a different sort, for instance suggesting a common *English* culture. His 'working his way towards a "new and substantial kind of socialism" draws precisely the same picture of the relationship between "race", national identity and citizenship as Powell' (Gilroy, 1987, p49).

Williams' optimism about technology and its potential to help break down elitist cultures and education, extending a range of knowledge and cultural forms throughout society, is subject to a further residual fear. If popularity overrides standards, it also standardises. Those who run our cultural institutions are 'interested not in the health and growth of the society, but in the quick profits that can be made from exploiting inexperience' (1961, p366). The masses that Williams speaks for are now merely inexperienced, while the technology which is their potential ally becomes a threat, because funded by capitalism. 'Shall we see, soon, a "British Chemicals General Election"?' (Williams, 1989, pp126/7). Crisis and revolution, the new language of the Right, are automatic responses. 'The matter is now urgent... We have reached a crisis... because it is by no means certain, in the short run, whether the new and constructive stage will be reached in time' (pp374/382).

Given this general background of wide-ranging cultural uncertainty around the 1960s it is hardly surprising that teachers too should have felt the need for a cultural bulwark. This is apparent in campaigns by commentators closely linked to or practising in education. The writer of a book called *The Uneducated English* could acknowledge that in 'a technically complex and rapidly changing society we need technically-minded, alert and adaptable people', and yet still despise the trappings of modernity, which produces a 'shallow and devitalized way of life which many teachers have regretfully noticed in their charges, and in the youngsters' parents as well' (Whiteley, 1969, p23-25). And television, with its 'hypnotic little screen which is taking over so many lives and sapping them of the initiative to do things and see things for themselves' (p23) is a part of the decline this suggests.

Reflecting precisely the same ambivalence, in 1960 the NUT held a conference 'to examine the impact of mass communications on present-day moral and cultural standards'. Here we have the NUT in pursuit of moral standards. The same Fred Jarvis who promoted the conference was later viewed by some as an agent of the decline he was opposing. In the publication which arose out of the conference, *Discrimination and Popular Culture,* edited by Thompson, a close collaborator of Leavis, the teacher is credited with a fundamental duty to promote English culture, and becomes a paragon (almost a parody) of virtue.

> Experts are needed in the sphere of 'cultural' health as much as they are for bodily health - to ensure that there is a range over which real choice can be exercised, that conformity of any kind is not imposed, and that our distinctive national culture is kept alive and accessible... Though not all teachers are willing and equipped to give their pupils lessons in discrimination, schools can still pursue one central purpose, and many of them do, supremely well. That is, to bring their pupils into as much contact as possible with the first-rate in art, literature, and music, all widely conceived (Thompson, 1964, pp18/20).

It is hardly surprising that this cultural manifesto goes on to speak of schools and teachers 'supplying the very best ... in ethics and in manners'. What is so remarkable about the NUT in this period of educational expansion is the way its concerns so closely pre-echo those of the Right in more recent years. Only very slowly did the sort of positive response to new media and new media content supported by Williams affect the teaching of English in schools. Williams was central to the development of the positive acceptance of mass culture as meaningful in its own right, even if this acceptance wavers uncomfortably between different foci: critique (mass culture as ideology), resistance (eg studies of youth sub-cultures), or celebration (support for working-class culture). But somehow or other mass culture always brings us back to crisis, as this is the only way that capitalist structures can be critiqued in an era of relative plenty.

> In the chronic instability of mature capitalist societies it can seem to offer a 'safe space', a reassuring refuge from the bewildering proliferation of institutions that seek to police the deepening crisis. This is the terrain of the popular media... (CCCS, 1980, p263).

The double act

Relative plenty is the source of the final paradigm of crisis and cultural loss, a paradigm represented in postmodernism. Here, the tensions over the significance of change in modern society reach a climax. How can we worry about skill shortages when we are undergoing a 'crisis of overaccumulation' (Harvey, 1990, p327), or, in Baudrillard's melodramatic prose, we live in an era of promiscuity, of 'superficial saturation, of incessant solicitation' (1990, p196). Culturally as well as politically, the Left have been undermined, as the 'struggles that were once exclusively waged in the arena of production have, as a consequence, now spilled outward to make of cultural production an arena of fierce social conflict' (Harvey, 1990, p63). The 'commodity fetishism' portrayed by the Frankfurt School as a threat to working-class consciousness now pervades all social communication.

Postmodernism is naturally contrasted with modernism, eg that of Le Corbusier, in which appears an optimistic belief in the power of change. I have argued above that this optimism about the future was in fact highly constrained by the social implications of change. Postmodernism, by contrast, takes the constraints for granted. 'The development of techno-sciences has become a means of increasing disease, not of fighting it... We are in this techno-scientific world like Gulliver: sometimes too big, sometimes too small, never at the right scale' (Lyotard, in Appignanesi, 1989, p9). The problem is not the anomie produced by modern forms of mass production of goods (the Marxist concern), but a permanent disorientation caused by unremitting consumption of *information* - what Baudrillard calls an 'ecstasy of communication'. 'Here things rush headlong to the rhythm of technology, including "soft" and psychedelic technologies, which take us ever further from reality, all history, all destiny' (Baudrillard, 1990, p164). The result is 'endless free time... which surrounds us like a bleak terrain... seeing that instantaneous communication has miniaturised our exchanges into a succession of instants' (p195). Despite Baudrillard's apocalyptic language, the crisis is not very different from the tired culturalist doubts of earlier times. The only difference is that we can go no further. 'We are already beyond the end. Everything that was metaphor has already materialised, caved into reality' (p198).

Even critics of postmodernism seem to accept some of its foundations. In a 'postFordist' period when mass production is being replaced by flexible production systems, the one thing that is lost is certainty. The individual's control over his or her surroundings may paradoxically diminish. 'Time-space compression always exacts its toll on our capacity to grapple with the realities unfolding around us. Under stress, for example, it becomes harder and harder to react accurately to events' (Harvey, 1990, p306). The loss for some is one of community.

> What is shared, then, is no longer 'culture': a living body, the actual presence of a collectivity (all those things which once comprised the symbolic and metabolic function of a ceremony or feast); nor is it even knowledge in the strict sense, but that strange corpus of signs, references, school reminiscences and signals of intellectual fashion called 'mass culture', but which could be named the L.C.C (Lowest Common Culture) (Baudrillard, 1990, p68).

But the new common culture (very different from that of Williams), with its 'correct answers' and certificates, produces an oppressive educational standardisation. With his description of game shows as popularised exams, Baudrillard, flamboyantly, but very much in the tradition of Leavis, undermines the significance of examination. 'Fuelled by a mechanical process of question and answer, this L.C.C nonetheless has many affinities with school "culture"' (p68). It is, after all, not too difficult to imagine the national curriculum tests administered over the mass media (cheating aside). Perhaps this is the vision of the future - everyone nationally tested and graded for quality. 'With our society, it would be the entire masses mobilised in an endless game of double or nothing, where everyone would ensure or put at risk their own social destiny' (p69). For Baudrillard, the source of social malaise is the same as for many other commentators. How can we get to grips with standards in an era of rapid change and intensified relativism? More information means less knowledge, just as the cramming encouraged by the national curriculum will reduce understanding. 'Modern, "overloaded" individuals, desperately trying to maintain rootedness and integrity... ultimately are pushed to the point where there is little reason *not* to believe that all value-orientations are equally well-founded' (Ashley, in Turner, 1990, p100). For Jameson this is an era of cultural schizophrenia. Culture, becomes 'the fragmentation of time into a series of perpetual presents' (in Foster, 1985, p125).

> The schizophrenic, however, is not only 'no one' in the sense of having no personal identity; he or she also does nothing, since to have a project means to be able to commit oneself to a certain continuity over time....
>> Suddenly, as I was passing the school, I heard a German song; the children were having a singing lesson. I stopped to listen, and at that instant a strange feeling came over me... It seemed to me that I no longer recognized the school, it had become as large as a barracks; the singing children were prisoners, compelled to sing (Renee Sechehaye, *Autobiography of a Schizophrenic Girl*).
> (Jameson, in Foster, 1985, pp119/120)

Perhaps the disorientation suggested here through school song is also possible through the collapsing of the functions of creativity and control. In Japan, when selection tests were replaced with more subjective confidential reports (*naishinsho*), this merely extended the threat of credentialism into the more internal lives of students: 'Teacher: Let's sing a song that everyone likes. Students: Are our performances going to count on the *naishinsho*?' (quoted by Horio, 1988, p356).

For some left-wing commentators, postmodernism is not an inevitable end to critique. We still have to decide that popular forms of literature such as 'the du Mauriers and le Carres are, of course, tosh, and [that] their formulaic repetitions do qualify them for assembly-line status' (Dunn, in Punter, 1986, p86). For, Habermas, postmodernism is merely an extension of modernism and a concomitant accentuation of right-wing angst, the sufferer of which 'attributes all of the following - hedonism, the lack of social identification, the lack of obedience, narcissism, the withdrawal from status and achievement competition - to the domain of "culture"' (Habermas, in Foster, 1985, pp6/7). Rational critique is not only possible but necessary.

Postmodernism nevertheless has its left-wing adherents, though the arguments still seem unrealistic. McRobbie can see in postmodernism neither nihilism, nor superficial glitter, nor instantaneous commercialism. It offers protest.

> The reason why postmodernism appeals to a wider number of young people, and to what might be called the new generation of intellectuals (often black, female, or working class) is that they themselves are experiencing the enforced fragmentation of impermanent work, and low career opportunities. Far from being overwhelmed by media saturation, there is evidence to suggest that these social groups and minorities are putting it to work for them (in Appignanesi, 1989, p178).

Even if there is really anything new about 'impermanent work' or 'low career opportunities', it is possible that a massive extension of cultural outlets will enable the proliferation of oppositional voices. Images, not facts, become the carriers of change. 'Images push their way into the fabric of our social lives. They enter into how we look, what we earn, and they are still with us when we worry about bills, housing and bringing up children' (p172). Some of this interaction has effect because pop culture is not only immediately appealing, but contains the seeds of subversion. And much of this effect, McRobbie argues, is generated through education - within cultural studies in further education (but also implicitly in schools). The end result is politicisation, but also a renewed socialism, now re-interpreted as a cultural force. 'There *is* no going back... Dallas is destined to sit alongside images of black revolt' (p177).

But images can be negative (depending on your viewpoint); elsewhere McRobbie continues the age-old left-wing concern with ideology. If an adolescent magazine such as *Jackie* offers 'a kind of *false* sisterhood' (in Waites, 1982, p265) generally submissive to men, but creating an illusion of freedom, it is necessary 'for feminist teachers and youth leaders to involve girls in the task of "deconstructing" this seemingly "natural" ideology' (in Waites, 1982, p282). If Reith wanted to teach high culture, others want to teach 'ideologically correct' culture. But for how long can cultural studies maintain itself as the new academy, sorting out combative communication from kitsch? The welter of images will make this impossible. Education cannot serve as a means of channelling change. If the main postmodernist view is a pessimistic withdrawal from the attempt to turn mass culture and education into a site of struggle, leaving this to cultural contrast alone is not an answer to social inequality.

Probably the most thorough-going assessment of the implications of postmodernism for education comes in Wexler (1987). Wexler strongly criticises the earlier culturalist schools such as the new sociology of education, which focused heavily on school processes, for ignoring the historical formation of these processes. One element of this ahistoricism is the establishment by academics of an 'inauthentic identification with "the working class" or with the triadic oppressed groups of "race, class and gender"' (p181). Oppressed social groups must speak for themselves. 'Classifying and romanticizing cultural emanations as "resistances" was a diversion from asking what contemporary forms might replace the clubs, societies, and coffee-houses that once served as the public social places and occasions for education' (p182). Postmodernist reorganisation again offers the space for expression previously denied by state control. Wexler continues the language of crisis (declining profits etc) but notes that the responses - a mix of libertarianism and authoritarianism - cannot square the circle. All that has happened is that this 'historical internal contradiction - market commodity exchange and family religion-integration - is surfaced and reorganized in the current crisis' (p62). In education, further control is one response, but this generates further alienation. Through a 'commodification of education' (tests and performance indicators), increased privatisation, and greater school discipline, education is being reorganised, and with it the relationship of the individual to society.

However, while there is an historical trend towards control of the content of education, and of its production, there is a simultaneous tendency on the part of the subject towards elusiveness. 'Now, the text and the subject, I suggest, are moving in opposite directions: the text to closure; the subject to opening' (p117). The production of knowledge is increasingly questioned, resulting in a 'postmodernist' means of reception.

> we can begin to think about knowledge production as a series of editings and recodings... Social montage, and not representation, reflection or reproduction may be the more appropriate metaphor with which to pursue a social analysis of school knowledge (Wexler, 1987, p105).

The media, far from threatening education, now either liberate or replace it, as they offer one means whereby the subject can regain control. 'The mass communications/individual relation now already better exemplifies the educational relation than does the school..' (p174). Indeed, as in the technocratic critiques reviewed in Part One, if for very different reasons, education is accused of falling behind technological advance. 'Educators are imposing on youths a mode of social relations that is contradictory to forces of interactional technology through which they are doing their work, which is the identity work of becoming somebody' (p176).

Wexler's aspirations appear to update Illich's deschooling. Indeed, as there 'is a kind of de-schooling occurring - a de-schooling from the right' - he reappropriates this agenda. This bears some relationship to notions of 'popular education' (eg CCCS, 1980) but adds to this the liberalising impact of new technology. However, there is no evidence whatsoever that new technology is in any way liberating. What is the real impact of 'interactional technology' on the lives of all but the most *privileged*? It is not even clear if Wexler's account is supposed to describe actuality, the future, an aspiration, or a means of critiquing the past. Not only is the real space for action highly marginalised, but the mythic way this is achieved continues the glamorisation of oppression (he gives graffiti as an example) that Wexler seeks to criticise. The attention to 'textuality' continues the culturalist tendency to fail to attend to the realities of technological and economic oppression. Belief in society's ability to renegotiate identity through new technologies of expression may give the academic relief, but it leaves the bulk of society unaffected.

Postmodernism is hardly empirically grounded, and may at the theoretical level mean many very different things. However, the nature of the complaint echoes and reinforces cultural concerns which have preceded it, bringing things full circle. 'Since we are beginning something completely new, we have to re-set the hands of the clock to zero.' (Lyotard, in Appignanesi, 1989, p8). There is, indeed, nothing new about the postmodernist condition: it follows the faultline between democratic ideas of mass access and cultural concern over standards. But it seems unlikely that this double act, refracted in ERA through the attempt both to establish standards and yet, irrationally, to ensure that they benefit everyone, can succeed.

Conclusion

Whether fear of or ambivalence to mass culture is a response to technology (liberals like Forster, but also many current right-wing culturalists), standardisation (in their own different ways, Leavis and the Frankfurt School), commercialisation (Williams), ideology (cultural studies), or loss of meaning and reality (postmodernism), mass culture has continued in a wide body of opinion to pose a threat to social order or social justice. This threat encompasses education, often irreversibly sewn into the fabric of cultural commentary. The critical element of this concern is perhaps how to arrange the contradiction between demand for mass access and the notion of standards. The broad left-wing solution to this, not unreasonably, makes mass access itself a standard, but this is now intensely opposed by the Right. Nevertheless, the Left has helped make the cultural question a central plank in educational thought. 'In insisting that it was culture and politics that mattered... it was unable to stop its own drift into ideological positions that were weak in contest with the new-found strength of the neo-conservatives' (Harvey, 1990, p154).

Why the obsession with culture? Is it just a proxy for 'what to do with' the young? Educational standards easily become moral standards.

> A simple change in the law to make sure that any periods of truancy were automatically added on, at the end of compulsory schooling, would rapidly reduce the rate of truancy. Until the extra period had been completed young people would not be eligible for work, training schemes or unemployment benefit (Howarth, 1991, pp64/5).

It would also only take a simple change in the law to make truancy a criminal offence. Control and constraint - an attempt to tie the young more closely to their desks - are now central components of educational philosophy. In commenting on a book about youth culture, Dyson wrote in the *Critical Quarterly* that in 'place of high culture, we have pop-culture: and pop culture, the culture of youth, is colonising all the institutions - school, universities and churches where high culture should reign' (1970, p99). He then went on to warn, continuing the imagery of the 'bomb through the window' highlighted at the start of this book, that the 'next decade is bound to clarify the divisions between those loyal to the traditional culture and those opposed to it, and we may be in for something very like cultural civil war' (p103). But wars have to be willed.

6 Doing English or being English?

A contributor to BBC radio - a novelist and retired Oxford college principal - complains that education, in (supposedly) simplifying the teaching of English to make it more accessible, is educating people to speak in 'monosyllabic grunts'. Words have 'lost their meaning'. Actors, concerned to make Shakespeare's plays more approachable, do not know how to speak his language. Yet language evolves. People speak it with a massive range of articulation and skill, and always will. Meanwhile Shakespeare is performed to more and more audiences in a proliferating number of styles. Other lovers of English therefore have a very different view: for instance, the Rosens once asked why we should baffle children in enforcing artificial forms of writing. And what do adults expect to gain from 'putting writing in the same category as potty training, kiss grandma and grace before meals' (1973, p83)? Much later, in 1991, English teaching materials developed through the LINC project (discussed below), considered that a slogan saying 'you can't hand out condoms willy-nilly' is worthy of consideration in class. LINC's recommendations were rejected by the government. Is language a form of control or an entry into adulthood?

In the last chapter it was argued that the attack on education has a powerful culturally basis. The Right have insisted through legislation on basically Christian assemblies, on emphasis on the family in sex education, on propagating Britain's 'greatness' in history lessons, on re-establishing stricter norms in English teaching. Much of this programme perhaps works at the symbolic level only. Thus, there is really no need to emphasise Standard English as social pressure in favour of standardisation is massive. There is no need, indeed it is absurd in a modern society, to teach or preach any religion in school: let us finally admit that religion is a private affair. And certainly no-one should tell teachers which version of history to relate. Outside education, but not necessarily without influence on it, local authorities have been banned from supposedly 'promoting' homosexuality, and a committee has been established to oversee television programming in order to impose standards on sex and violence. Again, while these impositions may have some real effects, their impact is primarily symbolic.

However, counter-symbols are hard to come by. In liberal and left-wing quarters there has for long been concern that education should overcome cultural boundaries, yet the arguments have often been shrouded in ambivalence. If Bernstein's 'restricted code' exists, does it mean that working-class modes should be protected from middle-class superiority, or that working-class children must be taught to sound middle-class? The former has socialist potential but is also linked to the progressive notion that creativity rather than control is the basis for improvement at the individual level. This is especially so for the intellectually less able.

> Society despises and rejects these children, because it values intellectual capacity, and not essential creativeness of being. Thus despair, envy, and feelings of persecution in a million children are deeply reinforced, and damage their psychic capacities.... All children have remarkable creative capacities.... But in this creative expression there is no quantitative distinction to be made between achievements (Holbrook, 1964, pp40/1).

But the alternative, culminating in the 'entitlement curriculum', has also had powerful claims.

> It is very important that a sentimental attitude towards working-class language be avoided. Undoubtedly it possesses a certain dramatic vigour and colour which should be preserved. But it should also be recognized that such language forms are in some important respects limited in range and control.... in the near future routine manual jobs are going to disappear and jobs which will become available in industry or in bureaucratic, welfare or distribution spheres will require a much higher level of symbolic control (Lawton, 1968, p159).

Lawton's views can perhaps be seen as proposing a merging of cultural forms into a commonly shared, less hierarchical model; proponents of the 'basics', on the other hand, while they restrict the codes of everyone equally, establish major distinctions between failure and success. Similar sorts of argument between English as opening and closing cultural membership persist, even if the concepts have changed (eg multi-culturalism, anti-sexism, knowledge about language).

English and culture

The core educational concern of the Right has not been technology, or maths, or science, but English. Time after time it is an imputed decline in the knowledge of the national language which has triggered the alarm bells. Not English alone, but meaning, must be fixed. This is partly in response to a left-wing interest in language, the core message of which is that all linguistic substructures reveal 'if you like, a fragment of ideology' (Barthes, 1967, p91). Meaning can never be fixed. Each sign is an accretion of meanings from the past, or from other social contexts. If the 'Leviathan connotes the Devil' and 'the Biblical tradition of the Middle Ages considers the adventures of Jonah as a journey to Hell' (Eco, in Robey, 1973, p66), it is 'entirely irrelevant to know if whales really exist' for the image of the whale to be effective. English is about meaning, not facts. As Stibbs puts it, writing for the National Association for the Teaching of English, the sort of educational practice required by the Right does not turn the student into an expert in English, even an able user of English, but into 'a good proof-reader' (1979, p19). Constraint is inevitable. Take an example (from Stibbs) of an essay headed *Lost in the Fog* and ending as follows: '*The name of the street I was in was called Middlefield Ave., then I knew that I wasn't fer away from home, it was only tem minutes walk, so home I went. Expexting only the worst.*' The teacher who marked this allowed some leeway in grammatical construction but noted in the margins that the end of the essay was 'not a sentence'; though it may be far more effective than a real sentence would have been.

If right-wing pressure towards standardisation has been strongly resisted by both teachers and educationalists - report after report has dismissed or highly qualified the grammarians' pleas (Bullock, APU reports, but also reports stemming from the National Curriculum process itself - first Kingman, then even Cox) - breaches are nevertheless made in this resistance. The development of the English curriculum since the establishment of the 1988 Act is in part a history of the redrawing of the battle lines. Both the Kingman and the Cox reports, commissioned so that attainment targets could be established (as well as the programmes of study which would flesh these out), threw both salt and balm on the cultural sores that have been developing in and around English for the last two to three decades. While the result was compromise (particularly over the role of grammar), one avenue was definitely closed: the extension of English to include the notion of cultural differentiation.

Kingman clearly rejected 'old-fashioned grammar' as a 'rigid prescriptive code rather than a dynamic description of language in use' (DES, 1988, p3). He also accepted the recognition of standard English as one dialect amongst many, and argued that children should study 'the ways in which, historically and currently, groups settling in Britain have enriched English' (p30). But that this should lead to any cultural questioning was less acceptable. The traditionalists had their impact, bringing Kingman to write, with some poetic licence, that the 'rhythms of our daily speech and writing are haunted.... by the rhythms of Shakespeare, Blake, Edward Lear, Lewis Carrol, the Authorised Version of the Bible', though it is more sensible to view language as formed and embellished by the people who use it every day, not by poets.

When this positive, if highly arguable, claim was combined with expression of cultural panic, the only possible outcome had to be the demand for cultural unity.

> It is possible that a generation of children may grow up deprived of their entitlement - an introduction to the powerful and splendid history of the best that has been thought and said in our language. Too rigid a concern with what is 'relevant' to the lives of young people seems to us to pose the danger of impoverishing not only the young people, but the culture itself, which has to be revitalised by each generation (p11).

Any glance round the number of bookshops now in existence, and the rows of classics or other 'good' books within them, would instantly dispel such myths. The truth is that an increasingly wealthy and educated population consumes not just more popular culture, but also more culture which is less popular. In giving credence to notions of panic, control through English teaching becomes more acceptable.

The subsequent Cox Report, 'under pressure from the DES, redrew the Programmes of

Study to mirror more exactly the words of the Statements of Attainment' (Barrs, 1990, p15). Kingman was rejected for not giving the government what it wanted. Perhaps its programmes of study did not conform adequately with its (over) detailed attainment targets, but more realistically, as was generally accepted at the time, the government took fright at Kingman's unwillingness to fully endorse the foundation of the English curriculum on a rock-hard definition of Standard English. Remarkably, in some respects the line wavered even more under Cox, who went as far as to make a clear plea for multi-cultural education. 'A major assumption which we are making is that the curriculum for all pupils should include informed discussion of the multi-cultural nature of British society, whether or not the individual school is culturally mixed' (1988, 3.7) And in its second report it demanded that teachers 'should recognise the intimate links between dialect and identity and the damage to self-esteem and motivation which can be caused by indiscriminate "correction" of dialect forms' (1989, 15.15). However, this demand received literally no expression in either the attainment targets or the associated programmes of study. As Cox says, the demand is indeed 'a major assumption'. This contrast between rhetoric and reality cannot be over-emphasised. The entire multi-cultural work of the national curriculum in English was boiled down to one injunction (a fragment of the Programmes of Study laid down in support of the 'speaking and listening' attainment target): 'Pupils should be encouraged to respect their own language(s) or dialect(s) and those of others'. This is quite obviously not going to be the case. There will be a fundamental reversal of the 'growing appreciation of the value of building on, rather than downgrading, children's existing linguistic repertoires and sensitivity to language' (Edwards, 1983, p77).

Even the National Association for the Teaching of English (NATE), who had for many years been oppositional to tighter control over English teaching, sounded a note of support for the proposals, though it also warned teachers that they might be 'lulled into feeling that much of what they contain meshes with much of your own current practice' (1990, p1). Cox brought the expected hardening of the central importance of Standard English (SE). Certainly he refused to list specific rules of language in the attainment targets, and was prepared to argue that SE should not be confused with 'good' English, as 'speakers of Standard English can use English just as "badly" as anyone else; they can write unclear prose, use words ambiguously, and so on'. He even recognised that 'Standard English raises large issues of the relation between language and social or national identity'. Nevertheless, as 'Standard English is the variety used in the vast majority of printed and published English', it must form the basis at least of the written English curriculum.

Perhaps the reality of that prescription is of relatively little moment. The main problem is the simple *reification* of the concept of Standard English, now conceived as a distinct cultural mode which can be switched on and off at will. No longer part of the natural language, it becomes an artifice. Thus the attainment targets can require children to 'demonstrate the ability to use literary stylistic features and those which characterise an impersonal style, when appropriate, using Standard English (except in contexts where non-standard forms are needed for literary purpose)' (DES, March, 1990, p14). This is a strange view of language, suggesting the use of SE along the lines of a mathematical formula. The flow between forms of langauge are much less rigid than that. Moreover, it all seems so unnecessary. If SE really *is* a standard, acceptable because it is so widely accepted, why does it need further standardisation? Virtually all educational expression is already broadly based on some version of SE, which is far from needing support or protection. SE is and has been for long thoroughly imperialistic and needs no assistance.

Dialects have for many decades been 'under continual pressure from the combined forces of education, the mass media, residential mobility and the importance of standard English in personal advancement.... Dialect speakers are an endangered species' (Kellett, 1992, pp2/3). Conservation, not destruction, should be the national concern. This involves no middle-class romanticisation. But nor should any assumption be made that dialect will become a working-class preserve, and thus inhibit career chances when competing against those who have abandoned both dialect and accent. In British schools 'great efforts are made by teachers to eradicate features of local dialect from the speech and, more particularly, the writing of their pupils' (Hughes and Trudgill, 1979, p11). It is difficult to see why there should be only one way of either writing or speaking. Should children in Yorkshire be taught not to say *while* (eg someone will not be back *while* 5 o'clock) instead of *until*? Is 'very good' really better than 'desperate good' or 'right good'? Yet these aspects of northern dialect must be rejected by SE. Hughes and Trudgill (1979, p21) give the following examples of regionally acceptable forms of SE.

Southern England	*I want it washed/It needs washing*
Midlands and north England	*I want it washing/It needs washing*
Scotland	*I want it washed/It needs washed*

All are equally comprehensible but should we in the end only accept the Southern forms? It is often argued that a single standard is needed as a clear lingua franca. But how often does one actually hear things like 'Tek mi advice, if shi pass nuh mek she goh to the same school as Jeanie gal Donna' (Jamaican Creole), or 'tha mun seeuit thissen' (broad Yorkshire) or 'if ye promise someone somic, divvent gan back on your word' (Geordie)? (These examples are taken from commentaries arguing the case for acceptance of dialectical expression.) We are not entering a tower of Babel, let alone a Rastafarian Babylon, as such language is by and large restricted to informal occasions. SE, sponsored as technically necessary, becomes not merely a technical but a moral norm: 'school success or failure is explained in terms of actual linguistic differences between children rather than society's attitudes towards those differences' (Edwards, 1983, p13). How far must the colonialism of the State intrude into the nation's communal and private lives?

It is of note that Cox refused to lay down what precisely is meant by SE, this being left entirely to teachers. While it is necessary to be grateful for this, perhaps the true reason is that the committee took fright at the real implications of any attempt to codify the language in this way - the end result of which could only be huge and public argument about which aspect of grammar or syntax has precedence over another. Cox knew this could not be done. To have initiated such a programme would have exposed the ultimate irrationality of the concretisation of SE. It had never been done before. Brought to the brink of eternally transfixing the language, and thereby also eternally transfixing conflict and irresolution, those responsible stopped short of the detailed codification this would entail and merely said: 'use Standard English'.

Of course, the Cox of the Cox report is radically different from the Cox of the *Black Papers*. Many of the report's recommendations are both sensitive and practical. Yet in his retrospective view of the development English curriculum Cox (1991) again reaffirms his fear that education might 'confine the Cockney or the Scouse to their own dialects', as we should 'grant every child the opportunity to speak and write in a manner comprehensible to everyone else who speaks English from whatever part of the world' (p153) - though Cox stops short of recommending export of the national curriculum to other, less fortunate English-speaking countries. And is Cox really talking about dialect or accent? He says the former, but what makes Scouse at times incomprehensible to Southerners is precisely accent, not the few words or phrases not common to both. Yet under pressure from SE not even non-southern *accents* are considered acceptable. How often does one hear a BBC regional news reader using an accent noticeably associated with his or her region? If the BBC does not trust Scottish people to understand their *own* range of accents, the goal of the English curriculum may not be clear communication but, rather, an act of control.

In attempting to reconcile the humanism of the bulk of English teachers with the right-wing demand for control and prescription, both Kingman and Cox faced insuperable problems. No statement of children's 'entitlement' or 'needs' at particular ages, and it is sometimes amusing how the use of these entirely different words interchanges in the Kingman Report and elsewhere, can translate without massive loss into the regular testing of output required by ERA. Attainment targets for seven-year olds as vague as 'Read passages of simple sentences (aloud as well as silently) with understanding', or 'Listen with comprehension to spoken language', or Cox's targets for those undertaking level-five work (half way through the required ten levels) such as 'use language to convey information and ideas effectively in a straightforward situation', would not be fleshed out by the programmes of study but by the tests. The tests are the attainment targets. All the preceding work by the two committees was little more than a smokescreen for greater control over how people marshall and express their thoughts.

The process is well underway in Japan where the Ministry of Education rejected a textbook poem describing the sounds of a river because these sounds were not standard Japanese, possibly out of fear that children would think of language 'as something belonging *to them* rather than as something whose use is controlled by the State *for them*' (Horio, 1988, p174).

Politicisation of standards

As Cox reports on the Cox Report, not only was the Kingman report swept under the carpet because the Conservatives 'wanted a return to the traditional teaching of Latinate grammar' (Cox, 1991, p4), but considerable pressure was brought to bear to ensure that the report appeared in the image of its political masters. On the other hand, their apparently cack-handed response was encouraging. In Cox's opinion,

> neither Mr Baker nor Mrs Rumbold knew very much about the complex debate that has been going on at least since Rousseau about progressive education, and.... they did not realise that my Group would be strongly opposed to Mrs Thatcher's views about grammar and rote-learning. The politicians were amateurs (p6).

One committee member, the popular writer Roald Dahl appeared to reject some of the committee's main findings, but failed to attend committee meetings. This gave rise to concern that 'if he expressed his adverse opinions to journalists he would dominate the headlines, and the Report might be irretrievably damaged' (p6). Cox himself set in train a process that would end with Dahl's resignation. On the other hand, when Baker found the report insufficiently in favour of grammar he readily turned to the media (eg a *Mail on Sunday*'s headline: *English report fails the test*). Cox himself was not invited to the press conference at which the Report was presented to the media as Mr Baker 'was determined to control the presentation' (p8). While the secondary report was being redrafted by the National Curriculum Council, the word 'grammar' had 'been inserted seven times without any indication of what it implied' (p10). Baker disliked the Report. 'He had wanted a short Report, with strong emphasis on grammar, spelling and punctuation', as a result of which it was uncertain the report would be published in its entirety. In the end it was published more-or-less back-to-front. Even then one final alteration was required. 'Use standard English, where appropriate' was changed to 'Use Standard English (except in contexts where non-standard forms are needed for literary purposes...)' (p12).

The attempt by the Right to make the cultural definition of SE more concrete continued with the furore over the Language in the National Curriculum project. LINC was funded by the DES to the tune of £21m. Yet the DES refused to publish the report, accusing it of being both biassed and an inappropriate teaching tool. The authors of the report claimed it was in line with the national curriculum and supported the use of grammar, though as a means of insight into the structure of language rather than as a system of rules. Despite the ban, a LINC reader had already been published (Carter, 1990), and a considerable amount of material distributed to the teaching profession. While Carter argues that the new approach is close to both Kingman and Cox it really used fairly suppressed themes within these as the basis for their subversion. Such conflicts and reversals are no doubt fundamental to the future of the national curriculum. The LINC reader incorporates the theme of the project within the title: *Knowledge about Language*, often abbreviated to KAL. Richmond notes the rhyme of KAL with pal. 'Seems harmless enough', he further observes, deliberately ungrammatically, and therefore deliberately symbolic. If a child had written that opening sentence in an essay it would have had to have been marked down.

LINC was supposed to provide materials for teacher training, and from that locus into the classroom. It was to provide real flesh for the conceptual, skeletal structures in Kingman and Cox, in particular through improving teachers' knowledge *about* language. Cox had failed to give full support to this concept as he feared abuse. 'Many teachers were ill prepared to teach language, and so might present the subject in an unenthusiastic manner' (Cox, 1991, p10), ie purely as grammar. Cox hedges about the issue while LINC unequivocally interprets grammar as KAL.

The authors of the LINC material were absolutely right insofar as they stated that both Kingman and Cox argued that English teaching could improve through an understanding of language, amongst both teachers and students. But this is a platitude which could in practice mean anything. Its inclusion in the reports was intended to satisfy the reality of demand in the teaching profession, while its inexplicitness satisfied the government. When educationalists sought to give it real expression, conflict was predictable. The moving of 'language variation' towards the heart of the new curriculum was obviously hardly in line with the linguistic incarceration desired by the government. It is perhaps not surprising that the government should jib at the following.

> Being more explicitly informed about the sources of attitudes to language, about its uses and misuses, about how language is used to manipulate and incapacitate, can *empower* pupils to see through language to the ways in which messages are mediated and ideologies encoded (Carter, 1990, p4).

To contend that a theory of language runs from Bullock, through Kingman and Cox, and is 'now central to the National Curriculum for English' (p9) is wishful thinking. There is no doubt that LINC material subverted the national curriculum, and was rightly intended to. The following is from Peter Nightingale, LINC co-ordinator for North and West Yorkshire.

> *'So the reading of a poem by Wordsworth could raise questions about the...*
> *nature of Cumbrian place names and topographical terms...' [Cox 6.20].*
> Well, it could, but the young verse writers and readers here seem more
> interested in other, more central issues (*ThinkLinc No 6*: Autumn 1991).

Yet the LINC report, however challenging in this formal sense, in its substance revealed little of concern. One of the reasons given for the ban appeared to be that the report relied overmuch on 'fashionable secondary agendas'. It is apparent that the minister was not merely concerned to be behind the times: 'Why do so many examples taken from the media deal with controversial matters in a biased way?' Such a question, suggesting direct censorship, can only result from detailed political scrutiny of educational inputs, such as the following two examples from LINC materials.

> The woman walks on with her second-hand fur
> Second-hand because rabbits wore it before her

> Who starts the wars? Well someone does.
> Who fights the wars? In the future - us?

Should we be frightened of being warned by young people that 'World War III will be won by no-one!'?

The LINC 'Materials for Professional Development' (1991) were introduced with the warning that at 'the request of government ministers and of DES officials, LINC has agreed to state that these materials are for teacher training purposes only' (ie *not* to be used in the classroom). But they are far from radical. Examples of texts that teachers could use for reading guidance varied considerably, from Dickens to a TV car ad, but in all cases the teacher is expected not just to teach the text but to encourage children to examine the function of the text or image, why it was created, by whom and for whom, and to consider any ideological underpinning (in the sense of coherence of ideas): for instance, the Volkswagen ad where students might be expected to note that 'the car, like the mother, is smoothly dependable' (p98). Another text shown was a poem by Sir Thomas Wyatt, published in 1557, coupled with a re-write of this by Gavin Ewart published in 1982. The following are the first verses of both.

> THEY fle from me that sometyme did me seke
> With naked fote stalking in my chambre.
> I have seen theim gentill tame and meke
> That nowe are wyld and do not remembre
> That sometime they put theimself in daunger
> To take bred at my hand; and now they raunge
> Besely seking with a continuell chaunge.

At this moment in time
the chicks that went for me
in a big way
are opting out;
as of now, it's an all-change situation.

As the commentary points out, through its series of hackneyed expressions the re-write suggests moral decline. The deliberate sexism of the later poem contrasts with a much more tantalising imagery in the earlier: 'Is the "liberation" of his sexual partners a source of excitement to the speaker, or of dismay?' Both poems are about 'time, change, fashion, betrayal' (pp89/90), but suggesting in a way that nothing changes. What is in fact a postmodernist reconstruction, creates within a set of teaching materials a double-take that brings in fragments of language change and moral questioning. Stimulating maybe, but 'dangerous'? Such appeared to be the fear of government. While one reason for the ban on LINC was the government's insistence that English is merely a matter of a simple set of rules - Tim Eggar, the Education Minister, noting in his own *TES* article that 'the main task of teaching children is to write, spell and punctuate correctly' - this was underpinned by a fear that cultural innovation entails a loss of control. It becomes

dangerous that ungrammatical or badly presented work should be understood and condoned... Knowledge about the structure and working of our language is too important for us to take the risk of this message being enshrined in a formal publication that could be used outside the context of in-service teacher training (*TES*, 28.6.91).

This official message was given fuller effect in another opinion article on the opposite page of *TES* by Janet Daley. This adds a further dimension to the issue. Censorship and social control now merge with a cultural and class imperialism. Continuing a by now perhaps rather tired right-wing argument that raising standards creates more winners than losers, Daley goes as far at to state that 'offering a child no exit from his [perhaps girls require no exit?] "social and cultural context" is a criminal abnegation of educational responsibility. It is tantamount to burying his mental feet in concrete.'

It is odd that with English like this Daley should criticise one of the report's authors, Professor Carter, for apparent infelicities such as 'extensively trialled': 'does he always write like this?' Does she? It is certainly questionable that a punishing understanding of grammar should be important to people who can misuse the word 'criminal' so wilfully. Form not meaning has become the issue. Is to be working-class, or a Moslem, to be interpreted as stuck in a 'social and cultural context', or tantamount to being aided and abetted by crime?

In the case of language (whose armature is grammar) any tendency to reinforce the self-defeating and self-limiting shackles of inadequacy, is unforgivable. Properly spoken and written language is the lifeline which any conscientious schooling system can offer to every child, from whatever background. It is the only possible path to real social equality. To talk of a grammar appropriate to 'working-class culture' is nothing less than educational apartheid.

It so happens that the LINC material did not talk of a grammar appropriate to 'working-class culture' (John Haynes, *TES*, 12.7.91), but that it should appear to have done so to some observers is more telling. Class imperialism is masked as progress.

> Guilt-ridden middle-class sentimentality has become one more excuse for
> complacency about the class system... To teach people how to speak and
> write their language properly and well is to give them a ticket to freedom.
> Being 'tolerant' of their 'differences' is another way of writing them off.

Standards means standardisation, and around a class-specific banner. However naively hopeful LINC might have been that the national curriculum could be hijacked, the notion that language is in part about variety and flexibility of use, that it should appear to students to be fulfilling rather than repressive, is a project which decent teachers will continue to maintain despite the depredations of the national curriculum.

Defining Englishness

It was suggested in the previous chapter that cultural arguments played a profound part in the movement towards change in education. Yet actual changes such as the insistence on SE are introduced in the name of efficiency and the technical demands of a modern economy: individuals need SE to get on in their careers; the country needs SE if communication in the new Information Age is to be effective. While it is not unamusing that the National Association for the Teaching of English, in commenting on the official reports on the English Curriculum - the foundations of the teaching of English for some time - should denounce it as 'written in a style which is often impenetrable' (Bibby *et al*, 1990), it also has to be said that it is not *real* efficiency that is at stake. Indeed, as one contributor to an ALTARF publication has suggested, it is perhaps speakers of SE who need to be educated in reasonable forms of communication. 'Why should we have to put up with convoluted, archaic forms of English jargon in order to provide business for lawyers etc, and to perpetuate the mystique of such professions - and their fees?' (ALTARF, 1984).

So what are the real goals of the English curriculum? One ultimate aim (seen in English and history) is to define more precisely what it means *to be* English. It has to be said that even on the Right, however, the source of concern is by no means always the same. For some it is the state of literary, for others of grammatical knowledge. If the first is wholly cultural, the second is in many respects, and certainly in the terms in which the concern is expressed, quite technicist. And so the cultural/technical dichotomy discussed earlier on persists here too, though again there are areas of overlap. The first is the rejection of English as self-expression. The Right generally opposes the notion that children should learn by doing, through understanding what they do, through individual experimentation, or through the satisfaction of achievement. They must either follow a higher model (the literary approach) or obey rules (those of the grammarians). The second major area of common ground sees the codification of both language and literature as necessary either for economic survival (the technical function) or for cultural survival (the preservation of 'our' heritage).

The English curriculum ostensibly attempts to raise standards. But what does that mean? Standards standardise, and that is certainly one objective of any national curriculum. But a standard is also a flag, a patriotic symbol. If the emotionalism which surrounds the generation and regeneration of language mixes poorly with the demand to cut and dry the language, the symbiosis between the two extremes is apparent enough. Both have had their impact on the attempted struggle of the Right to redefine what it means to be English. Efficiency is on the surface the key concept.

> Moreover, such a teacher will not have scorned the old-fashioned exercise of 'learning by heart'. He [many teachers are female] will have realised that, by learning to remember distinguished passages of prose and verse, children not only develop their general capacity to memorize, but also lay down for themselves a valuable stock of literary examples, which they can come to know intimately and which will help to form their taste (Marenbon, 1987, p36).

English is the forbidden fruit in the secret garden of the curriculum, something to fear. Children must not learn to think for themselves, as originality is a threat: the teacher 'should be sceptical of originality in response to literature because it is most likely to betray a failure of understanding'. Examinations should not tap motivation, effort, understanding or insight - even at A-level, where literature questions should be 'simple, designed to test range and precision of reading' (p37), leaving no room, in Marenbon's words, for 'self-criticism, tolerance, maturity or liveliness of imagination' (p34). Coketown's repressive modernity has come to town. Thus, 'in English as surely as in Mathematics and Chemistry, there is right and wrong' (p34). All that is needed are ticks and crosses.

However, language cannot be isolated from its broader cultural framework. The pamphlet by Marenbon quoted above appeared through the right-wing 'think tank', the Centre for Policy Studies, under the title *English our English*. (Compare to David Allen's NATE publication *English, Whose English?*.) English appears to be a matter of possession. Placing unusual faith in 'politicians and committees', Marenbon offers them a prayer: 'May God grant them sharpness of mind and firmness of resolve, for in the future of its language there lies the future of a nation!' (Marenbon, 1987, p40). His prayer appeared to be answered when asked to chair the SEAC committee on the English curriculum, though his subsequent resignation as things began to go awry may suggest that divine intentions lay elsewhere, and not in any parochial equation between education, culture and nationhood. The equation makes Standard English both a linguistic and a moral code: 'the language of English culture at its highest levels as it has developed over the last centuries' (p22). It represents the best of British.

Marenbon's insistence on antique aspects of grammar and on Britain's literary heritage says something about what it means to be - or not to be - British (or more precisely, English). National boundaries are being redrawn. Yet, almost standing the demand for concentration on English on its head, Marenbon claims that 'without some knowledge of Latin an Englishman will always remain, to an extent, a stranger to his own culture' (p38) - an interesting plea for multi-cultural education, even if only dead cultures may qualify, and living cultures, that is of people who have no Roman heritage, are disqualified. Despite the dryness of a chauvinism built on Latin, this sort of fundamentalism is easily politicised, as, for instance, in the *Sun*:

WE NAME THIS SWIMPOOL MANGALISO SOBUKWE
LOONY town-hall lefties were blasted yesterday for secretly trying to rename local landmarks in honour of black terrorists.

The same paper continued its concern for local people in an editorial on the same theme.

How long before they pop down for a quick one at the Queen Vic and find themselves in the snug of the Colonel Gaddafi Arms?

Here we have poor, simple British people addressed by a cosy vernacular - *pop down, quick one, Queen Vic, snug* - under threat not just by a foreign language and culture, but one which hides a deeper menace. Queen Vic is, in the space of hardly any words at all, invoked as a symbol of past security and glory - almost Marian in conception, with wings spread out in protection, while the 'snug' represents not just that shelter, not just our own cosy way of life, but the closeness of a foreign embrace that is clearly a threat.

At the same time as the above, an article appeared in the *Daily Mail* (by Paul Johnson), in which this time mother-tongue teaching is the focus of derision. It is not that mother-tongue teaching may or may not work, it is simply wrong in principle. Johnson's target is people of Bangladeshi origin who can only succeed in Britain through full mastery of English. It would appear that this facility alone will give Bangladeshis 'the capacity to become a fully integrated and useful part of the British people. Indeed, in 20 years time a significant proportion of our entrepreneurial millionaires may come from this group.' Indeed, they might also win the pools, without a word of English, but we are here quite clearly no longer dealing with merely educational issues. It has to be said that the belief in such alchemic miracles need not have racist connotations.

It is a business commonplace that if you teach £20,000-a-year people to speak and write so they can communicate their ideas, you turn them into £30,000-a-year people. It will be fascinating if the national curriculum in English is seen to contribute to a similar miracle for the country as a whole (David Skilton, member of the Cox Committee, the *Guardian*, 18.7.89).

But the era of miracles is over, and reform should not be based on the expectation of one.

Education and its cultural boundaries have now been pushed to the forefront of the battle over racism. Admission into English culture is made to appear a technical issue, dependent solely on achieving the appropriate pass. Even in the hands of an ostensible sympathiser with Islam (Hiskett, undated), someone with significant experience of Arabic studies, for whom the achievement of Islamic education is 'immense', it is still evident that there is a 'lack of understanding of the cultural problems large-scale Muslim immigration poses' (p3). Moslems can never *really* be British. 'Islam is a total way of life that permits neither the individual nor society any leeway' (p4). It is not long before this reduction of a cultural model to an everyday fact is bloated with threat. 'Equally disturbing for many conservatively-minded British people is the more immediate prospect of UK-Muslim intervention in British foreign policy... already a force to be reckoned with' (p33). When Hiskett quotes one Islamic commentator as believing that 'Islam endeavours to expand in Britain... It hopes one day the whole of humanity will be one Moslem community' (p19), echoes of earlier fears about Judaism are pronounced. And just as Jews had to be segregated before and during the war, whether for extermination or for their own protection, Moslems should also be kept apart, as there are 'major obstacles to integration of Islam in western democracy' (p32). Cultural exclusion becomes an almost technical issue. Islam is in contradiction with modernity, in inherent conflict with western cultural and political norms. Moslems, even if they know little about Islam, have 10 GCSEs, wear jeans, and speak with Yorkshire or cockney accents, can never really be British. Islam does not only, therefore, get in the way of individual progress (girls, constrained by the prohibition on exposure of the body, cannot learn to swim) but of modernisation itself. This does not mean that Hiskett proposes Moslems be allowed to avoid the national curriculum (maths, technology etc), but ERA's main contribution is in making segregation possible - though 'I do not pretend that this is a wholly reliable safeguard against the obvious dangers inherent in planting an alien, medieval, theocratic political culture in the incompatible environment of a Western parliamentary democracy' (p39).

It is hardly surprising that there should be bitter resistance to such cultural demarcations. The Indian Workers' Association, Southall, after commenting on a parliamentary statement by Roy Hattersley (then Shadow Chancellor) that in education the state should be

> providing extra visitors to remind parents of their new obligations in Great Britain. It is essential to make provision to teach these children: basic British customs, basic British habits, and if one likes basic British prejudices, if they are to live happily and successfully in an integrated way in this community (undated, p5),

went on to denounce various special policies supposedly designed to integrate 'immigrants' (Section 11, and 'the Empire of ESL: English as a second language'), as 'a specific linguistic environment backed up by legislative structures ...to formulate "numerical black Asians" as a deficit' (p5). The English curriculum was and is 'an all-white model based on a white norm' (p21), and thus 'the centrality of the oppression remains the same. The school denies us our childhood...' (p12). The *national* English curriculum makes a powerful statement about what it means to be English.

The attempt to convert colour to culture, to enforce a new segregation with cultural differences as a mask for racism, is often called the 'new racism'. One way of looking at this is through some sort of periodisation. During periods of economic growth black immigration is encouraged to assist the supply of labour, and an assimilationist philosophy develops to facilitate this. This philosophy is one-sided in its paramount insistence that the new migrants must adopt all aspects of English culture if they desire the full benefits of membership. Racism continues, of course, but public and political discourse is *de*racialised. However, with the rise in unemployment and competition for jobs from the late 1960s, racism became more overt, and cultural differences were more openly asserted. Later, when it was realised that repatriation was politically impossible, racism then turned towards the *internal* isolation of black people. The new racism derives from this process. It accepts the right of 'immigrants' to exist in this country but seeks to limit their citizenship. Segregation rather than repatriation is the outcome. (Hiskett's arguments above clearly apply this principle to education.) Perhaps the process could better be called one of 'depatriation': neither properly British nor belonging elsewhere, black people are treated as if in limbo. That black people have a 'right' to cultural distinctiveness then elides into the claim that these can never conform or converge with the rights of white people. They have different cultures, different interests, different ways of seeing things.

There can be little doubt that racism has changed course in such ways. However, this does not make the current ideological variant in any way new, even if there has been a change of emphasis. Nor is there anything new in the assertion of an immutability to cultural differences. Earlier obsession with biological differences always had as a corollary the notion that cultural differences were an automatic parallel. Because white cultural superiority is implied rather than stated does not mean that a fundamental change has occurred. What is new about current racism at the ideological level is the attempt to control the increasing political power of black groups and cultural organisations. Because black people in Britain *are* British, and therefore have certain ostensibly inalienable rights, the focus of attack has moved directly into the political sphere. Political barriers to black people are being erected, and political control of education is merely one aspect of this.

The Dewsbury affair brought these issues acutely to the fore. Interpreted as a prediction of how ERA will be used to further separate black from white in education, the rights and wrongs of the dispute revolved entirely round racism as a basis for educational choices. Despite protests to the contrary, the motivations of the Dewsbury parents who wanted their children not to go to a particular school, were in public never far removed from the understanding that this was because the school was predominantly 'Asian'. The authority made a terrible hash of the affair and had to concede the case (after massive publicity and the start of a judicial review). A subsequent victory account (1989) by Naylor, for PACE, the Parental Alliance for Choice in Education, made quite clear that the real community of Dewsbury was white and non-Moslem, symbolised by a ruined Cistercian monastery: such 'references to a Christian tradition are not without interest in the light of the events which will be described' (p8). The Moslem community is also positively, if patronisingly, described as 'a peaceful close-knit community of some 4,000 souls' (p9), but one that should apparently exist elsewhere, as a result of 'the almost universal desire of peoples of distinct cultures to preserve their identities' (p10).

But when Naylor kindly offers the services of PACE to assist Moslems in developing their own education away from white people, this would appear to be because of the success of the white Dewsbury parents. 'So far it is British culture that has been vindicated' (p175), though it is unclear how. While Naylor goes on to say that the 'ethnic minorities' now need defence, it is quite clear that the battle over culture is a zero-sum process: Moslems should be excluded from education with white people whether they want to or not. The 'new' racism is based, as before, not only on exclusion but on hierarchy, and is therefore racism pure and simple. Exclusion means inferiority. Flew, for instance, complains of 'the full outrageousness of the contention that no culture.... may be said in any respect, or with regard to any possible objective, to be either superior or inferior to any other' (1987, p122).

Oldman comments that through this sort of argument 'we are forced onto the back foot to argue about the instrumental value of cultures' (in Troyna, 1987, p40). This is a problem, but the point being made here is that the attempt to discuss the 'new racism' as a cultural artifact should not lead to the conclusion that there is no underlying conflict at all at the cultural level. It will be argued in the next section that unwillingness to tackle this dimension leaves free the ugly nationalism which underlies all racism.

The Left and the denial of culture

It is of note that Flew himself comments, perhaps ironically, on the Left's 'collapsing of the crucial distinctions between race and culture' (1987, p119). The reason, of course, is that there is no such thing as 'race', which remains therefore a cultural invention. The term 'new racism' is an anti-racist invention serving to suggest that *all* discussion of culture is unfounded. The main problem with this is that cultures *do* exist. Suppressing interest in culture means ignoring the webs that bind racism in place. This does not mean that racism is replaced by ethnicity, or a sense of community, ie that we have to worry about the '"we-ness/they-ness" character of the ethnic group' (Ringer and Lawless, 1989, p19). On such a criterion the members of a local cricket club could conceivably be considered an ethnic group. While other writers interested in ethnicity have written with a much sharper edge (eg Rex, 1983; 1986), the issue here is not cultural differences as such but how racism is used to underpin structural social inequalities. Acts of racialisation - the sorting out of 'ethnic' groups into hierarchies of control - are what count. These serve to 'define and construct differentiated social collectivities' (Miles, 1989, p75). The Right's claim that all cultures are equal marches in counterpoint to the Left's implied assertion that culture no longer exists. Cultural distinctions are used for political and social ends, and these have to be recognised.

This can be seen most clearly in the contrast made between multi-culturalism and anti-racism. In Troyna's case, for instance, multi-culturalism merely continues the assimilationist policies of an early era. Its apparent superficiality - the almost surreal adulation of 'saris, samosas and steel bands' (Troyna and Williams, 1986, p24) - avoids, through concentration on cultural surfaces, recognition of structural inequalities - inequalities which anti-racism exposes. However, even anti-racism is not enough. As in the case of Miles, racism also helps define class structures. Anti-racism must therefore take class into account.

> It is ironic, to say the least, that the current debate on antiracism reproduces many of the theoretical weaknesses supposedly associated with multicultural ideologies of educational change.... in order to develop policies which will undercut racial inequalities it is necessary to understand 'race' in a class context and consider racism as one of several mechanisms for the reproduction of class position (pp104/5).

Education must oppose the explicit manifestation of racism, undermine its ideological construction, and at the same time expose the connection between this and the operation of capitalism - and all in school time! Above all, the concern for class undermines the concern for culture. This is made crystal-clear in the distinction made between multi-culturalism and anti-racism. But there are several problems with the distinction:

1. Both multi-culturalism and anti-racism are ideal types - immensely fuzzy concepts which converge in reality. How, for instance, would teaching about the existence of craft industries in pre-Empire India be described? Is it anti-racist because it says something about the spread and impact of imperialism? Or multi-cultural because it draws attention to Indian achievements?

2. It tends to treat education as undifferentiated, taking little note of the ages of children or stages of education. Tackling racism at younger ages is likely to be predominantly multi-cultural, but as children get older the attempt to widen their understanding can be hardened by an understanding of racism itself.

3. It fails to assess the impact of its methods. This is by no means clear-cut. When white parents complain that their children are being taught to make chapattis rather than pancakes, this is because such multi-cultural teaching is a direct challenge to their own racism. Racists themselves translate multi-culturalism into anti-racism.

4. The policy imposes action and attitudes from above, denying the anti-racist impetus in young people themselves. A research report commissioned by the MacDonald enquiry in Manchester found widespread name-calling of a racist nature but also extensive friendships across 'racial' groups, while a similar study in London found that a large number of children opposed racism of any sort (Kelly and Cohn, 1988). Turning to such children for guidance, for a lead in the struggle against racism, is a different process from the imposition of a policy from above - with inevitably predetermined conclusions.

Alternative attempts to evoke the primacy of colour while not losing the notion of class, either by viewing colour as a class defined by power inequality (Sivanandan, 1986), or black people as a working-class within its own right (Ramdin, 1986), are no less problematic than the attempt to incorporate racialisation into traditional class analysis. While racialisation is undoubtedly part-structured by existing class relations, the attempt to incorporate both forms of division into one overall schema becomes hopelessly messy, whether at the theoretical or practical level. The MacDonald Report, for instance, strongly critical of the anti-racist policies in the school in which a 13-year old boy, Ahmed Iqbal Ullah, was murdered by a white boy in the playground, suggested that an understanding of class issues should have tempered the rigour of the school's anti-racist ethos.

> To deal with sex and race, but not class, distorts these issues.... This ostrich-like analysis of the complex of social relations leaves white working class males completely in the cold. They fit nowhere. They become all-time losers. Their interests as a group are nowhere catered for. That, surely, is a recipe for division and polarisation, particularly in the area of anti-racist policies (Runneymede Trust, 1989, p33).

Does this mean that white, male working-class children should be taught anti-racism, anti-sexism, *and* some sort of 'anti-classism'? That would be a tall order. Or that the concerns of white, male working-class children should be taken into account in dealing with racism.

> After hearing the evidence of the PEER (Parents' English Education Rights) group of parents in Manchester, one gets the sense of white working class parents who have little basis on which to root their own identity and whose education has given them little or no conception of the value of their own experience as English working class. They therefore react angrily and resentfully to a school which, in sharp contrast to their own experience, caters directly for the needs and preferences of Asian students (p35).

The committee made a powerful and important point in arguing that the social background of all actors should be recognised when dealing with social tensions, but there is a thin line between this and arguing that white racist children 'need support and sympathy' (Jeffcoate, 1979, p107) if racism is to be challenged, and an even thinner one between this and the argument that 'curtailing the National Front's legitimate entitlements is.... ideologically and strategically dangerous' (p106). Perhaps it is true to assert that positive discrimination for black people in some undifferentiated sense (ie including rich blacks) means discriminating against poor white people (Edwards, 1987, p33), but neither anti-racism nor multi-culturalism entail positive discrimination. The concern should be racism, not so much the well-being of the collection of individuals who make up a particular category defined by racist terms. The latter considerations may lead to an absurd weighing-up of gains and losses, with the advantages or disadvantages of being black or white, working-class or middle-class, female or male, all thrown into the weighing scale.

Even without a concern for class, anti-racism is of doubtful use, largely because of its denial of culture. This denial can be seen in Brandt's deliberate contrast of multi-cultural and anti-racist initiatives (1986), in which multi-culturalism is seen as an element of racism, as in the following hypothetical dialogue:

Schools:	We're all equal here.
Black students:	We *know* we are second-class citizens, in housing employment and education.
Schools:	Oh, dear. Negative self-image. We must order books with Blacks in them.
Black students:	Can't we talk about the immigration laws or the National Front?
Schools:	No, that's politics. We'll arrange some Asian and West Indian cultural evenings.

Multi-culturalism, in masking the reality of inequality, is made to appear paradoxically racist. This is put more starkly by Francis, writing for ALTARF.

> Where does multi-cultural education fit in here? It can be seen as part of the legitimisation of current inequalities - the presence of black people is sweetened for the white population by the more acceptable and consumable parts of their culture - multicultural restaurants, black tv comedies, black recording hits. The oppositional parts of the culture instead of being linked to inequalities in power, income, and discriminatory racist legislation and white racism, are instead seen as mindless outbursts to be soothed with community-police liaison (not community control of police) (in ALTARF, 1984, p90).

Brandt offers a tightly drawn typology: multi-culturalism tries to restructure a consensus between 'majority and minority' groups. Anti-racism, by contrast, directly tackles racist conflict and challenges state and institutional structures which promote racism (p121). Yet these distinctions are overdriven. A standard multi-cultural text such as Twitchin and Demuth (1985) might start with 'celebrating diversity' and the rather sickly-sweet 'getting to know each other', but the book includes discussion of the need to tackle Anglo-Saxon prejudices and arguments for an education that looks 'at the kind of views that the white people have inherited from the past' (p55). James, in ILEA's *The English Curriculum: Race* rightly warns against 'a superficial raree-show which emphasises the quaint and colourful aspects of exotic cultures', but 'fostering critical awareness of language... and of the arbitrary character of the social values' attached to different forms of English is a potentially critical elaboration of multi-cultural tenets. Above all, culture cannot be separated from language and dialect, or indeed any form of expression. 'Unilingual is unicultural' (Stibbs, 1987, p28). By the same token, denial of cultural differences, whether in favour of class or nation, can only serve to sponsor the standardisation of English as a dominant form. The identity provided by language, dialect and accent is a vital defence against the marching middle classes of the white south of England.

There are no cut and dried solutions to racism, and any attempt to invent these outside particular contexts (eg the need for black groups to form groups for collective defence against racist attack), can only do harm. The problem of attacking the sources of racism are far from simple. If the use of stories showing the impact of racism on disadvantage might run the 'risk of reinforcing the stereotype of black people as "problems"' (Schools Council, 1981, p134), what does multi-culturalism mean for young black people 'when the PC who regularly stops and searches their older brother sits in the school hall tapping his feet to the school steel band'? (Francis, in ALTARF, 1984, p90). The solutions will certainly not depend on simplistic distinctions. Different types of policy are required in different areas (eg the curriculum, school discipline, monitoring of school progress on the basis of colour and ethnicity).

All these are concerned with opposition to racism. The element most distinctively associated with anti-racism, the attempt to engage students in discussion of racism, is always likely to be a small part of any such action. It is sociologically naive to assume that through opening up issues like this within the classroom attitudes can be changed, let alone for the better.

> The discussion again began to fragment at this point and Jennifer Green told another story about a teacher she had met on holiday who she felt had articulated racist views. However, Beverley, an Afro/Caribbean girl seemed uninterested and started to fool around.
>
> JG - Well how would you have handled it Beverley? (numerous bids to speak and talking amongst themselves). I'm interested, how would you Beverley, what would you have done if you'd been me?
>
> AM - She wouldn't bother you know.
>
> V - You should have thrown your drink in his face.
>
> JG - (Many students now talking at once.)... Wait a minute... listen... one at a time. This is a good discussion. Beverley what would you have done?
>
> B - Me? (Inaudible.)
>
> (Foster, 1990, pp 90/91).

Anti-racism is a fairly limited catalyst with a possibly random effect.

Living culture

The real problem for multi-culturalism is that social inequalities based on colour have nothing (necessarily) to do with culture, making the latter an inadequate basis for opposing racism. But racism itself has a great deal to do with culture, and if the Left ignores the cultural cement that keeps racism together it is not doing a very good job. Through racism and anti-racism Right and Left join battle but also join hands. Both seek to racialise but both also de-culture society. 'Multi-culturalism often seems to argue that all cultures are

120

equally valuable (ignoring the fact that they are not equally powerful)....' (Francis, in ALTARF, 1984, p85). Both right and left-wing critics dislike the credence given to multiple cultures. Yet it is not collections but definitions of people which count. Anti-racism produces over-arching groups at the cost of actual social differences.

This could be age. For instance were the inner city riots of recent years black riots or youth riots? As Gilroy and Lawrence comment, they have been both, and each movement is in part formed by the other. 'Both Left and Right alike are unable to conceptualise "youth" as other than a transitory phase between school and eventual work'. If the Right seeks to 'transform "youth" into a stage of extended dependency', the Left, obsessed by structure, ignores the multi-faceted disjunctions within and interconnections between youth cultures. The discipline of anti-racism has little interest in the cultural strivings of youth. All the Left can manage is 'to mourn in moralistic fashion the non-appearance of sustained anti-racist policies' (Gilroy and Lawrence, in Cohen and Bains, 1988, pp144/5).

If Gilroy and Lawrence are over-optimistic in their view that youth cultures can become more spontaneously anti-authoritarian and anti-racist than the crabbed anti-racism described above, the argument that the need is for 'genuine forms of anti-racist education centred on the social practices and cultural preoccupations of youth' (p153), is surely right. The denial of culture is not just a denial of the sometimes prissy outcomes of multi-culturalism. It narrows the focus, for instance, away from the cultural strivings of young people. Anti-racism is ultimately always reactive.

> But anti-racist activities encapsulate one final problem which may outlive them. This is the disastrous way in which they have trivialised the rich complexity of black life by reducing it to nothing more than a response to racism. More than any other issue this operation reveals the extent of the anti-racists' conceptual trading with the racists and the results of embracing their culturalist assumptions. Seeing in black life nothing more than an answer to racism means moving on to the ideological circuit which makes us visible in two complementary roles - the problem and the victim (Gilroy, in Ball and Solomos, 1990, p208).

Anti-racism narrows the space in which a genuinely cultural activity can work. Culture 'is fluid, it is actively and continually made and re-made' (Gilroy, in Ball and Solomos, 1990, p208). It is not Williams' 'common culture' we need but a constantly evolving, and no doubt contradictory, set of cultures. If the reality of identity is suppressed by racism, it is not helped by the rigidities of anti-racism. Above all, it is precisely how culture is 'made and re-made' which should be at the heart of opposition to racism in education. By chipping away at the monolithic myth of 'Englishness', reinforced and set in concrete by the bureaucratic mesh of the national curriculum; and by celebrating not just diversity but diversification, much of the cultural cement which locks racism in place may be eased. Racism will never go away, but it can be marginalised and put on the defensive. This does not mean ignoring inequality. Study of all inequalities and the social conditions which engender them should eventually become a fundamental part of education. But it should not be forgotten that cultural definitions define and delimit the divisions that are used to maintain inequalities.

Conclusion

In the previous chapter it was argued that too much is made of culture. Fear of cultural loss or threat has fundamentally influenced the framework within which the campaign over educational change has been conducted in recent decades. It makes little difference whether the source of concern has been the nation, high culture, or working-class culture. It has been argued in this chapter that this cultural pressure has begun to have significant real effect, for instance through the national curriculum, which paves the way amongst other things for the further standardisation of the English language. The Left has failed to meet the challenge because of the strict interpretation of culture on class lines. It goes further in suggesting that culture is merely a racist artifact and thus sees culture as irrevocably contaminated, despite the fact that for a large part of society cultural identities remain paramount. These are not only 'ethnic' but relate to class, gender, age, region, and so on. The dominance of culture on the Right and the fear of culture on the Left suggests a two-fold reaction: first, the notion of cultural decline should be totally rejected - wherever it stems from, and whatever the parameters of the argument (eg nation or class); second, education must be allowed to recognise the reality of cultural difference. In this case neither harmony nor equality are the building blocks.

Part Three:
Education, power and equality

Education is being re-formed in the spirit of crisis. While this may be addressed as one of economic decline, it is often nevertheless given impetus by a violent fear of cultural loss. However, the real crisis is not one of economic or cultural decline, but of allocative principles. These come into question not as a result of decline but of growth. Growth produces a crisis for social groups who feel threatened by general educational advance, particularly in a period when, through intermittent recession, growth is no longer guaranteed. The fear is manifested in claims about falling standards, skill shortages, loss of leadership, and so on. The final chapters examine the battle over the redirection of education that this conflict entails.

One element which does not feature in this is the growth in business influence over education. Again this is a slight trend only. The influence is certainly tighter than before in training and FE provision, but in schooling it is fairly superficial. It is simply not in the interests of business-people to waste time or money on the highly intangible effects of increased involvement in schooling, whether this means funding CTCs or membership of governing bodies. Many particular initiatives designed to make people think that industry-school links are becoming significant are in fact highly marginal. The *Mini-Enterprise in Schools*, a DTI project supported by National Westminster Bank (MESP, 1991) purported to help young people understand business, although the actual operation of these trading activities quite clearly rely on charity (parents buying from children, local businesses patronising children with assistance etc). Indeed, while the MEs supposedly 'provide opportunities to explore wealth creation, marketing, finance, business organisation', it is hard to see how the organisational skills they might encourage are any different from those needed in, say, running a charity or public service. Moreover, as Shilling points out, real opportunities for self-employment are extremely limited. As MESP projects will have little relevance to the 'routine repetitions of manual labour' (1989, p122), at the ideological level such projects may well be counter-productive. Perhaps they are best seen as something rather like complex 'bob-a-jobs'. In the case of SCIP (the School Curriculum Industry Partnership), established by the CBI, TUC and School Curriculum Development Committee 'to promote students' better understanding of the industrial society in which they live', even if 'schools-industry organisations rely almost exclusively on managers' as adult facilitators (*SCIP newsletter*, Autumn, 1987), this hardly suggests an ideological battle. The London Compact, promoted by left-wing ILEA and gaining the support of major firms such as Asda and Barclays, had right-wing support, but was really a highly inflated account of what many schools have been doing as part of general practice. While special education courses sponsored by a well-known hamburger chain leave an unpleasant taste in the mouth, we have not yet quite made it to 'Kentucky Fried Schooling' (Hargreaves, in Hargreaves and Reynolds, 1989, p10). It is hard to believe this is the way of the future.

If political control has little long-term impact on educational spending, it is nevertheless central to equality of distribution. This can perhaps be seen in terms of rationalisation. The process is quite clear historically, starting with the first provision of public money in 1833 (£20,000 to supplement private subscriptions), through the Bryce and other Commissions, and the major Acts (eg 1944), the expansion of higher education in the 1960s and 1970s, and now the national curriculum. Even if government often lags behind demand, it appears it can be strongly associated with this process of rationalisation. However, this ignores major political cycles in development. Current institutional provision, for instance, is far from rational: county, voluntary aided, grant-maintained, private schools, assisted places within these, and CTCs; different relationships between primary, middle and secondary schools; sixth forms, sixth-form colleges, sixth-form consortia, tertiary colleges, FE colleges, and so on. Each is a survival from or an accretion on to an earlier epoch.

Such complexities, as old distinctions are dissolved and new ones developed, have a long tradition. In the nineteenth century educational provision was just as complex. For the aristocracy there were the major public schools like Eton, for the middle classes there were the lesser private institutions - some commercial schools, and the 700 or so endowed grammar schools (many of charitable status). However, there were also status differentials within this agglomeration:

> tiers of schools, with different curricula, leaving ages, staffs, fees and clienteles, for different levels of income and status and thus expectation, within the 'middle class'. It was a process of grading and differentiation which reflected one of the most widely accepted axioms of Victorian society - that education should reflect disparities of social class and should only slightly seek to transcend them (Digby and Searby, 1981, p11).

Rationalisation, eg through the 1868 Taunton Report, which sought to consolidate these differences with three distinct tiers of schooling, served a specific social purpose. The higher up the hierarchy the greater the salience of the classics. 'Never has a congruence between social class and the curriculum been more explicitly avowed' (Digby and Searby, 1981, p39). In public schools up to four fifths of the timetable would be devoted to Latin, Greek, and ancient history. The goal was not useful knowledge but an arcane credentialism. Middle-class schools were more progressive, but nevertheless only began their domination of education through aping the education of the aristocracy. Perhaps a similar relationship now exists between working-class and middle-class educational demands, or at least political perceptions of these.

The history of education is not one of simple expansion or rationalisation but of cycles of development, through which different forms of integration and segregation are developed. Now the critical issue is whether education is retained as a general service (like health), or a redistributive service (like housing). The comprehensive ideal - but also right-wing talk of national efficiency (justifying universal rules such as formula-funding and the national curriculum) - suggests the former, while choice suggests the latter. However, efficiency and rationalisation have nothing to do with equal access, and indeed usually mean the reverse. The 1858 Royal Commission, for instance, was asked to 'enquire into the present State of Popular Education in England and to consider and report what Measures, if any, are required for the extension of sound and cheap elementary instruction to all classes of the people'. *If any?* And Lowe's famous statement when payment by results was introduced through the Revised Code of 1862: 'If the new system is not cheap, it shall be efficient, and if it is not efficient, it shall be cheap'. Despite Victorian concern for morality, technical education (of little interest to the classically trained elite) had to be funded through a tax on alcohol, called 'whisky money', which therefore funded technical education 'in proportion, not to the educational needs but to the amount of drink consumed' (Lawrence, 1972, p27). Any increase in working-class abstemiousness had to be at the expense of the education of their children.

The same applies to more recent times. Development in Scotland has occurred round two core concerns, one expansionist, the other segregationist: the belief of the providers (teachers, local authorities, and the inspectorate) that education should be comprehensive, and a persistent programme in the Scottish Education Department (SED) within the Scottish Office to make education selective. This ended only with the establishment of Labour in power in the 1960s. The SED had until that time sought to maintain a twin-track educational system: a fast track for university aspirants, a non-certificating track for the rest. This could be the case even where the SED were apparently egalitarian, for instance when it sought to raise the effective leaving age after 1900 by three or four years.

> By lengthening the period during which pupil and family were required to invest in education and to forego earnings, the new definition favoured wealthier families.... Thus the policy of social efficiency was overtly universalistic, but covertly particularistic, favouring particular social groups and particular local communities (McPherson and Raab, 1988, p44).

Growth is possible under any Conservative regime, but is likely to be managed through segregation, eg tripartism after the 1944 Act, or the tying of expansion in higher education to higher fees and student loans.

Re-segregation, the purpose of current intervention in education, requires greater control over the supply of alternative definitions, in particular those of teachers and local education authorities (LEAs). The following chapters are about the change that is occurring in these areas, and their possible impact. The desire to control teachers stems from their ability to provide a professional definition of educational needs and educational standards. The removal of control over the curriculum through its nationalisation, direct imposition of pay awards and conditions of work, and the enforced switch from LEA to governing-body employment - all these result in the one of the most radical changes in status that teachers have ever been subjected to. All sources of professional direction have been suppressed. The replacement of the Schools Council (the basis for teacher influence on the curriculum and pedagogy at the national level) by the Secondary Examinations Council and the School

Curriculum Development Committee (SCDC) was bad enough, but the former was set up as a substantial body with much influence over the GSCE, whereas the SCDC was a puny, advisory body, enjoined to disseminate good practice: 'a kind of curriculum dentistry or pointing of the school brickwork' (Plaskow, in Morris and Griggs, 1988, p212). Of course, the government has not been able to introduce change (the replacement of professional by bureaucratic control) without the support of professionals at the highest levels and, as discussed above, this has resulted at times in near-fiasco.

A further source of substitution of bureaucratic for professional modes of control comes with the abolition of HMI and the establishment of the right to tender for inspection awards. These are governed by a strict definition of what constitutes a 'bad' school - ie one which could in the extreme be threatened with closure; in the *1977 Black Paper*'s euphemism: 'Schools that few wish to attend should be closed' (p9). It has often been argued that HMI itself was an element in the bid by the centre to establish overall control. Whether or not this was so, its professional stance made it at best an unreliable ally. While it called in the so-called *Red Book* (DES, 1978) for more objective methods of curricular provision and assessment of performance, its own judgements, stemming from typical teaching methods, were themselves hardly objective. The same goes for its own curricular proposals. HMI itself recorded teachers' comments that its proposed 'areas of experience' and associated checklists were 'too bland and general' (DES, 1981, p59). HMI's reward for its reconnaissance of the secret garden on behalf of the DES was abolition. And yet HMI's effort to establish a common curriculum and a means for assessing progress was at worst moderately useful and at best a means of gaining support from both LEAs and teachers. The 'frequently expressed fear that HMI's interest implies a plan which aimed to undermine the freedom of individual schools' (DES, 1981, p8) is odd now that both HMI and school freedom have gone.

The other main source of change is in LEA control. This has been important as it is the means through which educational justice has traditionally worked. While no claim can be made that LEA control of education has made it more equal, the ability to direct the flow of children into schools is a fundamental defence against the deepening of inequalities. This power has now been removed. This affects Conservative authorities too, of course, but this is less a matter of centralisation than of factionalisation. If political parties are each 'a complex set of plural institutions' (Rose, 1980, p254), then what counts is which subset gains central power. At the cost of much Conservative local government, the 'New Right' has nationalised minimal local authority. Whether this is seen as 'enabling' or 'disabling' local government is a moot point, though the use of the former term has great propaganda value. Possibly some changes have been mere expression of power, but even then, while there may as Hampton (1987, p237) suggests be 'an element of fantasy' in Conservative thinking and policy-making (such as the ban on gay 'propaganda'), this does not diminish the need to assess the social cost of entering the world of fantasy.

The control of LEAs has been undertaken in order to limit, or even end, the ability of local government to combat inequality. While the government dare not introduce selection directly, it has instead introduced a proxy: the 'good school'. The new parental inspectors, the comparison of test and exam results, the publication of truancy rates, the central definition of a 'bad' school - all these are designed to encourage a closer relationship between 'good' schools and 'good' areas. As will be argued in the final chapter, most notions of what constitute a good school contain a great deal of mythology. However, the importance of the concept is that it attracts attention away from what constitutes good *education*. The institution, not the practice, is being made to count: another reason for the suppression of professional definitions. At the same time, curricula on paper mean nothing without resources.

> technology (however defined) requires resources - equipment such as computers, electronics kits and modelling materials, expendable materials particularly for younger pupils, staff time in order to keep the size of teaching groups low, and in-service training perhaps of a far-reaching nature. Its introduction or expansion cannot be imposed by fiat, within existing limits of running expenses and staffing (Leonard, 1988, p41).

The national curriculum deepens control without necessarily releasing resources, while closer central control of education puts not just education, but even individual schools, within the gift of government.

Although there has been considerable conflict between teachers and LEAs, with central government sometimes siding with one and then the other, recent government intervention has driven the two sides into closer agreement. Right-wingers have lumped together teachers and their employers jointly as a vested professional interest (as the providers of education). While bearing little relationship to reality, this critique has served to provoke the two sources of provision into resistance to governmental attempts to become sole arbiter in education. Opposition started with ERA. Most of this was fairly conventional lobbying. For instance, the Council of Local Education Authorities (CLEA), jointly run by the Association of County Councils (ACC) and the Association of Metropolitan Authorities (AMA), established a lobbying forum which invited all interest groups to combine in opposition to the Bill. This, the Standing Conference on Education (SCE), at its first conference included the two local government associations, the teaching and some other unions, churches, and a wide range of pressure groups or professional interests such as the Campaign for the Advancement of State Education (CASE), NATE, the Islamic Council, the Association for Speech Impaired Children, and so on. As a spokesperson from the Voluntary Council for Handicapped Children put it, 'there's nothing like disaster for creating consensus'. Most of those present opposed at least some aspects of the legislation, but views were not always aligned. For instance, the Association of British Chambers of Commerce demanded that on the governing bodies of colleges 'at least one half of the total membership plus two must be employer representatives', and indeed, in order to exclude the public sector organisations such as LEAs, only 'representatives of employers who are industrial, commercial or professional companies or partnerships'. On the other hand, another manager described the proposal to take colleges out of LEA control, in view of close links in local training and recruitment, as 'madness' (CLEA, October, 1987).

A common theme was helplessness in the face of the government's populist propaganda over 'parent power'. Various spokespeople for parental or similar organisations, while acknowledging that LEAs have traditionally neglected parental influence, were bitter about the government's refusal to accept organisations such as the National Federation of PTAs as representative. The established parental organisations, traditionally slighted as an impediment to local bureaucracy, continue to be slighted but, strangely, as an impediment to decentralisation to actual parents. The concern to attempt to reclaim the link with parents taken over by central government led to further campaigns stemming from SCE organisations, such as the 'Parents Initiative', which aimed to mount a major briefing of parents and governors on the real implications of the legislation. Likewise, the NUT mounted a highly expensive but very poorly attended *Rally for Education* in the Albert

Hall, with actors reading quotations from educationists and philosophers, high-quality musical performances by students (to demonstrate the fragility of creative learning or expression under the national curriculum), and speeches from church and other representatives. One of the NUT's propaganda themes became *Campaigning with Parents*. All, of course, to no avail. Meanwhile, the Labour Party's 'Education Charter' proposed a voluntary contract under which teachers would offer more time to discuss children's progress with parents while parents would encourage homework, reading at home, and selective use of television. To some extent this is a class perception, with the Tories' ideal-typical middle-class parent pushing their children hard and wanting teachers to do the same, and Labour's ideal-typical working-class parent rarely visiting school and doing too little for their children at home.

Finally, while much of the press was against the 'providers' and in favour of moral panic (most tabloids and, if far less consistently, some Conservative quality papers), this was not so with broadcasting. For instance, the BBC's *Education Programme*, while balanced, ran many highly questioning items on the likely impact of the legislation. The same, if to a lesser degree, applied to Channel 4's *Promises and Piecrust* and *Education Extra*. Here, perhaps, professional broadcasters, also under threat from government attacks on supposedly vested interests, were suspicious of the political motives behind attacks on other public-sector providers. Programmes on open enrolment, testing, and local financial management did far more to examine the exaggerated claims of the proposals and their potential problems than did much of the press. For instance, in the *Education Programme* on parental involvement, representatives of the NFPTA and CASE argued that it is extremely difficult to involve parents in anything not explicitly to do with their children. A survey in Manchester found that 78% of parents attended parent evenings, but only 9% wanted to discuss broader matters; in Oxfordshire the figures were 67% and 17%. 'Reform' may even be predicated on parents doing nothing (not turning up to meetings, not opposing opt-out ballots). It 'suits the government that parents have no status.... They can pretend that people who have views are not real parents and that real parents haven't said anything' (Joan Sallis, CASE). It is of interest to compare the ideological use made of parents by the government in the UK to parental power *over* government in the USA.

> Sometimes the influence has been channelled through the elected school boards that have been the bane of many a school superintendent and have been the bludgeon forcing the incorporation of many lay concerns and non-academic functions into the schools. At other times parent groups have petitioned, lobbied and pressured the schools directly. But whatever the mechanism - elections and elected officials, confrontation of educators, court suits - the voices of parents and lay groups have long been loud and clear (Rhoades, 1989, p28).

In Rhoades' view one of the main reasons for this difference is the power of higher education in the UK, which puts parents into the position of jockeying for a good position in the race for selection. General or community interest is limited.

What, then does the government's populism mean? In an excellent *Panorama* programme on 2.11.87 (*The Class Revolution*), an adviser to Mrs Thatcher, Oliver Letwin, compared the opt-out proposals to council house sales, both policies the result of Mrs Thatcher's 'unerring instinct for what Englishmen really want'. While we clearly need not worry about what women or the Welsh may want, all the evidence suggests that one major ingredient in current change is not parental involvement but parental apathy. Who will take schools out of council control? Who will decide if a teacher is sacked?

> In classic Foucauldian terms the 'dividing practices' provided for by this discursive complex both *totalise* and *individualise* the social-subject, the concerned parent. All parents are taken to have shared interests in opposing liberalising reforms in education but they compete individually, via their children, for the scarce rewards of educational success (Ball, 1990, p34).

While the professionals attempt to attack the Right's pseudo-populism failed, the issue was not (and still is not) a conflict between professional and populist (or parental) interests, but between professional and political interpretations of these interests. The government cannot, in the meantime, maintain its reforms without professional support. Conflict is therefore unavoidable. One way round this is ever larger doses of bureaucratisation. Whether it will ever go as far as civil servants marking exercise books is perhaps unlikely, but symbolically speaking we may be close to this.

7 Teachers

Various pressures have come together in recent years to compress the role of the teacher: strict spending limits, distrust of the public servant, belief that worker organisation is inimical to efficiency (or consumer rights), and fear that mass schooling cannot provide moral development. The teacher is at the heart of many right-wing shibboleths. It is not just that progressive education, teacher-led, is seen as making teaching easier and learning harder, but, in the words of Mrs Thatcher, if children are 'being taught political slogans' instead of English, and being given 'an inalienable right to be gay' instead of moral values, children have to be protected both from excessive ease and from indoctrination. Referring to the usual HMI report which finds teaching good, middling and poor in roughly equal proportions, Flew seeks to undermine the entire teaching profession.

> Nor must we ever forget that if Labour's *Charter for Parents* and the wishes of the NUT were ever implemented, then idle or incompetent teachers - who were under this particular inspection actually in the majority - would, through pupil profiles uncheckable against the results achieved in independently assessed public examinations, become the ultimate judges in their own causes. Having first ruined the wretched pupils, they could then commend their own work in producing what they chose falsely to say were superlative results! (1987, pp136/7)

Here we have not just a minority but the bulk of teachers posing a threat to social well-being. It is clear in much of this sort of writing that the impact of the teacher is far from being within education alone: 'Adolescent violence has increased ten-fold in 20 years and it would be both difficult and naive to absolve the schools of all responsibility' (Boyson, 1975, p13). But let us not worry if such an accusation has a negative impact on teacher morale. Their high turnover 'cannot simply be blamed on low salaries which themselves

130

reflect over a number of years the low esteem in which teachers are held by the rest of society' (Boyson, 1975, p28).

A similar attitude can be seen in the case of social workers, another core element in the public sector (more specifically the welfare state). This is apparent, for instance, in the media reporting of child abuse. Like teachers, social workers are somehow always wrong, often cast in the role of either 'wimps or bullies' (Franklin and Parton, 1991, p14): social workers may be 'butterflies in a situation that demanded hawks' (*Daily Mail*) and 'easily manipulated, disgraced, browbeaten, conned and bearded' (*Sun*), but also may 'seize sleeping children in the middle of the night' (*Sunday Telegraph*) and be 'abusers of authority, hysterical and malignant, callow, youngsters who absorb moral-free marxoid sociological theories (*Daily Mail*) (quoted on pp14/15). It would be possible to replace 'social workers' with 'teachers' in some of the above passages to reproduce right-wing vituperation of the profession fairly exactly. Ultimately, the issues are neither education nor social work but the role and extent of the welfare state.

> In this process, social workers have become vehicles for a more general discussion (typically a critique) concerning the role of the social democratic state in the post-war period as a provider of goods, especially welfare goods; about the nature and priorities of state functionaries in the private sphere of the family... (Franklin and Parton, 1991, pp10/11).

When teachers reasonably asked why women, as crumpet, a tart, a dish, or sweetiepie, are compared to food (ILEA, *The English Curriculum: Gender, Material for Discussion*), *Today* was concerned that if 'teachers will spend so much time worrying about their sexual Ps and Qs that they forget the three Rs' (21.1.87). In a *Mail* article on Bangladeshis, Paul Johnson blamed teachers - 'self-appointed spokesmen... largely middle-class ideologues... anxious to promote a "multi-cultural"' society for the failure 'to concentrate on teaching English'. At about this time, while I was interviewing Haringey's PR manager, a journalist rang about a book for under-fives called *Jesse's Dream Skirt*, in which a young boy likes to dress up in his mother's clothes. The PR officer pointed out to the journalist that the book was on a reading list circulated to libraries by a local group. It was not a part of the school curriculum required by the council. He added that his own boys liked to wear his wife's clothes occasionally! The next day the following article appeared in the *Sun*: 'BOYS TAUGHT TO WEAR DRESSES BY LOONY LEFT... Tory MP Terry Dicks said: Haringey are encouraging children to turn into transvestites. "The nutcases who put forward these ideas will mark the youngsters for life"' (17.8.87). Of course, the book would have no effect on their lives whatsoever, but what parent would fail to be concerned? At around the same time the *Daily Express* sought to evoke the same fear when it wrote that in Ealing 'schoolchildren, some as young as eight, to be taught that homosexual relationships are as equally valid as heterosexual relationships, with gay and lesbian switchboard numbers to be displayed in their schools and youth clubs'.

Such reconstructions of truth pave the way for incoherent 'reform' at the national level but also make it harder for teachers to deal with sensitive issues. While in its advice to teachers the Assistant Masters and Mistresses Association acknowledges that 'caring teachers... will seek to avoid imbuing the nature of sexual feelings and behaviour with the kind of guilt which prevents young people from developing into self-aware, mature and responsible adults', it also warns that if a governing body decides against the teaching of sex education, even advice in response to a specific question (eg about contraception) could be regarded as a breach of school policy and therefore a disciplinary offence. Teachers, like social workers, have responsibility for the welfare of their students, and have been accused of being both educationally soft and ideologically hard with children, both weak and authoritarian. Thus the Hillgate Group called for the acceptance of teachers without teacher qualifications 'who have not had their brains stuffed with the dubious material now taught in so many teacher training courses' (1987, p27). This is not the case solely in the UK. In France, Stal and Thom have described teachers in much the same light. 'Pedagogy and ideology are as thick as thieves' (1988, p73). The critique may not be subtle but, whether expressed in publications funded by the Right or in the mass media, it evokes a powerful unreality, and an inevitable demand for 'reform'.

Improving the educators

'Good teaching, as researchers are discovering, is complex' (Fullan, 1991, p312).

Teachers have perhaps always had an ambivalent position in society. In the nineteenth century they were regarded with suspicion in many urban schools, which working-class children sometimes attended unwillingly, reacting violently to the new representatives of authority. But at the same time, village teachers might be seen as representatives of the community against local authority. The central government also viewed the teacher with ambivalence, sometimes expecting her to be the state's moral agent but at other times a mere relay-station for top-down methods and content. In 1862 the Revised Code required that schools and teachers receive pay according to pass rates in simple exams ('the basics'). This was linked to what was in effect a national curriculum: 'Every scholar for whom grants are claimed must be examined to one of the following standards', with arithmetic at standard two requiring a 'sum in simple addition or subtraction, and the multiplication table'. The desire for change was associated with concern about poor teaching methods, following on directly from the 1861 Newcastle Report.

> we have seen overwhelming evidence from Her Majesty's Inspectors, to the effect that not more than one fourth of the children receive a good education. So great a failure in the teaching demanded the closest investigation....

But actual change was linked to deskilling.

> The New Code abolished payments direct to certified teachers and made them to managers instead, in a single grant, thereby opening the system of grants to schools taught by teachers with poorer attainments. At the same time, it instituted a lower class of certificates than those previously existing and raised the regulation number of pupils allowed for each teacher (Maclure, 1965, pp74-80).

The comparison between current change and these nineteenth-century reforms has often been made.

For much of history teachers have had low pay and status, and indeed this was considered necessary to a form of teaching where control of the wild working classes required strict control over classroom management. The new system prevented differentiated treatment. Change in this role can be interpreted in Foucault's terminology of 'moral technologies'.

> Strategically, the insistent demand for more efficient education disguised a latent conflict between a utilitarian and a medical norm of assessment. The universal utilitarian principle of annual examination opposed the medical psychological discovery of defective and imbecile populations that required segregation. The medical norm achieves efficiency by pathologizing and excluding the defective, thereby establishing the external limit of the normal (Jones, in Ball, 1990, p69).

If in the 19th century the fear was what to do with the bottom 80% or so, this has merely been reduced to the bottom 30%. In both cases teachers were held to be failing. Much British policy of the 1980s derives from the USA where, in some areas 'widespread doubt about the efficacy of specific techniques, combined with a lack of confidence in teacher dedication, has encouraged managers to feel that school programs - not individual teacher's skills - are what counts' (Kerchner and Mitchell, 1988, p211). For 'school programs' in the UK read national curriculum. The result is that teachers must be the vehicles not the motors of improvement. But while there are grounds for not relying solely on teachers' expertise, it is odd that this curricular pressure should actually be more apparent in the UK. Poppleton (1990) reviews survey data which shows that teachers in England have a far higher degree of specialist skills than their USA counterparts. For instance, 42% of American teachers of maths and/or computers were qualified in their area, compared to 81% in England (p187). Yet American teachers now possess greater curricular autonomy.

Even if there were a fundamental problem with the quality of teaching in the UK, it is far from unclear that restriction of the teacher's pedagogic role is the best means of improvement. There are several ways in which educational reform through teaching can be attempted.

1. Technical transfer from higher education to schools, eg in the setting of standards, preparation of teachers, or management functions in education. An Educational Assessment Centre at Oxford Polytechnic provides senior teachers in management positions profiles of their own strengths and weaknesses (Tomlinson, 1992, p192). France has extended university-level involvement in teacher training, while in Britain it is being eroded.

2. Professionalisation: in 1986 in the USA, *A Nation Prepared*, produced by a task-force on education, advocated 'greater teacher control over the teaching process and a share in school-level decision making' (Hess, 1992, p157). Alternatively, some USA districts have introduced or are considering measures such as higher paid mentor or 'master' teachers, or a separate certification system for supposedly outstanding teachers. Such schemes have been discussed in Britain on both the Right and the Left (eg Barber and Brighouse, 1992).

3. Client empowerment: various options are available, such as vouchers, open enrolment, and/or the transfer of power to governing bodies. Various American districts or States have adopted one or more of these, though parents there have always had more influence.

4. Performance-related pay - through one-off bonuses, extra increments, or pay enhancements somewhere between the two. These can be linked to student performance or general judgements on merit or performance. Appraisal itself has many variants: eg self-appraisal, the production of a checklist of traits a good teacher is supposed to have, a report on achievement, or the extent to which teachers reach management objectives.

5. Minimum competency testing: performance indicators working through students' tests or exam results. This 'is often heralded as a viable means to exercise hierarchical control over teachers' curricular choices' (Rosenholtz, in Lieberman, 1990). In Tennessee, children are subjected to a vast battery of tests which puts great pressure on teachers, but a survey of Tennessee teachers showed that the pressure was making 20% consider leaving the profession. This approach is at the heart of ERA.

These strategies offer different prospects for the teacher, with the first two increasing the status of the teacher, the third diminishing it, the fourth having a variable effect, and the last leading to intensified control. However, even then none of these strategies is straightforward in effect. Greater professionalisation may extend teacher control over the teaching process while the mentor concept, which takes this process further, may divide the profession into an elite and an underclass subservient to this. On the other hand, there is even some left-wing support for the latter, for instance in the proposal from Ross and Tomlinson for the creation of a new class of 'senior teachers' to enable teaching 'to use its best and most highly paid talent more effectively' (1991, p23). The same policies may have different purposes. Various forms of American teacher empowerment reviewed by Johnson (in Clune and Witte, 1990) indicate that even the most liberating version, which accords teachers some professional rights over recruitment (or dismissal) can perhaps be interpreted as extended control, not dissimilar to the power of head teachers under LMS, for instance when a junior high school 'cut eight full-time positions and bought outside hourly instruction in special subjects' (pp352/3). On the other hand, the establishment over teachers of a more parochial level of control through increased say for parents or governing bodies is a matter of degree. In Britain this is accompanied by loss of curricular control, but in Chicago 'it is clearly expected that schools will adopt dramatically different curricula in seeking to improve the educational achievement of their students' (Hess, 1992, p166). The same applies to performance pay. Teaching unions in Britain favour appraisal as an aid to professionalism, but linked to performance it becomes a form of control rather than of career guidance. Appraisal on the basis of possession of qualities or traits is clearly the most ideological form of appraisal and the strongest form of control.

It would be wrong, therefore, to assume that a reduction in the influence of the teacher is necessary to any conception of educational reform. There is really nothing inevitable about this. While there are attempts in this country to reduce the number of teachers or, alternatively, the qualifications or experience of new entrants, in France a major expansion in the profession is underway, partly as a result of an attempt to get 80% of the school population to stay on in school to take the *baccalauréat*. An entirely new institution has been established to provide teacher training at university level across the board - the *Instituts Universitaires de Formation des Maîtres*. An explicit goal in this change, supported in a report submitted to the Education Ministry in 1989, is to try to raise the academic status of teacher training without losing the vocational element traditional primary teacher training entailed. 'Together these constitute what the Report calls *"professionnalité globale"* (all-round professionalism)' (Blondel, 1991, p201). While France is one of the few countries to link increments to performance, involving competitive appraisal by head teachers, additional duties bring contractual rights to higher pay (Le Metais, in Tomlinson, 1992).

The concluding argument of this chapter is that current change in Britain may well be the reverse of much longer-term developments. On the assumption that recession is overcome and the economy continues to grow, albeit more slowly than some others, then education is likely to take its share in the benefits this provides. To ensure that these benefits are reasonably distributed, and at the same time to supply thorough-going information on educational processes which parents and students themselves may increasingly demand, pressure on teachers is likely to grow not just to provide facts, let alone simply credentials, but a much broader service. The current attempt to limit the teacher is likely to prove counter-productive.

Bringing the teacher to book

The pressure to make teachers account more fully for their activities now *seems* irrevocable. Control may be in the form of greater emphasis on contractual specification; increased supervision by employers (performance evaluation schemes); legislative determination of hours worked; removal or curtailment of rights over the curriculum; the imposition of centralised tests on students (inevitably also a test of teacher performance); or the monitoring or publication of school outcomes. However, these pressures have not all been consistent, partly because accountability is itself an ideological term. In the case of teachers the term is in fact meaningless, as none of the changes underway actually make teachers more accountable *as individuals*. The influence of the occupation as a whole is being reduced, but that is a very different matter.

Ranson, Hannon and Gray propose two simple forms of accountability which determine the outer framework within which the struggle is likely to operate (in Walker and Barton, 1987), one being the 'professional' mode in which teachers remain the prime judges of student performance, which is assessed broadly and not solely on examination results; the other is the 'market' mode in which teachers are accountable to consumers (parents), who need to compare performance on the basis solely of examination results. They compare the response of three LEAs to the requirement of the 1980 Education Act on LEAs to publish information on secondary school performance. One LEA promoted a professionalist ethos: while information on students was increased through portfolios combining exam marks, graded assessment, and personal records of achievement, schools themselves were assessed only through dialogue with the LEA. 'The tacit agreement is established that in exchange for a restricted public language, a more elaborate, extended code is developed between professionals' (p11). This is in marked contrast to schools (in an affluent area) which fitted into a market model - explicitly compared in terms of exam results and with spare capacity in schools maintained to facilitate parental choice. The third LEA suggests a new type of accountability based on neither professional nor consumer sovereignty, but on community participation and citizenship. Schools in this authority, apparently with a high concentration of black people, are encouraged to negotiate the learning contract with both students and parents. The writers do not describe how this occurs, but argue that this is a more genuine accountability than the competitive system of the market model, 'which fragments and destroys the public as community' (p20).

In practice, accountability can mean many things. While the national curriculum and tests impose accountability from outside, many teachers welcome aspects of the change: partly because it offers new ways of thinking about teaching, but also because it reduces *some* of the burdens. And there is no doubt that this potential responsiveness has always existed. Hamilton's account of a local attempt to introduce testing for informal and diagnostic purposes, a development which required considerable skill and commitment, describes a successful subversion of the scheme by teachers for the purpose of classification by ability, thus routinising and simplifying the task (in Reid and Walker, 1975). History and habitude also play a part. A survey of primary teachers in France and England showed French teachers

> strongly supporting the need for a centralised system as the basis for equality of opportunity and English teachers manifesting an equally intense belief in the importance of institutional and individual professional autonomy in order to provide most suitably for different pupil needs (Broadfoot, 1990).

Nor are alternative influences from outside the teaching profession necessarily straightforward. There has, for instance, been persistent left-wing distrust of teachers, seeing in them either a potential source of unwelcome conservative influence on children, or alternatively, through a commitment to a professionalist ethos, a threat to the principles of trade unionism. The Labour Party's failed to oppose the principle of the national curriculum in parliament, which has widespread support, if for various purposes, for instance as a means of transmitting 'values embedded in liberal democracy (O'Hear and White, 1991, p9). Control and prescription are generally popular. This ambivalence to the teacher on the Left has a long pedigree, of course, going back at least to the 'new sociology of education' (eg Young, 1971). While making teachers an active vehicle for ideological change theoretically gave teachers a central social role, there was little doubt that this was because of prior inadequacy, and that change would itself be inspired by cadres of (ideologically) effective teachers. A related ambivalence relates to the target of curricular reform. Following from the seminal work of Bernstein (1971), if middle-class homes give their children educational superiority because they prepare them better for (middle-class) teaching processes, should the working class become more middle-class, or should it be not children but the system of education which should change?

A different form of ambivalence affected other writings from the 1960-70s. Illich's diatribe against schooling (as opposed to education) was certainly radical, but in confusing liberation with accountability, his message is uncomfortably right-wing, for instance sneering at the waste implied by the cost of investing in 'twelve years of schooling in New York City (a condition for acceptance of a worker into the Sanitation Department) - almost fifteen thousand dollars' (1973, p21). Illich even proposed an equivalent to education vouchers with his 'edu-credit cards'. The libertarian agenda failed to understand that doing away with schools is hardly likely to reduce inequality. The left-wing task has been not Illich's libertarian deschooling but a reschooling, in which teachers become more not less important. Young's injunction to question 'categories like teacher and pupil or even what counts as education, ability and achievement' (1972, p201), while sounding like Illich, requires distinct action if schools are not to maintain the class structure 'of which they are a reflection' (Young, 1972, p210). Marx replaces Freud as liberator. But if reschooling provided teachers with a script, it also startled them with a powerful spotlight, and the Right were watching closely from the wings.

Teaching centre stage

Despite the above pressures, the teaching profession had developed a fairly coherent, liberal-humanist approach - if considered unchallenging of standards by the Right and unchallenging of the status quo by the Left. Perhaps the main formal achievement of the teaching profession has been the establishment of the CSE and the successor GCSE (though both achievements were qualified). CSE Mode 3, based on teacher assessment, led to a significant expansion of the curriculum and of teaching styles, inducing from the Right the claim that 'we cannot afford to become a CSE Mode 3 nation' (quoted in Whitty, 1985, p131). Nevertheless, assessment continued into the GCSE, and there can be no doubt that this exam bucked the trend, even if the original idea has been altered and ever since its adoption there have been demands for its demise. For instance, the Institute of Economic Affairs (1988) has called for abolition and, failing this, the establishment of an alternative O-level type examination for the top 15-20% of children.

The period around the establishment of the GCSE represents the final flickering of teacher influence over the direction of education. In 1984 the Schools Council, with statutory responsibility for disseminating new ideas and best practice stemming from teachers themselves, was abolished and replaced by bodies in which the teachers had no fixed say. At the time the Council was developing major new curricular proposals, as it happens in parallel with the DES. According to Plaskow the DES asked the Council to delay publishing its *Practical Curriculum* so that the DES' *School Curriculum* could appear first. 'They were both published in April, 1981, with coincidentally similarly-coloured covers. That was the only similarity between them' (in Morris and Griggs, 1988, p210). A later teacher-influenced report, the Low Attainers in Mathematics Project (LAMP), commissioned by the DES and strongly influenced by Cockcroft, was also wholly rejected.

> Mathematics can be effectively learned only by involving pupils in experimenting, questioning, reflecting, discovering, inventing and discussing. Mathematics should be a kind of learning which requires a minimum of factual knowledge and a great deal of experience in dealing with situations using particular kinds of thinking skills (LAMP, 1987, p9).

LAMP's aim was to improve the teaching of maths through a wide network of teacher co-operation. The report, at just the wrong time, was a straightforward claim 'that expertise lies in teachers' own experience' (p38). Its main theme made an inseparable link between progressive ideals and efficiency, with individual approaches to problem-solving seen as improving the performance of both teachers and students. The findings were rejected as irrelevant to standards. The following satirical comparison from a college lecturer sums up well enough the impasse reached between political demands to commodify the teaching process and professional resistance to this.

> JUNK FOOD... All the preparation is done for you by someone else... It does you little good; it tends to pass through you quickly.... All the real nutrient is removed and substitutes have to be added... JUNK MATHEMATICS... This is done by the author or teacher... It looks well structured and appears logical, but is dull and lacks substance. Pupils are unable to retain or apply it in new contexts (LAMP, 1987, p15).

Perhaps not unrelated to this, following a television programme which claimed that children who eat junk food perform poorly at school and, further, that vitamin tablets improve IQ, there was a run on vitamin supplements in the shops. Certainly teachers need to be worried when they can be replaced in part by vitamin pills.

Proletarian teachers?

While the claim of teachers to be a profession has always been weak - they neither deal with clients in the strict sense nor have rights to self-regulation - one major factor which gives the use of the term some credibility is the substantial curricular autonomy teachers have enjoyed. But with the loss of curricular control and a combination of actions intended to undermine teacher organisations - the removal of bargaining rights and the transfer of employment to governing bodies - the teachers' loss has been two-fold.

Faced with this double decline, are teachers being proletarianised? This also suggests deskilling - a paradox, if true, for those trained to teach skills to others. It is well enough known that white-collar work does not necessarily signify middle-class status. Clerks are an obvious example. The proportion of clerks in the workforce increased from less than 5% in 1911 to 16% in 1979, but at the same time their status plummeted from one of privilege to inferiority, and this decline was accompanied by a large drop in relative pay. In 1913/14 average male clerical pay was 122% of the average for all occupations, but 93% by 1978. In the case of women, who by 1971 formed 70% of the clerical workforce, there was a rise from 56% to a giddy 69% (Callinicos and Harman, 1987, pp14-17). Callinicos and Harman include teachers - 'white-collar employees who are actually members of the working class' - in this apparent proletarianisation. The pay of teachers declined significantly against average national earnings from 1975 to the early 1980s (Jones, in McNay and Ozga, 1985, p234).

In addition to the suspension of teachers' negotiating rights, the nationalisation of the curriculum, and the imposition of nationally devised testing procedures, a further threat has come through the introduction of new means of teacher accreditation. A smallish element of the change is the introduction of 'licensed' teachers (mostly teachers with qualifications and experience from abroad who would previously have had to obtain an appropriate British qualification to enter the profession), and 'articled' teachers (graduates who may avoid the standard teaching qualifications by training for two years within schools under a 'mentor', but with 20% of this training period spent in college). Both may diminish the sense of a 'professional' route into teaching, but do not remove it. Take-up is slow, with only 842 teachers entering the profession by the above means in 1990/91, compared to nearly 24,000 doing a B.Ed/BA or PGCE (Gilroy, 1992, p11). It may also be that such schemes enable a mode of training which is interactively geared to the demands of students themselves: which Lumb, Mason and Price call the 'empowerment of articled teachers' (1991, p218). Ultimately, however, the move towards accreditation in terms of 'competencies' - a predefined set of traits which trained teachers are supposed to have or to acquire - which is closely linked to the notion that college education is not as necessary as previously thought, suggests an attempt to switch from professional to bureaucratic criteria of success. Many of the proffered definitions are, like the SATs imposed on children, predictably vapid, eg the need to 'produce coherent lesson plans' formulated by the Council for the Accreditation of Teacher Education (quoted by McNamara, 1992, p277). Licensed teachers in particular may be judged largely on the basis of 'competencies'. McNamara points out that this change serves to shift the emphasis from *process* to *outcomes*, just as national testing replaces a method with a measurement. Above all, as 'a competency statement means whatever anyone wants it to mean' (p278), the change puts teachers in the hands of bureaucrats and politicians who can change the definition of a good teacher at whim.

To break 'the hold of the dogmas about teaching methods and classroom organisation', as Mr Clarke as Education Secretary of State in 1991 put it (quoted in Gilroy, 1992, p6), the PGCE is also to be 80% school-based. While this element had been increasing in teacher training through voluntary agreements between higher education institutions and schools (with most PGCE being over 50% in the classroom), Clarke's imposition clearly suggests a substitution of practical for professional status. Trainee teachers will be marginalised in their schools, be forced into routine work, be cut off from those learning elsewhere, be given very little time to reflect on their methods or experience, and be inculcated into a narrow departmentalism. 'It cannot be anything but bad if trainee teachers are to be isolated in schools and never have the opportunity to develop the broader perspective the profession requires' (Poppleton and Pullin, 1992, p129). The general move away from graduate status suggests that thinking teachers, as opposed to practically competent teachers, are seen as a problem. Having a degree does not make a good teacher, but being able to place your job in the context of teaching methods, child development, and the broader social issues, is hardly likely to arise if teachers are merely required to have a 'knack' of teaching. It should also be pointed out that while entry into the profession has for a long time required graduate status, even by the end of the 1980s only half of teachers trained in the UK had degrees or an equivalent qualification.

The move towards 'alternative certification', following various American experiments (school-based training, competency statements, mentor teachers), has been initiated in a period of falling rolls, a situation which naturally weakens the possibility of resistance. But perhaps the changes have also been introduced with an eye to future growth. The impact of birth rate changes will be to increase the number of primary age children in the 1990s, but at the same time reducing the number of young adults to teach them. Weakening the status and influence of teachers now will therefore serve to prevent any growth in influence when demand for teachers increases. In the USA it has been asserted that the demand for new teachers in the 1990s will be double that of the 1970s. 'Alternative certification is then a response to the shortage of teachers in urban areas' (Fullan, 1991, p310). On the other hand, of course, this could backfire at the point when the market for teachers improves. Fullan blames a turnover rate of 30% in the first year of teaching on excessive reliance in field-based teacher-training, where induction is short-term and the teacher feels unsupported.

Performance-related pay probably has the same non-educational focus. While Tomlinson argues that this 'is part of a necessary change to school and college culture, if standards are to be raised significantly' (1992, p2), the evidence is pretty non-existent. Tomlinson's claim that schools need to acquire leaner management structures like other, more industrial organisations, with 'smaller numbers of highly skilled and skill-flexible workers' (p13) appears, paradoxically, to be related to the need to attract more staff, 'to help solve the consequences of the demographic timebomb' (p14). So, again, proposed changes to the teaching profession are geared less to improved school performance than to overcoming shortages (without requiring across the board pay increases). Indeed, the claim that paying for performance automatically means improved educational standards is too tenuous to be worthy of discussion. Rewarding for 'excellence' may well reduce creativity in others by encouraging teachers to copy solely what others are doing (Freedman, in Walker and Barton, 1987, p56). All that can be said is that performance pay is extremely limited in Europe and even in the USA it has become marginal, with one national survey revealing only 2% of public-school teachers getting individual awards for performance (Jacobson, in Tomlinson, 1992, p48). This is because the system has many inherent problems: performance criteria are difficult to settle; aspects of achievement as measured by output (eg exam results) are out of the teacher's control (ie depend on intake); resentment and demotivation arise amongst those who fail to receive extra rewards; and extra pay becomes an expectation which cannot easily be cut back. Thus far the government has fought shy of performance-related pay across the board, but only with great reluctance. It seems not unlikely that the principle will creep in on an incremental basis.

Control of pay is only one aspect of a possible proletarianisation. Another is reduced security of tenure deriving from schools having cash-limited budgets. Here again Britain is following in the footsteps of the USA, where in some areas teachers have been treated much more ruthlessly. Between 1979 and 1983 many thousands of teachers in the USA were made redundant, the state of Massachusetts, for instance, losing 8,000 in one year alone (Freedman, in Walker and Barton, 1987, p41). In the view of Webb and Ashton the process of control sets in train a self-reinforcing circularity. Teachers' lower status reduces motivation, further reducing the right to esteem. In extreme cases teachers may be considered to be 'burnt out'. The effect of this on performance is then taken as a cue for the need for greater control. They report USA surveys which show a considerable decline in teacher morale. In 1961 57% of female teachers (and 35% of males) said they certainly would choose teaching again if they had another career choice. By 1982 the figures were 25% and 16% respectively (in Walker and Barton, 1987, p22), although other factors such as declining demand must have been a further factor behind this slump in interest.

Teachers are increasingly subject to bureaucratic control, whether of work processes or of pay and conditions. But this may not be tantamount to proletarianisation. Certainly the scope for initiative has been reduced, but the range of tasks to be undertaken has actually increased (some stemming directly from the national curriculum). The loss of control suggests deprofessionalisation rather than deskilling. The ambivalent position in which this puts teachers can be seen clearly in a central aspect of their working environment, the issue of discipline. Teachers have often claimed they are vulnerable to violence and abuse, though the Elton Report (DES, 1989) put some of the blame for discipline problems back on teachers, for instance noting an HMI report which claimed that teachers were inadequately prepared for classroom control, partly as a result of over-theoretical initial training. The implication is that practical rather than professional preparation is the answer. However, a mass of practical advice exists on how to cope with difficult classroom behaviour (eg Robertson, 1981), but such advice can only be implemented through the opportunity to rethink practice, for instance through INSET, and through long-term experience. The immediate experience trainees get will be fairly useless in the long term.

There are certainly many proponents of reversion to firm methods of teaching: teaching the class from the front with limited attention to individuals, using fully prepared materials, and so on. The national curriculum and associated tests are clearly designed to force this approach. However, while good preparation is obviously beneficial, the evidence that teachers fail to maintain control as a result of adherence to a specific pedagogic theory, is extremely weak. Even empirical studies such as that of Rutter et al (1979) can tell us very little. For instance, the finding of a correlation between more time spent in teaching and better student behaviour (p115) is a very poor index of actual classroom interactions.

Discipline and control are in reality far more complex issues. As parental and student rights increase, for instance with a growing awareness of child abuse placing both a duty and a danger in the path of teachers (as many as 30 heads or deputies alone have been suspended pending accusations into alleged sexual or physical abuse: *Guardian*, 2.6.93), or with the proliferation of threats and counter-threats over racism, the question of discipline is not just a simplistic one of classroom control but of dealing with complex and ambiguous situations where no easy answer may be apparent.

The ambiguity of some disciplinary issues is brought out clearly in Booth's sensitive analysis (in Booth and Coulby, 1987) of a crisis in a Manchester school in 1985, when large-scale graffiti appeared on school walls saying things such as '[name of teacher's] mum sucks niggers cocks'. The LEA overturned the suspension of five fifth-year children and eventually suspended 47 teachers for refusing to teach them. Strike action followed across the LEA, and support for this action came from normally cautious unions such as the SHA and NAHT, but also from parents. So, with teachers being offered a new placement away from the stigmatised children, the punishments they felt should have been meted out to the children were visited on them - suspensions and (prospective) transfer. The conflict had no simple resolution and ended only when the children eventually left the school. Of real note was the astonishing balance of positions. In the view of the NUT publication, *The Teacher*, 'The issue is about the right of teachers to teach and pupils to learn in a sexist-free, racist-free and violence-free environment' (quoted on p16), while one councillor 'argued in turn that the visions of violence were motivated by a desire to see the reintroduction of corporal punishment in schools'. The authority was apparently concerned to protect the interests of the disadvantaged from heavy-handed treatment, yet one member of the Parent Action Committee accused the authority of ignoring the views of the community: 'This is a working-class area and the dispute has affected the prospects of working-class young people' (p18).

While recognising the teachers' right to dignity, Booth himself argues that in 'common with other professional groups such as shopkeepers, doctors and social workers they are not free to exhibit preferences for one client over another' (p19). Yet in reality, and like social workers especially, teachers have little professional status. It is understandable, therefore, if they insist on more formal protection. AMMA's position (in *Assaults on Teachers*) quite rightly asserts that teachers, not just parents and students, have rights; unwillingness to 'tolerate abuse by pupils is not an admission of professional weakness'. It is rather, the right of any worker to be protected against abuse. It is difficult to see how in current circumstances teachers would get any reward or credit for turning a blind eye to abuse by students. The public sector in which teachers, like social workers, cannot put a foot right, is at the moment hardly conducive to recognition of such achievement.

Professionalism and industrialism

It seems apparent that in recent years teachers have been subject to deprofessionalisation rather than to deskilling. In this case then, do teachers benefit from professionalisation or unionisation? There is certainly considerable evidence of militancy on the part of teachers and their unions. The teaching unions were established during the period of the 'new unionism', with the NUT quickly becoming one of the country's biggest unions. In 1910 it was the fifth largest overall, but the biggest white-collar union, and also the biggest union in the public sector (Seifert 1987). Seifert's historical account of industrial action reveals considerable militancy directed specifically to improved pay and conditions in the early part of this century. In 1919, 300 schools in Yorkshire were closed through strike action. During the war most areas of the country were affected by disputes. In Lowestoft, in 1923, when the authority insisted on doubling the pay-cut agreed in Burnham, over 1000 children were kept away from school by their parents in favour of their regular teachers.

On the other hand, hankering after professional status (in fact returning to the era of craft unionisation) may have impeded the advance of unions. In the USA the National Education Association (NEA) is the second largest union, but it has strong professionalist leanings, as evinced in the following statement from a senior NEA figure in 1957.

> Unionism lowers the ideals of teaching. By emphasizing the selfish, though necessary, economic needs of teachers - salary, hours, tenure, retirement - unionism misses altogether the finer ideals of teaching and the rich compensations that do not appear in the salary envelope (quoted in Kerchner and Mitchell, 1988, p57).

While many of the major teachers' strikes in Britain have from the start been about bread-and-butter issues, Seifert suggests that one of the most vital concerns was the goal of professional status, resulting in 'various struggles over registration, a teachers' council, uncertificated teachers, and control over training' (1987, p17). Professionalisation has always been a strong union demand. One cause of the Rhondda dispute of 1918, when 1,200 teachers resigned, was the low pay of uncertificated teachers: the NUT had until then not allowed uncertificated teachers membership of the union. However, the value of reducing the ability of the authorities to employ uncertificated teachers as a means of cutting wages, along with the additional benefit of an extended and unified membership, together were worth more than attempts to maintain a professional differential. The inclusion of uncertificated teachers in 1918 added 11,000 to the membership of 100,000 (Seifert, 1987, p41). When, more recently, the NUT opposed nursery classes attached to schools staffed primarily by unqualified nursery assistants, its concern 'to promote opportunities for its members' conflicted with its 'genuine desire to obtain more nursery provision, especially for the disadvantaged child' (Lodge and Blackstone, in McNay and Ozga, 1985, p222). This conflict of interests between provider and client has, of course, become a fertile source of right-wing insistence on control of union influence (though this promotion of the rights of consumers still appears to exclude increased nursery provision).

It has been argued by several commentators that professionalisation and union militancy are by no means necessarily distinct processes. Roy (in Kimber and Richardson, 1974) describes two conflicts which reveal either side of this balance. In the Durham dispute of 1950-52 the Labour local authority had insisted that all teachers (and other public servants working for the authority) should join a union. Remarkably, even the NUT opposed this measure, apparently objecting to enforced politicisation. The NUT put out a statement asserting that 'the policy of compulsory membership is deeply repugnant to professional workers' (quoted on p95). At the request of the union nearly 5,000 teachers in Durham County went on strike and the authority backed down. The second case was an offence to teachers as trade unionists. In 1952 the government sought to impose greater pension contributions on teachers, and again the union endorsed strike activity. Attendance at branch meetings jumped from 30% to 80% (p100). Roy concludes that teachers and their unions may act like a professional association in certain circumstances but predicts that as pressure grows on conditions of service, militancy is likely to increase.

Lauder and Yee reveal the reverse of deprofessionalisation in New Zealand, where teachers have been under as much pressure as in the UK and USA, but have successfully used their union strength to resist de-professionalisation. The two occupational forms are therefore mutually supportive rather than contradictory. Analysis of wage trends in New Zealand suggests that strike action (the union mode) had been successful in raising wages while teachers' assessments of change in their own control over the curriculum (a professional concern) had not decreased (in Walker and Barton, 1987). In addition, it seems reasonable to argue that increased administrative control can potentially release creativity. For instance, the more the head becomes a manager, the greater the reliance on the teaching staff to perform adequately. No change is one-sided in its effect. This is also implicit in Bernstein's concepts of 'collective' and 'integrated' education (1971). The former consists of compartmentalised, self-contained subject specialisms, producing hierarchical knowledge and control of staff (as fact-giving limits independence and the scope to innovate). The integrated curriculum (teaching thematically across subject specialisms) decompartmentalises and therefore encourages co-operation between teachers. This further suggests a professional ethos which can support collective action by teachers disposed to it.

Views also differ as to the significance of the undoubted militancy the early years of the century revealed. It can be seen as part of a wider movement of labour unrest and therefore as an aspect of class conflict. Nevertheless, with post-war expansion the unions became an important part of the educational Establishment, negotiating policy with the DES and LEA associations. While, in Seifert's view (1987), this incorporation 'into educational subgovernment remained partial' (p48), the unions were nevertheless incorporated into 'respectable professionalism' (p31). The NAS/UWT, perhaps the more aggressive teachers' union, has made it plain that its long-term strategy is to raise the professional status of teachers - including for instance their right to control the curriculum.

The political cycle

The implication of much of the above is that there is no inevitable *trend* towards loss of teacher autonomy or status. Part of the change is cyclical. In a period of declining rolls and recession, the Centre, currently strongly opposed to the public sector, has taken advantage of the weakness of the profession to undermine its long-term market position. After the last war the teaching profession rose in influence, pay and esteem as a result of growth in the education sector as a whole (and therefore without the need for significant strike action). The two decades after the end of the war saw the establishment of equal pay for women teachers, a fairly stable process of negotiation through Burnham, a substantial increase in the demand for teachers, and nearly a doubling of education spending as a proportion of GNP. Teachers also acquired considerable autonomy in the determination of the curriculum - partly because the government could not have managed expansion at the same time as extending control. All seemed plain-sailing. In the words of Max Morris, ex-NUT President.

> Every improvement in teachers' conditions is inevitably an improvement in the education of the children of our schools. Equally every improvement in educational conditions within schools improves teachers' conditions. The two things go together like that (quoted in Shipman, 1984, p84).

However, as circumstances declined, the unions were forced into action. The imposition of public sector pay restraint led directly to the first really national teachers' strike in Britain, the ultimate result of which was Houghton. In 1970 the NUT followed the NAS into membership of the TUC. From 1974 to 1987 education's share of public spending fell from 13% to 10% (Morris and Griggs, 1988, pp15/16). While for much of this time teacher numbers did not fall significantly relative to rolls, reduction of teacher pay is certainly a government target. In 1981, 22% of scale one teachers were at the top of their scale, compared to 44% of scale two teachers and 53% of scale three. The increase over the previous three years had been 6%, 8% and 10% respectively (Walsh, in Ranson and Tomlinson, p129). The pressure on individual schools under LMS to reduce these costs is immense, and this is perhaps beginning to take effect. An Audit Commission survey of 100 schools revealed a small trend towards increased student-teacher ratios in schools which have been managing their budgets for some time (Audit Commission, 1993). In addition, it seems that cheaper teachers are being appointed, possibly 'irrespective of whether they are the most appropriate people for the job' (p10). While government control over numbers is constrained, it can act to reduce costs. According to the Day report (DES, 1993, p9), after a period of shortages, planning targets for recruitment have been exceeded, and it now apparent that recruitment is being used to lower costs. 'Only 22 per cent of retirements were at the normal age in 1991-92, compared with almost twice that proportion in the early 1980s' (DES, 1993, p12).

However, the government's hands are still loosely tied as it is by no means certain that shortages have been eliminated. In secondary schools there remain problems in subjects central to the national curriculum, especially mathematics, which in 1990 was 37% below targeted recruitment (Ross and Tomlinson, 1991, p23). In addition, recently increased recruitment is partly explained by recession, as teaching offers relatively high security. If the recession ends, 'the current attractiveness of teaching might then be expected to abate'. With rising rolls and the demands of the national curriculum, supply problems 'remain a distinct possibility for the medium-term' (DES, 1993, p15). The national curriculum also creates more pressure to match teachers to posts by qualification, experience or age. In 1984 the number of CDT teachers aged over 50 was twice the average (Merson, 1989, p172). While they may be excellent teachers, the likelihood of recent training in technology is reduced. It has also to be said that with a sluggish market (through falling rolls), specific rationalisations (leading to ring-fencing), and an ageing profession, mobility is already highly limited; yet the entire structure of recent 'reform' is geared to reducing mobility even more, eg through 'weakening local authority discretion in the deployment of teachers' (Merson, 1989, p171).

In summary, pay and status in teaching are more vulnerable to cyclical changes than other public-sector professions, however ideologically determined the government's attempt to sponsor a trend towards decreased pay and status for teachers. For much of the post-war period circumstances have been in favour of teachers, but this was ended by a combination of falling rolls and continued recession. With any significant alteration in these conditions, many supposedly necessary teacher 'reforms' would be difficult to maintain.

Working in the public sector

Even the Right like to assume that trade unions should be professional bodies. 'Many of the NUT's policies are virtually identical with those of the Labour and Communist parties and are anti-educational in that they have not led to more boys and girls learning more and better' (Naylor and Marks, in Cox and Marks, 1982, p119). On the other hand, while some on the Left persist in opposing professionalist pretensions and in arguing for 'an alliance on educational issues... complemented by an alliance with the Labour movement on broader questions of social and economic policy' (Jones, in McNay and Ozga, 1985, p249), it really seems very difficult to separate issues of industrialism and professionalism. Saran reduces the distinction between trade-union and professional leanings to a 'moot point' (in Morris and Griggs, p147). In the view of Kerchner and Mitchell, teachers in the USA are caught between the model of commercial, client-service relationships and a model of general public service, with neither fully appropriate. Teachers need to move beyond traditional trade-union concerns, replacing industrial unionism with 'professional unionism' (p18).

However, this is not straightforward. The ideal underplays the significance of two factors which produce the tension in the first place. One is the impact of politicisation. Kerchner and Mitchell acknowledge this insofar as they see professionalism as a necessary antidote to politicisation, but fail to see how entrenched political interference may become. The professional model cannot assume any shape outside a political framework. Their own 'Educational Policy Trust Agreements' between unions and administrators would be marginal without political support. However much the NUT may claim to be a profession, or to put the interests of users above those of providers, it is difficult in the current political climate to see this taking root. The second problem, which again makes direct action in support of the professional model a hopeless task on its own, is the fact that most teachers are public servants dependent on public sector pay determination. This dependence severely limits both the status and the obligations of teachers. They have little control over the rewards they receive. Similarly, Fullan's argument that the future for improvement in pedagogy is an 'interactive professionalism' (1991, p290), which encourages much more interaction and support between teachers, simply begs the question. The status of such peer support is politically defined. Teachers cannot adopt a professional mantle. Whatever the conflict between professional and labourist goals, professionalism is denied by the position of the teaching process within the public sector. This brings us full circle to the argument at the beginning of this chapter that the attack on teachers is not motivated on educational grounds but is based on their vulnerable position as public-sector employees.

It will be argued in the remainder of this chapter that what is at issue is not the tension between professionalism and labourism, but the equivocal role of teachers as public servants. Disputes have become more bitter since 1969 neither in response to an attack on teachers' sense of professional status nor, alternatively, as a rejection by teachers of the latter in favour of militancy over pay. The problem has been the vulnerability of the public sector to interference from central government. Seifert comes to similar conclusions on this issue and on the national politicisation of teacher conflict. 'The central issue, then, was not the inhibitions of a false definition of professionalism, but the reality of teacher power in a decade of rapidly centralized control over more and more aspects of state education' (1987, p118). This centralisation undermines the professional autonomy of the teacher, and with it the claim to improved pay and conditions. Equally critical to teachers is the fragmentation of their power base. Current policy is a deliberate attempt to break the unions, to dismantle national agreements and pay structures, to tie job security to the popularity (and implicitly viability) of individual schools, and to transfer employment responsibility to shifting and idiosyncratic governing bodies. The result will be a fundamental decline not only in conditions of service, but in status and autonomy, with the teacher's wider network of influence greatly diminished.

Two common but conflicting views of the impact of the public sector on the teaching profession exist, neither adequate in itself. The first sees the public sector as vital to the extension of education, and through this the economy. The history of trade unionism in education is in part one of the struggle for such an expansion (eg in the face of Treasury representation of the interests of the taxpayer). This is apparent in the above quotation from Max Morris, ex-NUT president. The second view reverses this by arguing that the growth of the public sector directly impedes economic growth. Human capital can develop only at the expense of private capital. However, many on the Left also view this rightward shift as inevitable because it perhaps presages the decline of capitalism into chaos. Left-wing asseveration of right-wing policy at least confirms that the Centre is hollow.

> To read the educational output of the National Union of Teachers is to experience the power of the past over the present. Looking back, the union emphasizes its overriding aim of securing expansion of opportunity; it stresses the reasonableness of its cause and the supporters the cause has attracted, across the political spectrum.... This outlook is plainly that of a body which claims not simply trade union status but co-responsibility for the education service (Jones, in McNay and Ozga, 1985, p233).

Jones implies that this view is vapid rather than broad, and the professionalist stance obstructive of wider action in support of labour. 'The problem with this approach is that it is not at all symmetrical with government policy. For the government, education occupies just a few degrees of a wider arc of vision' (p242). And with the slits in the vizor apparently becoming narrower it seems reasonable to be at least mildly apocalyptic: 'cost discussions about how best to spend a growing budget are over' (Lodge and Blackstone, in McNay and Ozga, 1985, p218).

However, the underlying problem for teachers, previously shielded by consistent economic growth and rising rolls, is their peculiar role in the public sector. One aspect of this is the extreme weakening of the teachers' position through formula funding. Allowing only average staffing costs forces schools with expensive teachers to look elsewhere. Yet the tying of cash to bums on seats rather than to experience or ability has no obvious educational advantage. It is also a contrast to more economically successful countries. In France the links between the major unions and the socialist government have brought considerable protection. And though something like licensed teachers were established - the *professeurs d'enseignement générales des colleges* - these are mostly ex-primary teachers given a back-up course and a year at university, as well as being recruited by exam. They are not very different from other teachers. In Germany there has been a long-term attempt to remove non-professional teachers - the number remaining is negligible - and to increase the proportion of specialist teachers, now nearly 70%, in secondary schools. It seems unlikely that this will be reversed. Moreover, as civil servants they cannot be dismissed. The position of teachers has been affected by cuts, but largely through highly reduced chances of entering the profession. In 1986 91,500 teachers were not appointed to a position in the public sector; only 12% of applicants succeeded (Weiss and Weishaupt, 1989, p43). Britain is in fact following an American rather than a European model, with a similar impact on teacher motivation.

British teachers are therefore under an extraordinary double pressure as *commodified public servants*. They face the worst of both worlds as they simultaneously grapple with the power of the state and the power of the market. They have, of course, nearly always been public servants, but their status has changed at critical junctures in the formal definition of this functionary role - for instance, in passing from charity to board status, and thence to employment by an LEA. More recently, the central state has begun to take control. The initial stages of each change is a benefit to teachers, as increased centralisation pools their bargaining power and rationalises pay and conditions, thus reducing the scope for arbitrary action by the employer. Before the war, unions and central government were sometimes allies against local authorities, as the establishment of a framework of national public sector pay bargaining was necessary to teachers for effective trade unionism. The state's interference was a result of a desire partly for control, partly for rationalisation (including of pay). Even when central government helped set up the Burnham machinery a number of authorities refused to be bound by its agreements (until the state made the agreements statutorily binding). The state also, if intermittently (eg through Houghton) ensured considerable increases in teacher pay. This later sometimes transcended partisanship. In the 1980s a number of Labour authorities not only sought cuts but took harsh action against striking teachers, such as docking pay for teachers refusing to supervise at lunchtime. Employers asked the Clegg Commission on pay comparability to take into account 'the limited nature of managerial tasks' undertaken by teachers (Seifert, 1987, p155). But over time the advantage of central intervention diminished as the central authority began to flex its own muscles: the unions became bigger but took on bigger opposition too. The government abolished Burnham repeating, with a degree of insouciance, a previous Labour Secretary of State's statement, that no government 'could put itself in a position where it could hand over the power on the global sum to someone else other than itself' (DES, 1987, p7). In reality, it was now interfering not only in the 'global sum' but in teachers' pay and conditions, which was Burnham's central task.

In the final stage the rationalisation of conditions initially wrought by the central state brings with it the nationalisation of conflict, though the State has now succeeded in shunting actual direction of teachers' employment on to governing bodies. However, shuffling off responsibility for rationalisation to the school level may strengthen the hand of the unions as the employers also become fragmented. While attempted redundancies have so far been few, teacher unions are already 'cashing in' on the danger: *When the chips are down... you can rely on AMMA/If your job were under threat, would you know what to do about it? NASUWT does!* This may be one reason why the government has recently considered removing the immunities granted to unions in the public sector. This would give any school (or any parent) the right to take a union to court for any industrial action. In the long term massive conflict is inevitable. The stupidity of all this is that it will not help education. Finance rather than quality will determine the careers of teachers, and a good but expensive teacher will in general be far more vulnerable than a cheap but inadequate teacher. This does not mean high pay signifies quality, only that low pay is becoming the chief determinant of employment and career prospects.

Conclusion

At the 1993 NAHT annual conference Mr Patten 'was heckled and booed' by heads bitter about plans to publish exam league tables. 'The Education Secretary later said he did not know what he had done to deserve such a reception' (*DES*, 4.6.93). If true, that is an odd admission for any politician claiming to be in touch with feeling on the ground. The government's populist tirade against teaching is already beginning to rebound. The only way forward is to expose further the shallowness of this populism.

An international survey of teachers (Poppleton, 1990) strongly suggested that the more centralised and programmed the pedagogic system, the less fulfilled the teacher. Looking at three countries only and taking Japan as the most centralised and pre-programmed, the USA as the least so, and England as midway, the following examples show a very distinct pattern. (The scale ranges from 0 to 1 and the scores given below are the means.)

Table 7.1: Teacher job satisfaction in three countries

	USA	England	Japan
Considering all things, and thinking now about the teaching post you currently hold, how satisfied would you say you are with your present job?	0.64	0.50	0.40
In general, how much do you enjoy teaching as an occupation?	0.80	0.69	0.54
To what extent is success at work important to you?	0.94	0.87	0.69

Source: Poppleton (1990), p188

It would also appear that American teachers have most scope to experiment and most freedom to decide how to work. English teachers come between these and Japanese teachers. While some of these differences may be cultural, it appears that the less centralised and controlled the teaching process the greater the teacher's job satisfaction. However, in a number of districts in the USA strict controls have been imposed, though producing little evidence that the impact on education is positive. 'Intensification-type reforms focusing on narrowly defined and imposed curriculum and teacher competencies repel good people from entering and/or staying. Bureaucratic reforms may be able to guarantee minimal performance, but not excellence in teaching' (Fullan, 1991, p332). There is other evidence that teaching, fulfilment, commitment and *quality* tend to go together.

If, as this implies, teachers must resist a narrowing of their role, this is unlikely to occur either through an appeal to professional status or through heavy industrial action. The refusal to comply with some of the national tests already shows the way. Each task may have to be contractually supported. In the past, teachers have used contracts to break free from an imposed professionalism requiring more duties without pay or privilege. For Boyson the 'end of teaching as a profession was signalled by the determination of the NUT in London from 1973-4 to cease to "cover" for absent colleagues after three days' (1975, p28). However, the notion of a *contractual* professionalisation is not too much out of kilter with other right-wing proposals. Thus Sexton acknowledges that extra duties should be paid for and also that some sort of professional status such as a Fellow of a College of Teachers could be established. In return, responsibilities would be tightly specified. But this pseudo-professionalism is again a form of control as 'there would be a presumption of professional status and therefore no strike' (1987, p19). The limited membership of PAT, the right-wing 'union', suggests that this model is far from central. Sexton's 'fellowship' would be little more than the gold star teachers give to students.

Nevertheless, 'the primary motivation for using contract language to rationalize tasks comes from teachers who see rationalization as a mechanism for securing and protecting their interests' (Kerchner and Mitchell, 1988, p214). While this poses risks, alternatives are also Janus-faced. Johnson (in Clune and Witte, 1990) reviews several American attempts to empower teachers: eg through extension of influence beyond the classroom, reduced hierarchical structures within schools, and professional responsibility for peers (eg various types of peer review). The latter has some left-wing support, for instance in Ross and Tomlinson's proposal (1991) for the establishment of 'senior teachers' in Britain earning 'competitive salaries' (p26) and the professional representation of all teachers in a General Teaching Council. However, this matches quite closely demands on the Right for greater differentiation within the teaching profession and for the use of 'mentor' teachers, with more lower level work being undertaken by licensed or articled teachers. Barber and Brighouse (1992), again on the Left, specifically propose the establishment of teaching 'associates' and 'assistants' to support main grade teachers. But if this invents the elite teacher it also invents the dogsbody teacher. It should not be forgotten that there is already huge variation in the pay and status of teachers, with senior teachers earning more than double a novice's salary.

The other two elements mentioned by Johnson seem more viable. Perhaps the most important is strong union definition of professional rights and obligations (excluding peer review). While not widespread in the USA, 'joint committees for planning and oversight are increasingly common features of their negotiated contracts and trust agreements' (in Clune and Witte, 1990, p363). The advantage is that teachers' rights can be protected at the same time as goals important to schools or the wider area can be negotiated. Where conflicts exist these can be resolved more easily than through more restricted collective bargaining. Teachers might thus gain from tighter specification where this would clearly enunciate professional duties rather than general submission to direction. This could, for instance, include a stronger advisory and counselling function, currently undermined by the national curriculum and testing requirements. Some European countries pay specifically for professional commitment. An eight-week strike in Belgium occurred partly through inter-regional pay disparities after devolution to the regions in 1989, but also as a result of 'the reduction in paid hours for counselling and class councils' (Verhoeven, 1992, p101). All such renegotiations are far from easy, of course.

> For those professionals not billing clients for their time, professionalism frequently means working to the needs of the job, regardless of the time involved.... By contrast, most unionized blue-collar workers sell their time, and negotiate over what they should be expected to accomplish during that time. Additional time is sold at an additional price. How teachers and school systems resolve this conflict over time will indicate much about the potential for professionalization approaches to school improvement (Hess, 1992, p168).

This should extend to dissemination, as this involves the best teachers (but as ambassador rather than as 'mentor'). This does not mean campaigning, in the sense of the NUT's 'campaign to save education' in 1988 (*For all our Children*), but professional dissemination related to performance can have impact. In the USA, the NEA 'has launched an ambitious school reform project', involving 2,000 teachers. Called the Mastery in Learning Project, it is based on 'research-based approaches to learning and teaching' (Kerchner and Mitchell, 1988, p161). In the past, in the UK, involvement of teachers in reform at all levels - the school, the authority and the state - has been profound. Traditionally this has worked through teacher centres, specialist organisations such as NATE, and the Schools Council. This has been swept away by others who believe they know best, but in the wish to standardise they disseminate not best but average practice. This fails to fit in with the range and complexity of the educational experience. 'No two schools are so alike in their circumstances (history, resources, clienteles) for prescriptions of curricular activity to adequately supplant the judgements of those who work in them' (Simons, in Lawton and Chitty, 1988, p6). Simons may slightly romanticise the possibility of internal teacher accountability, if only because a significant core of teachers may be impermeable to such pressure; nevertheless, teachers are better placed than anyone else to learn from experience and adapt research or policy initiatives. In the USA Fullan too argues that 'interactive professionalism' can be significant to performance (1991).

In the meantime, as the Right seek to ensure that teachers may never again innovate on their own initiative, schools 'are faced with considerable "innovation incoherence" and in many cases "innovation overload"' (Ball, 1987, p268). One result is that 'the strategy of "omissive action" (like non-cooperation with tests) is becoming an increasingly powerful weapon in teachers' political and union struggles' (p268). This is a pity. A recent survey of primary teachers reactions by Bennet, Wragg and Carre suggests great gaps between what the state demands and what teachers can provide. Only one in seven felt competent to teach technology. In fact, this was the only subject other than science in which confidence has not dropped - 'but that is only because it has hit rock bottom' (*TES*, 18.10.91). Where teachers have a choice of tasks for tests, for safety many are using well-worn material rather than new material. The policy of teacher control is already showing its inherent hollowness, which can only be masked by removing attention from pedagogy itself to obsession with attainment targets and key stages.

In conclusion, it seems best to view the current position of teachers in the UK as the result of a combination of cyclical factors (political and economic) rather than of some inevitable trend to reduced status, influence or autonomy. It seems reasonably likely that, as education becomes more responsive to various social demands in the long-term, the teacher's role should expand into a much broader professional remit, and there is no obvious reason why this should be interpreted in elite rather than industrial terms. Professional rights and duties can be negotiated in the same way as pay and conditions. There is really very little difference.

While there is very little or no evidence that education is in crisis or that teachers are to blame for this, there are of course bad teachers, just as there are bad performers in all occupations. There may well be a need to deal with inadequacy, but the government has failed to do this. For instance, performance pay cannot remove bad teachers. It can only make them suffer. Current policy is not designed to remove those really incapable of teaching. Open enrolment, opting out, tighter per capita funding, and publication of exam and test results are all designed to define certain *schools* as bad. There can be many sources of school inadequacy, of which teachers are only one. Creating unpopular schools is going to do nothing to remove the worst and retain the best teachers. These issues are dealt with in the final chapters.

8 Local authorities

Educational systems, and their control by local government, 'have never captivated the sociological imagination' (Archer, 1982, p3), though for Archer herself local government is just one of the vested interests which unnecessarily bids up educational provision. So, perhaps if only out of lack of interest, centralisation must appear inevitable. On the other hand, many commentators see current centralisation as an inevitable rationalisation of haphazard standards. As an example, the percentage of the population receiving pre-school education in 1986 varied from 86% in South Tyneside to 14% in Dorset (Statham *et al*, 1989, p61). Perhaps the key point of this chapter is that reform of such anomalies has little to do with rationalisation: there is a substantial difference between standardising the nation at 14% and standardising at 86%. Under current conditions the former is the more likely outcome. However, this does not mean that LEA control is being weakened simply to reduce overall spending. The costs of administering LMS, of reduced school closures through opting out, of the national curriculum and tests, and of the CTC programme, of TVEI, all strongly argue against cost reduction as a prime motive in reform. The government is willing to spend where it, if not where local government, sees fit. The issue is far more one of power, itself tied to a restructuring of the balance of social advantage.

Choice and decentralisation

Reform of local government has been given effect through parental choice and decentralisation to the school level. Both appear as a form of liberalisation. However, choice has many potential forms and functions. It is highly misleading to describe these solely in terms of liberalisation. Certainly there are conflicts between consumer and local bureaucratic preferences. For instance, a USA survey in 1987 found that 68% of district superintendents and 60% of school principles opposed choice, while another survey found that 76% of parents wanted choice (Bennett, in Clune and Witte, 1990, p125). Nevertheless, this does not mean than choice is capable of providing fair and efficient education at the same time as liberalising access. More generally, below are some of the chief strategies open to authorities seeking to expand the role of choice.

1. The most radical variant is the voucher, enabling the owner to buy education from any institution, private or public. Kerchner and Mitchell label it a form of 'disinvestment', resulting from a lack of public confidence in established institutions (1988, p180). But vouchers raise costs, as the State in effect pays for a substantial part of private education. 'Whereas the entry of the bourgeoisie into public schools was financed privately, the incorporation of the working class could only be accomplished by the provision of state funding' (Salter and Tapper, 1985, p53). In addition, Treasury control over educational spending would be restricted. Seldon (1986), a central figure in the voucher lobby, complains that both the Treasury and the DES opposed vouchers as they would remove not only local but central control over education.

2. The adopted UK policy of open enrolment, extensive too in the USA. However, this can take different forms. It can be controlled to maintain quotas based on criteria such as class, colour, or, in the case of ILEA's banding system, to ensure a comprehensive ability intake. 'Controlled choice' is favoured in some USA districts. For instance, in Boston it has been used to maintain a balance between 'races', allowing complete choice as long as this balance is not breached (Alves and Willie, in Clune and Witte, 1990). At the other extreme would be completely free choice, which in the UK would require going beyond the recoupment system (where one LEA pays another for teaching its children) to the abolition of LEA boundaries, and therefore logically of LEAs.

3. Institutional variety. This is supposed to be British policy but thinking is chaotic, and highly constrained by ideological limitations at the political level. Recent extension consists of grant-maintained (GM) schools and CTCs. However, the difference between the former and their predecessors is merely a change of paying authority (except where the school is allowed to change to a selective status). Meanwhile, the intention that all schools should opt out makes the notion of extended choice simply laughable. As for CTCs, the requirement that these should be primarily business ventures has ensured a highly stunted growth. Above all, the British policy of seeking and supporting the 'good school' implies that all schools should follow an ideal model, thus reducing variety even further, a process massively aided by the straitjacket of the national curriculum.

4. Curricular variety. Despite some moves towards a national curriculum in the USA, curricular variety has always been a powerful element in education, and is even being increased in some respects. One extremely important variant, the growth of the 'magnet school' is also an element of institutional variety. In this case schools are set up to offer high-quality specialist curricula. (CTCs are a bowdlerised version.) Magnet schools can be elite schools or a means of attracting the less able through a more varied offering (Blank, in Clune and Witte, 1990). Insofar as they become elite schools, they may nevertheless have the opposite effect of vouchers in attracting parents away from private provision. Curricular extension need not depend on organisational proliferation, however. It is also possible to establish 'schools within schools': where there are too few schools for real choice they can be subdivided by programme (Boyd, 1991).

5. The transfer of choice from parents to students. This is probably only practical and meaningful at the upper secondary level. It requires a major increase in the size of schools in order to offer effective choice for students within them. It would be most apparent in the replacement of sixth forms by tertiary colleges. Increasing the size of schools inevitably means reducing the number of schools, and thereby limiting the choice open to parents. Indeed, this transfer of choice from parents to students is the only truly meaningful choice programme, not only on ethical but on practical grounds. It is not automatically obvious that merely being a parent endows a human being with common sense, let alone understanding, or why an age superiority gives parents rights over their offspring's current well-being or future destinies.

Choice is in practice often not an end in itself but a means towards particular political objectives. The American experience, from which British developments derive, is instructive. The pursuit of 'racial' equality in the 1960s led to a reduction in choice through the policy of bussing. This added to inequality as black people were the most frequently bussed. The Supreme Court nevertheless required policies which established 'racial' balance. The result was a series of programmes in which choice was used to achieve desegregation. However, schemes devised to put the court requirements into effect were often designed as defensive reactions. In Boston, for instance, the first (1975) plan devised catchment areas small enough to ensure a balance between black, white, Hispanic etc. Choice did not operate in these but did through the establishment of 22 city-wide magnet schools. These got extra funding and were linked to universities. 'Like most desegregation plans, the primary purpose of Boston's magnet schools was to provide an attractive educational alternative for the white middle class' (Alves and Willie, in Clune and Witte, 1990, p44). However, dissatisfaction led to major court involvement. The replacement plan added the concept of 'controlled choice' by allowing choice within large zones as long as social balance criteria were not breached.

Magnet schools offer institutional and curricular choice but also potential inequality. A study of 45 magnet schools in the USA found that 13 were very selective, 27 at least 'somewhat' selective, and only five non-selective (Blank, in Clune and Witte, 1990, p92). There is probably an additional self-selectivity. In Dallas, although only the school for the 'talented and gifted' had selective entrance, the average scores on maths tests at entry for seven other specialist schools ranged from 85% to 97%, compared to 70% in the district as a whole. District enrolment of whites was 20% compared to participation in magnet schools of 55% (p92). However, middle-class blacks also obtain entry to 'better' schools through these. For instance, in Milwaukee black parents are nine times more likely to choose a non-local magnet or similar school than are white or Hispanic parents (Bennett, in Clune and Witte, 1990, p144). While magnet schools promise educational enhancement, in the USA they have been introduced in the first instance to manage desegregation, not to improve educational outputs. 'We do not burden the "effective schools" strategy with the obligation of access equity (desegregation), and we would unfairly burden the choice strategy by asking it to solve all the results problem' (Bennett, in Clune and Witte, 1990, p145). Whatever the reform strategy, choice is usually limited. For instance, many states require parents to provide reasons for transfer, partly because 'opposition to racial segregation operates as a powerful constraint' (Bondi, 1991, p132), but also partly because of the political importance of local autonomy, which is still seen as an expression of community action.

This survives the anti-statist ideology of the New Right because local school districts are too small, too limited in purpose, and exist within a political culture deeply hostile to the collectivism with which local government in the UK is sometimes associated. Much of the debate about choice policies in the USA revolves around whether parental choice will enhance or undermine local community control, defence of the latter being nearly universal (at least in the rhetoric) (Bondi, 1991, p132).

If in the USA choice has been used to aid desegregation, though the impact is sometimes the reverse, choice in the UK is explicitly geared to resegregation. Mrs Thatcher herself explained that one purpose of choice was to 'make certain that anyone who has the talent, who wants to build up something for themselves, wants to take responsibility, to get out of the socialist queue approach, shall be able to do so' (*Daily Mail*, 15.9.87).

Choice is one aspect of the loss of LEA control. The other is decentralisation, seen especially in the transfer of most spending decisions to schools. This policy also has some history in the USA, though again the implications there have often been very different. American district boards have greater powers than British LEAs, including tighter control over the curriculum and powers to levy taxes specific to schooling. With a loss of small districts in recent years they have become increasingly significant, and this is often effected through Superintendents who have more power over education than any individual in British local government. 'School-based management' has in some areas been conceived as a broad freeing of those working in education at the chalk-face, so that 'teachers have greater opportunity to function and the boundary line between labour and management becomes less apparent' (Cline and Graham, 1991, p49), while in Britain those responsible for 'chalk and talk' have suffered a loss rather than a gain in control. A further aim in some American reforms is to ensure that 'students and parents can obtain substantive decisions related to their own concerns. Placement in classes, retention within the same grade, enrichment activities... are not simply made in blind compliance to the rules established by a higher district power' (p48). This is heavily underemphasised by British legislation, with accountability relying instead on publication of test and exam results.

With the 1988 Act, choice and decentralisation become much the same thing - removal of the right of LEAs to allocate educational resources. The devolution of financial responsibility to schools makes planned rationalisation very difficult not only in terms of overall provision but of balance within schools. For instance, as school rolls fall, staff may not be replaced as they leave. 'If there are no replacements, the curriculum can only be preserved if there is local authority action' (Shipman, 1984, p57). Through agreements between unions and LEAs, in 1980/1 over 1% of the teaching force was redeployed in 85 authorities (Walsh, in Ranson and Tomlinson, 1986, p127); while fairly small, even this capacity has now been virtually eliminated. The trend is therefore not towards rationalisation, as some commentators on change in local government have suggested. The last 10 years have ushered in a period of pronounced irrationalisation - not in any figurative sense but literally as an expression of opposition to planning and value for money. Thus, even while it appeared to be rational for government to use grant related expenditure as a spending limit rather than as an allocation of grant based on need (in order to bring down spending), local authorities 'responded rationally to these uncertainties by seeking to create a financial cushion against them. The result is that rates over the past three years have probably been higher than they need, by some £400m a year' (Audit Commission, 1984, p27). The imposition of a formula defined by average pay regardless of a school's actual staffing costs, when over 75% of its budget is on staffing, must 'reduce, not increase, local management flexibility' (Moncks and Kelly, 1992, p13).

Decentralisation is unlikely to increase administrative rationalisation. This is already apparent in what little survey evidence there is of the effects of LMS. An Audit Commission's survey (1993) found that the amount of time heads spent administering the budget varied from 3% to 70%. Out of 79 schools, 10 spent 40% of their time or more on the budget (all in primary schools). Schools are spending a great deal of money on administrators, with many schools paying for 40% or more administrative hours than in the past. For schools with less than 100 pupils on roll, the cost of administrators per pupil could be over £300, while for schools twice the size it might be less than £50 (Audit Commission, 1993, pp12/13). If schools could reduce the proportion of the budget which they spend on administration by only a small percentage, many million of pounds 'could be redirected into other areas' (p15), implicitly more useful. The purpose of decentralisation is less to save money than to destroy LEAs. Administration has been transferred, possibly proliferating, while 'the school has an additional task of ensuring that its own records and those of the local authority tally. This is a waste of time and money' (p14). Finally, very specific irrationalities arise out of LMS of a more disturbing nature. The Audit Commission found that a number of schools held very substantial balances. 12 out of 82 had balances of over £100,000, and in three cases this was nearly £200,000. This was worst in schools which had opted out, with five out of 12 having over £130,000 (p17). At the same time, around 9% of local authority schools have a deficit. In terms of actual spending, some decisions 'are of questionable probity' (p29). Governing bodies have very limited control, with even on paper only 10% of heads reporting limits on their authority to spend (p22). The decisions the Commission highlights include allocation of repair work to the husband of a member of staff (even though the quotation was £2,500 higher than the lowest), a head employing her daughter for administration at expensive rates, the award of a contract for electrical work to a teacher without other quotations, a head awarding a £3,000 contract to her husband (p23). Decentralisation would appear to have little to do with either efficiency or morality.

Certainly variation in educational provision occurred before LMS, which may suggest that local administration is inconsistent, leading 'to enormous inequities in funding of schools across the country' (Winkley, 1991, p16). However, this can still occur under formula-funding. It is not clear, for instance, that when some schools receive more than £1,600 per pupil from the LEA, whilst others get £800, either equity or consistency has improved. Not only can LEAs vary the overall education budget but they can set elements of the formula. For instance, while some authorities increase the weight for pupils of different ages when a child moves up one year to secondary school only marginally from the baseline of 1, some raise it as high as 1.7 or more (Monck and Kelly, 1992, p12). Irrationalisation has almost become a game as LEAs devise strategies either to discourage opting-out (through increased spending), or to cut losses on the assumption that nothing can be done to prevent this. Expecting to lose such resources, 'which LEA is likely to want to increase its schools' budget'? (Brighouse, 1991, p10). This probably reinforces traditional spending patterns, with left-wing authorities determined to maintain control and right-wing authorities hampered by historical underspend. Other irrationalities are apparent. For instance, where an authority finds it difficult to negotiate transport contracts in unpredictable conditions it may offload more of the cost on to parents, thereby discouraging moves to more distant schools - in clear opposition to the principle of greater choice and mobility (Thornthwaite, 1990).

Some aspects of the decentralisation process are, of course, in name only, enabling power to be removed from LEAs without it residing in any specific location. The applies especially to governing bodies. It is not known how far governors understand their responsibilities, and there is no doubt that many schools operate for a time with less than the full body. The AMA reported that soon after the 1988 Act resignations from governing bodies pushed turnover well above the usual 10% per annum, with nearly half those authorities replying to a survey saying the rate had gone up three to four times (*Guardian*, 10.9.90). However, 'governing body', like family, or community, is a sacrosanct term. The British love of the amateur survives from highly anachronistic modes of operation. It perhaps appeals to people such as Rhodes Boyson, producing a hardy, nineteenth-century individualism. For Boyson (1972, p37), the twentieth century

> has replaced a 'do-it-yourself' community by a spectator society expecting someone else - government, local authority or social service - to solve people's problems and regulate their lives. It is interesting to speculate how far compulsory state education has contributed to the cultural decline.

But in real life governors simply lack the legal and financial expertise that schools need. It is not parents that help schools but the chance that high level skills might exist on a governing body. While Stubbs was head of education under ILEA,

> they had experts from many walks of life on the governing body. There would be barristers and union leaders and education specialists arriving on governing bodies through various nominating procedures. Some bodies found that to be an enormous strength and some head teachers were enormously supported by that. Unfortunately and sadly one couldn't say that about every governing body or indeed a substantial number of them (in Bush *et al*, 1989, p163).

Unless experts arrive on the now much more pressurised governing bodies, all that happens is that the head feeds the body with the facts and policies they need, which adds nothing to local democracy but a huge burden to head teachers. Again, it is the schools with privileged intakes that benefit, as more expertise is likely to be forthcoming. The response of parents also varies vastly by area. As a chair of a board of governors in a difficult inner-city area, I experienced an annual general meeting attended by two parents. This was despite several efforts to encourage attendance (which did at least double the attendance from the previous year - before I became chair!). Such outcomes are common. The government does not seek to publish data on the impact of decentralisation as to do so would undermine its basis in myth.

The local lead

In 1981 LEAs were required to have a curriculum policy, as it was believed that their earlier lack of interest was a source of irrationalisation. But this extension of responsibilty appeared to be a blip. Within a further seven years LEAs were required to abandon virtually all policy-making in education. The local authority lead in education has now been killed off, and with it all potential for local innovation. While Nicholas Ridley, as

Environment Secretary, appeared to feel that local government's purpose had more or less been served, he could acknowledge that: 'Many of the most successful government policies which affect local authorities began from initiatives taken by local government which have been promoted in national legislation by central government: council house sales and competitive tendering to mention two' (Ridley, 1988, p32). It is indeed possible that in difficult times it is often local rather than central government which provides a policy lead. Blunkett and Jackson aptly note that: 'During important periods of social and economic change, local politics has moved in advance of Parliament' (1987, p69). In its early years local government often led central government, for instance pushing the latter to allow it to provide sanitation, which the government itself felt was the job of charities or private industry. At the turn of the century the ideological conflict was between the 'improvers' and the 'economisers'. The latter were mostly Tory, but there were Tory improvers - such as Liverpool, who expanded utilities with some fervour.

In the case of education, early in the century the Boards often expanded provision beyond the remit allowed by the centre, while growth since the war had been managed, as the Layfield Report put it, 'without any change during that time in the basic statutory requirements which were laid down in the Education Act of 1944' (Layfield, 1976, p404). Most major educational policies derive from or through local government. Comprehensive schools (Middlesex, Coventry), middle schools (West Yorkshire), tertiary colleges (Devon and Lancashire), publication of exam results and financial delegation to schools (ILEA), the use of a common curriculum (Croydon) - all these policies were started by LEAs before being supported by government. The government, of course, likes to portray LEAs and teachers as out-of-touch, but reforms introduced by both LEAs and teachers in fact stem from response to direct local pressure (Kogan, 1983). Central government rarely innovates. Even CTCs 'seem to have more in common with innovative comprehensives of the 1970s' (Edwards, Gewirtz and Whitty, 1992, p102). Government initiative in areas of local authority responsibility are by no means unequivocal improvements. Central training strategies designed to nationalise priorities, in particular through the removal of control of further education from LEAs to national agencies, may seek to transcend local disparities, but they may also damage the ability of FE colleges to respond to local needs. 'Ironically, a national training initiative whose express purpose is to close the gap between vocational training provision and employers' needs, is, in many localities, making it wider' (Rees *et al*, 1989, p238). FE colleges are generally innovative in finding new markets.

Change may of course fail, as apparently in the case of the Leeds Primary Needs Programme (PNP). Designed specifically to bring change to an underfunded primary sector, deemed also to be generally old-fashioned in teaching styles, it spent about £13m, the largest component of which was the employment of at least one PNP co-ordinator in each school whose task it was to encourage and support change. The authority itself commissioned a study which turned out to be highly critical of the project. In one account (Alexander *et al*, 1989), each element of the project's aims was deemed to have been a partial failure. The attempt to broaden the curriculum failed because resources went into the main traditional areas of language and maths, with science doing fairly badly. Attempts to broaden the teaching environment also failed. There was very little adaptation of classroom lay-outs to include areas for specific types of study, and the growth of team-teaching was patchy. The project had some similarity to the national curriculum in being a top-down initiative which specified in considerable detail what teachers and schools were meant to deliver. It failed to build on what primary schools were currently achieving. However, the real difference is that the PNP's failure was local while ERA's will be national. Indeed, even if the PNP had been a success it is unlikely that much of it could have survived through LMS and the national curriculum. For example, the project drew attention to the nearly total constraint on teacher time in primary education, with the average teacher getting only a few minutes non-contact time each day. The co-ordinators were expected to introduce change partly through freeing time for teachers to plan and introduce change, and team-teaching was an essential element in this process. The national curriculum constrains this free time even further.

It may also be the case that in many LEAs the potential for innovation has for some time congealed into a bureaucratic paternalism (Hoggett and Hambleton, 1987, p15). For Cockburn, 'our local councils don't spring from some ancient right of self-government but are, and under capitalism always have been, an aspect of national government which in turn is a part of the state' (1977, pp1/2). After the war Liverpool was run for nearly two decades by a Labour machine - 'less than a dozen people few of whom had any great interest in local government policy questions' (Gyford, 1984, p62). The Labour group in Birmingham in the early 1960s resisted pressure from the local party to introduce comprehensive education until the Labour government made it national policy in 1965 (p62), while in 1956 a Tory administration in the West Riding had promoted comprehensives ahead of their time.

However, periods of quiescence may themselves produce change. The Left critique of traditional Labour local politics eventually produced the new urban Left, its policies including anti-racist and anti-sexist programmes, closer links with the voluntary sector, decentralisation, and measures to boost local employment. Perhaps the main feature of this new approach was a willingness to innovate, if less radically than critics suppose. Wainwright quotes Ken Livingstone, as GLC Leader one of the leading innovators, merely shrugging his shoulders: 'There was nothing that a good social democrat couldn't do on a warm day' (1987, p97). The focus of innovation in this case was the ability of local authorities to act in response to various newly defined inequalities. It is this that resulted in the massive anti-local government campaign of the 1980s. The following analysis is of coverage in five tabloid newspapers during an entire month of the 1987 election campaign. (It includes news, editorial, features, letters and cartoons.)

Table 8.1:   Tabloid coverage of local government

	Mirror	Today	Express	Sun	Mail
Column inches devoted to local government	42	539	673	837	1055
Percent of above claiming authorities incompetent etc	4	6	56	65	77
Percent 1st line devoted to 'race', gender, sexuality	50	---	69	51	68

Note: Column inches=area taken up by item

The *Mirror* coverage probably reflects the standard amount of coverage likely to be expended on parochial local government by a tabloid paper, and this can therefore be taken as the norm. In fact, the only Conservative authority making an appearance in any of the papers was one in Cornwall doing too little to prevent dogs fouling the beach.

Papers over this period produced various cycles of the following... *big-spending loony left-wing councils...a minefield of race relations and feminist propaganda... race spies... hard-hit ratepayers... some areas face financial ruin, mob rule... municipal lords and masters... hard-left socialist republics... jobs for the boys... black people have been brainwashed... racism witchhunts and political interference... corrupt the morals...* and so on. Education took its full share of this apocalyptic vision, confirming the already existing image of crisis in education... *extremist councils have infected our school system condemning many thousands of children to a bad start in life... loony left-wing teachers... education chiefs who try to enforce homosexual and ethnic rights in the classroom...*

Many of these tabloid reports were shown to be mere fabrication (Curran, 1987), but they were particulary important in this electoral period. A publication potentially available in libraries about gendered make-believe (mentioned in the previous chapter) reveals, in the view of a 'think tank' publication informed by the national press, 'a Labour controlled municipality promoting transvestism amongst toddlers' (Regan, 1987, p49). One of the most widely publicised incidents was the (presumably highly limited) circulation of a reading book designed to explain why some children may live in single-sex families (*Jenny lives with Eric and Martin*, Bosche, 1983). While the fear appeared to one of encouraging homosexuality, it makes one wonder what power a few photos of a gay couple asleep and a five-year old child complaining about her 'sleepyhead' father can have to turn infant children from heterosexuality. Like most books for children, the book ended with common-sense sentimentality: '"Can you and Dad have babies?" she asks. "No, you silly," says Eric, grinning.... "So it's lucky you have me," says Jenny. Eric thinks so too.'

Some authorities were certainly politically inept. However, being inept is not the same thing as being wrong. While the Haringey manifesto required that 'lesbianism and gayness are treated positively in the curriculum', for a previous Chief Education Officer such statements were no more than 'heroic and vapid assertions' (quoted in Bush, Kogan and Lenney, 1989, p126) unrelated to the reality of social change. While the recognition in Greenwich's Equal Opportunities statement of lesbians and gay men as 'oppressed people' is not an especially helpful statement, it is difficult to see why a local authority should not 'act to eliminate discrimination' or 'campaign against laws... which discriminate against Lesbians and Gay men'.

An Audit Commission report (1987) appeared at the time of the above campaign and happened to look at those Inner London authorities the tabloid press had targeted. The report contained valid criticisms but also revealed an odd extension to the auditor's armoury of accounting techniques, enabling it to suggest that excessive spending may result in

> poor housing and education, high crime rates much of it drug-related, large scale immigration and associated racial tension, an exodus of jobs and the more well off to the suburbs, high youth unemployment and welfare dependency and the break-up of traditional family structures (Audit Commission, 1987).

Of course, the Commission report did not say that 'mismanagement by councils was resulting in appalling levels of homelessness and crime, disappearing jobs, and falling standards of education' (*Daily Mail*, 19.1.87), though it made that an easy media claim.

Despite 'the absence of any independent and objective view of what a standard mainstream service might involve' (Home Office, 1989, p9), equalities work may now be sufficiently extensive to be considered a general local authority phenomenon. An AMA survey of its members found that all of the 53 responding authorities had or were developing equal opportunities policies in employment, over half in service delivery and about one third in the award of grants (AMA, 1988). In 1989 I sent a questionnaire to virtually all local authorities in Britain asking about resources, structures and work in the area of 'race' and ethnicity. A separate questionnaire was sent to Education Departments, excluding ILEA. 49 replied. The following summarises the results (though few authorities provided all or most of these).

Table 8.2:   Equalities provision within education departments

	%
Equalities policy specific to education	60
Encouragement of multi-culturalism or anti-racism	58
Provision of 'race' advisers	41
Courses on racism	57
Multi-cultural courses	42
Support of mother-tongue teaching	44

On the other hand, of course, such action may merely result in incorporation of dissident black organisations (eg Ben-Tovim *et al*, 1986, p144). Indeed, many of the comments from officers replying to the survey acknowledged the difficulties from the inside.

> As equal opportunities has been a carbuncle on the backside of LAs for so long I think it's about time it became more mainstream. There is a case for saying that equal opportunities units almost have an inbuilt self-destruct button because they are rarely accepted by most LAs and they are easy to sabotage.

> Fundamentally this is a deeply racist/sexist/disabilist/homophobic authority which I have no personal stake in and do not intend to become involved in but remain on the outside as a catalyst.

Alternatively, it may also be the case that 'leaks to the right-wing and, in the main, racist press which so dominates the media in this country, have consistently come from officers whose comfortable existence has been threatened by the challenges posed by council who have been elected on a policy of equal rights and opposition to institutional discrimination' (*Asian Herald*, 17.11.87).

Equalities work perhaps reveals the final area of innovation in local government. This is important in itself, but above all the conflict this has generated indicates the profound link between local government and social welfare. It is local government's potential ability to redistribute welfare that has been the source of centrally imposed constraint.

Centralisation or decentralisation?

It is difficult to review current change in education without reference to a more long-term restructuring of local government. ERA could as well be described in a book about local government as about education, which would then be just one element in a fundamental re-ordering of the central-local relationship - including stringent financial controls; the abolition of the GLC, ILEA and metropolitan counties; enforced sale of council homes; the pressure to reduce labour costs through competitive tendering; and constraints on local government publicity. A major part of the government's legislative programme in the last few years has been taken up with local government, with the 1988 Housing Act becoming the 50th major piece of such legislation in the first ten years of Tory rule (Gyford, 1985, p1). The changes have also been accompanied by a string of bitter legislative battles and publicity campaigns.

Explanations are various. There is little evidence for a major reduction in spending, including in education (Ball, 1990, p80), and some anti-local government activities such as the poll tax have been very costly, both politically and financially. Political objectives, with Labour's control of the big cities and declining Tory loss of control over the districts, seems to be one cause. This is obvious enough in selective ratecapping or control over local government publicity, or in new legislation to encourage opting out when the Tories lost control of the shires in 1993. Nevertheless, this is only a partial explanation. For much of the lives of the metropolitan counties and the GLC, for instance, their party control was different from that of the centre (Flynn *et al*, 1985, pp56-76). Conservative authorities have also felt the pinch of central intervention, including the loss of controls which even the most laissez-faire might wish to retain (eg county control over planning, often used to preserve the green belt). Nicholas Ridley, as Secretary of State for the Environment, explicitly included Conservative authorities in criticism of local government resistance to loss of powers: 'Inside every fat and bloated local authority there is a slim one struggling to get out' (1988, p26). Policies important to the centre have often clashed with local authorities under the same party control. Macmillan forced house-building on unwilling Conservative authorities, and the Wilson government forced cuts on unwilling Labour authorities.

Right-wing ideology itself suggests decentralisation as a motive for reduction in the local government role, regardless of partisanship. Many on the Right see local government as an unnecessary intermediary between the state and the family. Thus Kenneth Baker, if with a shaky grasp of engineering, described current change as moving power from the hub and the rim, *through* the spokes. In 1988 Mrs Thatcher lectured to the Church of Scotland to this effect: 'The family is the building block of society. It is a nursery, a school, a hospital, a leisure centre, a place of refuge and a place of rest' (*Guardian*, 26.5.88). Not much left for local authority here. The objective is not decentralisation as such, anyway pretty superficial, but a *destructuring* of society. There will be just the government and lots of schools and colleges: intermediate agencies will merely pass on funds and the family becomes the agent of government.

The Left has also called for decentralisation, for instance in the community movement in the 1970s and through the New Urban Left in the 1980s. At the most extreme, abolition of LEAs might release black or working-class communities from local paternalism. More prosaically, various initiatives have sought to enfranchise, if not empower, the local consumer, for instance through decentralisation of housing services (Boddy and Fudge, 1984). Theoretical support for such work, which goes beyond the apparent political convenience of the 'rainbow alliance', can be recognised in the concept of postFordism. As industry moves into a supposedly postFordist capitalist cycle in which mass production is replaced by small-batch techniques controlled by information technology, public services must follow. 'Public services should move beyond the universal to the differentiated service' (Murray, *Marxism Today*, October 1988). This includes equalities policies geared to specific groups. After all: 'Capitalist retailers and market researchers make these distinctions in pursuit of sales.'

However, neither education nor local government, largely because of their labour intensiveness, are under pressure from technological innovations deriving from production. If there is a demand for change in the public sector it is from consumers, not producers, and that implies a political not a technological imperative. It may be that technology is the only means of replacing obstructive bureaucrats and professionals, who have to be dragged '"kicking and screaming" into the latter part of the twentieth century' (Hoggett, in Hambleton and Hoggett, 1987, pp223/4), but technology does not make policy. In education, professionals have been replaced not by technology, largely impossible, but by bureaucratic formulae. LMS, for instance, has seen the demise of LEA advisers, special needs providers, psychologists, and managers of services. This solution is again political and ideological. It is neither a technological nor organisational imperative.

It has also been suggested that current change is in reality one of centralisation - in the view of Newton and Karran bringing UK government 'within sight of a form of government which is more highly centralised than anything this side of East Germany' (1985, p129) - and of course East Germany has moved on since then. Centralisation is recognised by some to be essential to efficient modernisation. Perhaps it was never a desirable statement of educational goals for a secretary of state to assert 'that he was only able to find money for the demolition of Second World War air-raid shelters' (Taylor, in Ranson and Tomlinson, 1986, p152). Nevertheless, it is unclear why centralisation should be equated with efficiency. Logically it may serve to extend inefficiency nation-wide. But some do make the equation between central control and efficiency. In Rhodes' characterisation, government is an institution which must manage both escalating social demands and a fragmenting political-administrative system, without which government 'will appear wholly directionless' (Rhodes, in Goldsmith, 1986, p20). Greater control is sought over competing sources of power, eg local government, whether through incorporating leading elements of such power sources in central government (the period leading up to 1979), or through total exclusion (post-1979). 'As policy-making becomes increasingly differentiated, the "logic" of the process generates imperatives to co-ordinate' (p20). Yet this explains little. Life has been getting more complex since the Stone Age, but such an observation is hardly a sound basis for understanding political change. The 'Rhodes framework' (Rhodes, 1981) can describe but not explain.

An alternative framework is provided by the notion of economic crisis. Ranson and Walsh (in Ranson *et al*, 1985) relate changes in central-local relations to changes in economic need. In most of the postwar period the concern of the state has been to 'transform and modernize the social structure' (p18). This initially required centralisation ('paternalism') - to establish the welfare state. A period of devolution followed (the 'social democratic state'), when local government gained new powers, especially over education, to manage growth and accompanying social change. Then came a period of corporatism in the 1970s as the state sought to manage not growth but decline, though this was merely a disguised centralisation. 'Local government was being co-opted by the centre to legitimate its own diminishing scale and status' (p12). Finally, as decline became more severe, the state, controlled by the Tories, has centralised in order to decentralise (in favour of the market). However, there is no particular reason why economic decline (or growth) should compel either a corporatist or a laissez-faire system of management. Sharpe (1979), for instance, has argued that modernity encourages not greater central control but decentralisation (eg in the old USSR). When the Conservative Party came into power in 1979 its first Environment Secretary, Michael Heseltine, defined efficiency in terms of less central interference, promising 'a bonfire of 1,000 *central* controls' (*Local Government Chronicle*, 5.5.89, my emphasis). While it is not impossible that failure to deliver was itself a response to economic need, in general too little attention is paid to political definition of economic crisis. For instance, it has been argued that fiscal decline and crisis in the 1970s, most spectacular in the case of New York, was 'fundamentally a *political* event' (Gottdiener, 1987, p126), in which the centre played a major part. A state of emergency is defined by the state.

As just mentioned, it has been noted that the government is both centralising (acquiring more power) and decentralising (bringing the market into the public sector). Which is primary? One view is that it is decentralising in order to centralise, eg using local financial management of schools and 'parent power' to fragment LEA resistance to central direction. But it can be argued in reverse that the government is centralising in order to decentralise - using political power to extend economic laissez-faire (this being a resource rather than a power argument). This ambivalent relationship between trends to centralise and decentralise is less apparent elsewhere, where the latter may be more predominant. In France, a highly centralised country, the 36,000 communes in the lowest tier have prevented rationalisation into larger, more efficient groupings (in contrast to the British changes of 1974), and this local strength is institutionalised though political representation by the same individuals (eg *commune maires*) at higher levels. At the same time, reforms encouraging decentralisation have weakened the power of the *préfet* (the centre's local administrator). France is now more corporatist than centralist (Garrish, 1986). Other countries are decentralising to local or regional level. Belgium has passed control of education to regional and language groups. All the Scandinavian countries have introduced experiments in 'free local government', in which local authorities apply for exclusion from central regulation in order to encourage innovation and democratic accountability. In Sweden about 25% of the proposals concerned education - even though in 1985 Swedish local government already spent 22% of GDP (Stewart and Stoker, in Crouch and Marquand, 1989). In Norway, local authorities are allowed much local leeway in national curriculum plans (including such things as peace studies).

> In the recent moves towards *dirigisme* in this country it might be argued that the Secretary of State is merely moving into line with our continental neighbours. He appears... to perceive that Europeans have 'tended to centralize and standardize' whilst our 'maverick educational system' has 'gone for diffusion and variety'. His perceptions are clearly not entirely accurate, nor are they up-to-date (Haywood, 1989, p168).

Goldsmith notes that 'unlike other countries, Britain has adopted a centralising strategy to deal with the crisis, whereas most others have tended to follow a decentralising solution' (1986, introduction), but the reason given for British centralisation is not an inexorable impetus to manage the state more efficiently so much as the political strength needed to change the social structure for *ideological* reasons. Even Rhodes, moving beyond concern for administrative adaptation, accepts that 'the limited state required decisive state action for its realisation' (in Goldsmith, 1986, p21). It is not centralisation per se that is significant but its ideological focus. It is unreasonable, therefore, to argue that there is an ineluctable trend towards either centralisation or decentralisation, or that while 'the motives might differ.... the forces often combine in the same direction' (Hargreaves, in Ranson and Tomlinson, 1986, p164). There is no compelling reason to believe that local government reform is related to national exigencies, whether political or economic, let alone educational. The tension between the centre and locality is purely ideological, and this will no doubt vary over time.

The rest of this chapter will argue that local authority of education is vital, though it may not matter how this is distributed. Brighouse, for instance, proposes that educational policy should be established at a regional level (around 5m population) with education in practice run at the district level. Either way, central government must be freed 'of its present substantial and increasing role in governing and directing detail of so many of its citizens' local services' (in Ranson and Tomlinson, 1986, p179).

Local government and redistribution

In one sense there has been neither centralisation nor decentralisation but, rather, a process of the periphery leading the centre. Laissez-faire local government, in calling on the centre to divest it of unwanted obligations, has nationalised itself. For instance, the right to buy a council home was pioneered by Conservative authorities like Birmingham and Leeds (when under Tory control) 'thereby fuelling the demand at succeeding Conservative Party conferences for this to become national party policy' (Gyford and James, 1983, p13). Wandsworth has gone further than ERA in several ways since the abolition of ILEA. Cambridgeshire pioneered Local Financial Management in 1980, which formed the basis for LMS schemes required by the 1988 Act, but going much further, for instance setting up services for the physically impaired as businesses. 'Some businesses are beginning to identify "unprofitable" schools. For example the music service has identified the small rural primary school as a potentially unprofitable customer' (Gale, 1991, p35). By 1988 just over 40% of authorities responding to a survey of competitive tendering had contracted out some services. However, the impact on authority employment varied enormously, with the bulk reporting (whether accurately or not) either no or negligible redundancies. Kent claimed 2,500 redundancies - all in the schools cleaning service (*Local Government Chronicle*, 8.7.88). Sir John Grugeon as leader of Kent County Council 'was involved in all major decisions taken by the first (1979-83) Thatcher government' (Holliday, 1991, p53). Kent's attempt to provide choice between *types* of education (11+ and 13+ comprehensives and 11+ and 13+ grammars) rather than between *schools* introduced a far greater level of overt segregation than the centre dared move towards.

Holliday generalises to a new approach which he describes as the New Suburban Right, which, like the New Urban Left, seeks to politicise and extend local initiative, but around choice and financial prudence rather than around local social and economic strategies. It harks back to old Conservative traditions of 'common sense', non-political local government. As always, 'it is something of a paradox that the very people who... support a view of local government as 'non-political' are those who mobilise most strongly in defence of their economic interests (Saunders, 1979, p271). The motto of the London Municipal Society, formed in 1884 out of conservative and ratepayer groups, was (at the helm of its journal *The Ratepayer*): 'This is not the cause of faction, or of party, or of any individual, but the common interest of any man' (Young, 1975, p130). But of course this depoliticisation is more apparent than real. Nicholas Ridley as Environment Secretary hoped to see 'my colleagues in local government become more politicised', apparently out of fear that with 'too much localism... the political interpretation of the Government's voice is not heard'. If he also expected to see local-taxpayers' representatives 'coming back as alternatives to the main political parties' (Ridley, 1988), this would serve the same function of centralised laissez-faire.

This is a distributive issue, therefore. After the Transport Act 1985 had removed monopoly control over public bus and coach transport, Nicholas Ridley was reported to have said at a Bus and Coach Council annual dinner: 'You are now free to run your businesses without the constraints of a social conscience' (Blunkett and Jackson, 1987, p80). It has been the redistributive power of local government which has been the source of the most bitter local-central conflicts, from Poplar (over payment of poor relief), through Clay Cross (over rent rises), to recent battles over jobs and services. The expansion of local government, first in the hands of Liberals then through the Labour Party, was redistributive, and in the minds of many was intended to be. 'Whatever the future may hold for our economic system, local government is likely to remain firmly established as the most effective instrument of social welfare in our national life' (a contributor to the 1935 publication *A Century of Municipal Progress*, quoted by Dawson, in Loughlin *et al*, 1985, p26).

This has continued ever since. The GLC (and ILEA) used their control over the business rate to fund women's, black and ethnic minority causes, the Greater London Enterprise Board, hugely increased grants to voluntary organisations, and aid to poor boroughs under the Stress Boroughs Programme, together totalling nearly £120m in 1983/4 (Forrester *et al*, 1985, pp48/9). ILEA's policies included 'phasing out of "clocking in" for basic hours' and introducing 'pay deals benefiting the lower paid; midday supervision arrangements leading to better pay and training for 5,000 low paid meals supervisors' (ILEA, P6019, 15.10.86). Given the importance of local authority employment in some boroughs, when Hackney claimed to have raised black employment from 11% in 1980 to 26% in 1985 (London Research Centre, 1986, p140), even if most of these jobs were low paid and unskilled, they must have had significant social impact.

This power to redistribute has been local government's problem. *Half a Century of Municipal Decline* (Loughlin, Gelfand and Young, 1985), published 50 years after *A Century of Municipal Progress*, makes clear that even by 1935 the writing was on the wall. The nationalisation of profitable utilities and services of universal scope (particularly health) had left in the hands of local government more exclusively redistributive services such as social services and cheap housing - which 'benefit not the community as a whole but specific groups within it' (Jackson, in Loughlin *et al*, 1985, p153). As the need for these occurred most acutely in areas of low rateable value, forcing further dependence on central funding, suppression of local government activity had a straightforward redistributional impact.

It is less obvious how education can be viewed as redistributive in this direct sense, but it is certainly a source of private competition, which must therefore be strongly affected by adjustments to its *collective* distribution. The two processes are in fact closely linked. The charitable status of fee-paying schools increases their attractiveness relative to state education, but while rules requiring publication of exam results may make the sector more or less attractive as a whole, they will also make one private school more or less attractive relative to another. While opting-out sets up a competitive relationship between local state schools, it may also make state schools seem increasingly viable alternatives to expensive private education.

The competitive element is generally confused with notions of human capital. When an individual beats others in the competitive process of acquiring qualifications, this is considered an addition to the nation's stock of skills. This confusion of collective and private aspects of education makes it increasingly difficult to place. In the 'dual state' thesis of Cawson and Saunders (1983), the central state looks after investment interests - expenditure of most concern to capitalism, as well as such things as law and order (called 'social expenses'), while spending on 'social consumption' such as education is often left to local government. However, such distinctions now seem inadequate. 'Education, for example, could be seen as a legitimation form of social expenses, or as social investment in human capital, or as a type of collective consumption' (Dunleavy, in Boddy and Fudge, 1984, p71).

Whatever the function of local government in education it is clear that this must have redistributive impact. It is tempting to see this in terms of urban distribution, in particular of urban patterning. One of the earliest major approaches to study of the urban, that of the Chicago School, was explicitly spatial. Cities are divided into quarters or circles based on income, and compete on that basis. It soon became apparent, however, that this sort of analysis fails to explain the cause of urban distribution of resources. To avoid models which posit the existence of individuals prone to cycles of deprivation, and areas which collect such individuals, it is necessary to see how residential patterns relate to production. An account of such effects is given by Buck, Drennan and Newton in a comparison of London and New York (in Fainstein, Gordon and Harloe, 1992). For instance, while manufacturing employment declined at the rate of 4.4% for much of the 1970s in inner London, in the outer metropolitan area it declined by only 1%. The less labour-intensive financial and producer services increased by 4% and 5.1% respectively. From 1987-89 these last rates were 5.8% and 10% (pp85/6). Such massive shifts in welfare are more pronounced in London than elsewhere in Britain as a result of property prices and the cumulative impact of the loss of externalities: big manufacturers take the small ones with them. Such change could be seen in terms of skill cycles, even if the only *local* externalities which the new financial services may generate may be sandwich bars. If computer and communication technology 'has eliminated out of the two cities tens of thousands of routine clerical jobs' (p99), it is by no means the case that the generation of new jobs is anything more than marginal. The redundant clerk is more likely to serve than eat in the adjacent sandwich bar.

What makes current urban sociology distinctive is not spatial analysis of the sort espoused by Park but its concentration on the provision of collective goods, including education. As such, local government rather than the urban will become a central focus. For Castells (1977, 1983), the local state is a crucial vehicle for collective *consumption*. Capitalism in decline requires increased social expenditure; state intervention politicises people around consumption demands (while Marx' concern was solely with production). The localism of this collectivisation can combine communities across class divisions, producing widespread urban protest movements against cuts in social spending, and may therefore transform the class structure from within. It is easy to see how struggles over the distribution of education - eg the siting of popular schools - can fit in with this thesis. Nevertheless, the relation between class and political action is far more complex and actual

166

evidence of multi-class protest is extremely limited (Lowe, 1986). In addition, while urban areas and local government control of these might well be sites of conflict, there is no reason to think that this is necessarily going to be left-inclined or in any way subversive of the status quo. Protest may well come from middle-class groups. In his study of Croydon, Saunders (1979) describes powerful 'community' pressures on local government, including middle-class resistance to comprehensivisation. The type of pressure group then formed ('Save our Schools') has now almost become stereotypical. They are least likely in deprived areas. Why then should struggle over collective consumption reinforce and not weaken the class consciousness of the working class?

This suggests some spatial competitiveness over *collective* goods. This is perhaps clearest and most central in the case of housing, itself linked to education, as choice of school is constrained by residence. For instance, the sale of council houses transfers wealthier working-class people away from estate schools. People caught in declining areas are subject to cumulative deprivation. As jobs go so do schools. There are no such things as housing classes uniting people across social classes through sharing tenure (Ball, 1983), but people lacking access to advantaged housing, whatever its tenure, are likely to be marked by vulnerability in other areas of collective consumption, and local government has been a central factor in the distribution of both education and housing.

The local distribution of education

> 28% of the fathers had been convicted of some offence and eight per cent had been in prison. Eleven per cent of the children were living in homes broken by death and divorce, another seventeen per cent were part of families characterised by severe marital discord, and official statistics show that the rate of children in the care of the local authority was 12.5 per 1000 (Rutter *et al*, 1979, p33).

> Journalists, politicians and broadcasters now find that their children are going to schools alongside youngsters who would always in the past have been hidden from sight and sound in some back-street sink school (Wright, in Finch and Scrimshaw, 1980, p106).

Comprehensive schools tend to equalise social class intake. In Scotland, class segregation in education varied greatly by region prior to comprehensivisation. It was highest in Edinburgh but declined considerably with comprehensive schooling, and thus 'the politics of Edinburgh schooling may have been a factor in the Education Minister's decision to introduce a policy for parental choice' (Echols *et al*, 1990, p210).

Choice is as much a social as an educational act. For instance, exam results appear to have little weight in school choices. Looking at choice in Scotland since 1981, when parents chose reasons for selecting an alternative school, 'the school has a better examination record' takes up less than 3% of reasons given (Adler *et al*, 1989, p133). Similar findings occur in a survey in Sheffield (Boulton and Coldron, 1989). While the long list of options in the Scottish survey encourages fragmentation of response, the salience of non-educational factors is still pronounced. The table below tentatively regroups Adler *et al*'s categories to compare reasons for rejecting a school with reasons for selecting an alternative, but along two broad dimensions only (discipline and convenience).

Table 8.3: **Reasons for choosing an alternative secondary school** (% of all reasons)

	Burns City	Burns NT	Maxton	Watt
Discipline				
Rejection	33	31	30	45
Selection	15	8	10	15
Convenience				
Rejection	8	10	7	9
Selection	19	26	22	23

Source: Adler, Petch and Tweedie (1989, pp126 and 133)

Discipline here includes concern about type of children at a school. It would therefore seem that an important motive in avoidance may be fear of a 'problem' school. Parents do not search for a model school, but once avoidance has been managed convenience may be a prime determinant of an alternative selection. The above cannot prove such a motivation, but the negative associations of the discipline-related factors are pronounced.

Adler *et al* found (in the case of primary schools) that 'the odds of moving from the schools where most of the children lived in local authority housing to the school in which fewest of them did will increase by a factor of 3.1 compared to the odds of movement between schools with identical percentages of children in local authority housing' (p176). This applied far more to moves from outside a catchment area. In one town, 50 out of 55 such moves were to schools less strongly linked to council housing. To exaggerate perhaps, where parents perceive a means of escape from 'estate' schools, they do so. This was supported by the finding that there was movement away 'from schools serving areas where the unemployment rate was high and there were large numbers of low income and single-parent households' (p178). While the movers 'may have benefited, those who have remained with the district school may have had to pay a heavy price if they and their schools have become even more stigmatised than they were previously' (p215). While all social classes take advantage of choice, its distribution is far from equal. For instance, one study of choice in Scotland found that 17.7% of professional people chose private education while 11.5% of the remainder of professional people chose a *non-local* state school. For an 'intermediate' class the figures were 10.4% and 6.4%, while for skilled manual people they were 1.2% and 5.2% (Echols *et al*, 1990, p213).

It is of note that significant movement to or from a school may say little about that school's popularity. The study by Adler *et al* gave considerable credence to the notion of a 'bandwagon effect', whereby movement becomes self-reinforcing - partly because siblings and friends follow first choices, partly because schools perceived to be in decline, and therefore losing resources, social variety and curricular enrichment, become decreasingly attractive. Declining local populations, the bandwagon effect, and differences between areas in historical over-provision all effect rolls in ways that are outside the control of the school itself. It is worth quoting one secondary head's despair in full from the account given in Adler *et al*.

I had an outstanding staff, highly motivated. We were a model of primary-secondary liaison. We had primary teachers and children attending our music and art classes. We went into local primary schools and put on exhibitions and did reprographics for them. We operated an 'open door' policy and had 60 adults attending our classes. We started a homework policy. We used local newspapers to spread good news about the school. You'd have thought being a football manager would have helped, wouldn't you? It didn't help any.

The first-year intake fell from 164 to 58 in five years (1989, p217). The ex-CEO of Haringey gives a not dissimilar account.

There were headlines in a national paper about copulation being on the curriculum and subsequently the head of that school successfully sued the paper concerned. But it was very hurtful and damaging for the school at the time. Recruitment went down significantly and the school needed temporary protection in terms of the number of staff which were allocated. And we were able to do that, and it was educationally right and proper that we should (Lenney, in Bush, Kogan and Lenny, 1989, pp135/6).

The question whether quality is a factor in popularity can also be looked at in terms of flows across catchment area boundaries. The following is based on figures for transfers at ages 9, 11 and 13 provided by the CEO, Tim Brighouse to Oxfordshire's School's Sub-committee in September, 1987. Oxfordshire's policy of allowing choice had already resulted in over 99% of parents achieving their first choice of school. Given this, and the fact that the county was willing to expand capacity beyond the formal planned admission limit (PAL), it might be expected that a popular school would attract more people from both within and across catchment boundaries. Taking intakes of over 85% of PAL as a dividing line between 'popular' and 'unpopular' schools produces nearly equal numbers of each out of the total of 47 (though, especially in rural areas, low utilisation does not necessarily indicate true lack of popularity). The highest percentage of PAL taken up was 108% and the lowest 31%, with the average in the well-used schools 95% and that of the less used schools 68%. While the average proportion of actual capacity used which was taken up by 'insiders' was lower in the more popular than in the less popular schools, suggesting some influx of 'outsiders' in such cases, the difference was very small (81% against 87%) compared to the variation in overall capacity taken up.

The supply of choice

Choice in education is determined by available spare capacity and its distribution, not by ethics. It only became an issue with falling rolls, which had also encouraged the last Labour government to legislate to extend choice, if in limited form. In the period of growth after the 1944 Act, when demand exceeded supply, it was far from easy to give effect to choice. In fact, choice depends not on demand, which can be taken as a given, but on supply. The government cannot extend choice significantly without the spare capacity to play with. In the same way, if falling rolls increase the scope for choice, rationalisations (closures) reduce this. While there is demand for greater choice - for instance, in the late 1980s secondary school placing requests in Sheffield were between 24% and 28% of all transfers - there are still major inequalities in the amount of choice available. Boulton and Coldron asked their Sheffield sample how many secondary schools their child could easily travel to: while 36% could get to three or more, and 34% to two, 29% could only get to one (1989, p42). Closure of less popular schools could therefore add to the relative deprivation of those with little or no choice.

Closures reduce both costs and choice. This problem puts the government in the strange position of both demanding and preventing planning, creating yet further irrationalisation. The Audit Commission at an early date strongly criticised the government for turning down one in three closure proposals 'even where the LEA has prepared a reasoned and substantiated case for closure on education grounds and has completed the arduous (two year) consultation process' (1984, p56). It is also probably the case that authorities are slowing down closure proposals in order to discourage applications for opt-out, though this policy does not receive support from organisations such as the AMA, partly because failure to close schools may damage the principle of comprehensive education. Major LEA closure programmes are probably broadly rational in the criteria used, eg capacity rather than organisational factors (Bondi, 1989). While Labour, for instance in the party's manifesto in Ealing, could oppose school closures 'to ensure that the effects are borne equally by all schools', mainly by 'planning intake levels to bring about a fair distribution of numbers, courses and facilities' (Ealing Labour Manifesto, 1986), this still suggested a rational attempt to balance social justice and cost. This is very different from the protection given under ERA to excessively small schools resisting closure. This inefficiency redistributes resources away from schools in poorer, inner city areas - an inevitable result of formula funding - to small schools in 'good' areas. Some Tories such as Michael Heseltine, in the Commons debate on ERA, also saw this clearly enough.

> Expectations will have been raised and indeed possibly encouraged by local politicians anxious to divert attention from what they know must happen by suggesting that somehow or other ... the Secretary of State will have a pot of gold to keep the school in existence.

For Rhodes Boyson opting out was clearly a means of resisting rationalisation.

> I would like to see schools in my constituency opt out. Primary schools may opt out only if they have more than 300 pupils, but small village schools may wish to opt out. When I was a Minister, delegation after delegation made representations for the preservation of village schools.

When a Secretary of State is viewed by a local authority to be acting 'contrary to the requirements given by his department and advice given by the district auditor' (*Local Government Chronicle*, 21.4.89), it is hardly surprising authorities might be afraid to threaten a school with closure.

Of course many LEAs have been dilatory, partly out of fear of parental opposition, but the government has colluded with delay, possibly in the hope that unpopular schools will somehow disappear as demand falls. However, short of internal combustion, perhaps sometimes thoughtfully provided by disaffected children (with £33m in school damage through malicious fires in 1990-91: *Guardian*, 27.1.93), it is difficult to see how this can happen. Once the 300 size limit was set aside by the government, schools as small as 12 pupils balloted to opt-out. With parents threatened by school closures arguing that 'we fight for our own, don't we?' (*Guardian*, 25.1.91), it appears that educational provision may eventually be determined by clout rather than by need. The same goes for the use of choice by public authorities to avoid investment decisions. Where a school is in a state of disrepair and in need of funds it is easy to imagine it 'being offered choice instead' (Bennett, in Clune and Witte, 1990, p151).

Choice is always supply-constrained. For instance, of 17 secondary schools in Lewisham in 1988, five (including the Haberdashers Askes single-sex schools) were oversubscribed, while two more were virtually at published capacity. This left only 10 schools where significant choice was possible, with rolls ranging from 38% to 88% of published capacity (Lewisham Development Plan, para.112). Even then there is no necessary relationship between relative and absolute disparities. For instance, the 38% school, Catford, had on one definition 60 extra places, while Sedgehill with 72% had 120 spare places (para. 368). As Catford was a boys school and Catford County (53%) was a girls school, this leaves even less real choice.

As rolls rise choice will be reduced even more. The rise will be slow but will gradually flood out most empty spaces. Choice will be replaced by competition, and this is undoubtedly the aim of the legislation. Such competition is hinted at in the 'push' factors discussed above, but will become intense. There are already signs of excess capacity being used as an excuse to introduce selection. For instance, a 'CTC' set up by Conservative Lincolnshire with funding from 40 firms, the Lincoln School of Science and Technology, is one of the first schools to apply to change its comprehensive status and adopt selective entry. However, it is important to note that this is not a response to popular demand. Under the Tories, an attempt to convert a comprehensive into a grammar school was forced out after fierce protests. 'People threatened to stand on an "Against secondary moderns" ticket in Conservative wards.' In the words of the head: 'We have got to do something. Any school that is over-subscribed has to select its children' (*TES*, 4.6.93). Popular demand therefore works against itself and open enrolment really means closed enrolment. Local authorities now find themselves acting *on behalf of* choice in seeking to minimise the impact of oversubscribed schools selecting children.

The government has thus used a period of falling rolls, when choice is easy, to introduce it as a principle which in later years will have an utterly different meaning, to reintroduce segregation. It is worth remembering that the tripartite era, much lauded by the Right as a period of freedom and choice, actually offered far less than has been available in the last 25 years in most of the country, as parents could not select schools outside the sector which had selected their children. The supply of choice is always ideologically limited.

The cost of borough competition

The most important actual reorganisation of recent years, the abolition of ILEA, derives directly from the 1988 Act. The purpose of the abolition was to end ILEA's redistributive power (though borough rivalries were also a factor, with even Labour boroughs unhappy with some aspects of ILEA provision). As demonstrated in chapter one, the quality of education could not have been a real factor in ILEA's abolition. The cost arguments also appear to have been little more than propaganda, however relatively high ILEA's spending happened to be. No adequate consideration was given to the possibility of splitting ILEA into either vertical segments grouping several authorities together, or horizontal layers so that there could be an overall authority dealing with each level of education, as proposed, for instance, by Lightfoot and Rowan (1988). Most boroughs simply became costly mini-ILEAs. The average size of an LEA in Britain is just over 70,000 primary and secondary students, while the biggest of the new London LEAs, Greenwich, had just over 26,000 at the time of abolition. The high cost of the transitional arrangements, the continuing cost of the 13-fold replication of administrative structures, and reduced ability to deploy teachers to outer London where rolls had begun to stabilise, must significantly limit savings.

The main cost impact will in fact be distributional, as ILEA provided a cross-subsidy from rich to poor boroughs. ILEA itself was explicit about this, eg in a propaganda leaflet for Southwark residents. 'The ILEA is spending more than £97m on education in Southwark this year. How much of this do Southwark ratepayers have to raise? Less than £47m... This shows graphically how the ILEA is able to draw on the wealth of central London to subsidise education services in less well-off areas'. In 1987/8, only 26% of ILEA's rate precept of £943m was demanded from householders. Thus, Lambeth council, opposing abolition, claimed the borough got £100m and paid £47m. As the biggest net exporter of children to schools in other boroughs, it stood to lose even more if these boroughs, as they promised to do, sought to restrict such imports. As a relatively poor borough, abolition almost undoubtedly meant greater long-term inequality. There are already substantial differences between the boroughs. The most extreme differences are given below.

Table 8.4: **Social characteristics of five inner London boroughs in 1987/8 (% primary pupils or their parents)**

	Lewisham	Wandsworth	West-minster	Hackney	Tower Hamlets	ILEA
Eligible for free meals	38	41	49	59	72	49
No wage earner	18	20	32	35	44	27

Source: ILEA Education Statistics, 1988-89

While Conservative Wandsworth campaigned for independence, having many young parents it had gained from ILEA's cross-subsidies. However, as an 'over-spender', ILEA had been penalised through loss of all block grant from the centre for nearly the last decade of its life. Wandsworth hoped to recapture central government grant. In one year it levied a nil poll tax and thus gained funds through progressive taxation without charging for local services, a route previously closed. With cuts in services which previously generally benefited the less well-off, the relatively well-off in the borough would therefore receive a cross-subsidy from tax-payers in other boroughs.

Given the existence of a unitary education service in Inner London for nearly 120 years, no account of borough boundaries had been taken in the distribution of facilities. As Ouseley, the outgoing ILEA Chief Executive, put it at the time: 'Luck and geography will play a big part in determining the sort of education pupils will get after ILEA's abolition' (*Local Government Chronicle*, 26.5.89). This became apparent very quickly with some boroughs refusing to take children from other boroughs. Each borough could lose or gain from these swap arrangement. ILEA's own survey of swaps (P9035, 5.5.89) suggested that about 24% of Inner London children attending ILEA secondary schools went to schools outside their borough. As the cost of providing education was greater than the cost recouped from boroughs (though renegotiations can change this), 'a borough which is a net exporter of pupils will be at a financial advantage over one which is a net importer'. The main importers were Camden and Westminster, the main exporters Lambeth and Hackney. On the other hand, while the importers would lose out in revenue terms if this continued, the cost of excess capacity is high. Thus, in its development plan Wandsworth stated its intention to maintain as many schools as possible through 'a phased achievement of a 30% reduction in net exports' (para 5.2). Insofar as they were successful, the reduction in choice and efficiency would be considerable. Lambeth, by far the biggest net exporter, stated in its Development Plan that it intended to minimise exports to reduce excess capacity but also because of 'the financial burden of paying other London boroughs to educate Lambeth children' (para. 5.10). This was impelled by the imminent *raising* of recoupment rates. As around half of Lambeth's secondary students are taught outside the borough, any rise would be significant. Its net recoupment cost represented 9% of its education budget (para 5.22). Yet, as a Hammersmith report prior to abolition put it, with inadequate secondary capacity in Kensington and a net outflow to Hammersmith, any shortfall in recoupment would mean that Hammersmith 'will be subsidising Kensington and Chelsea' (STC 2028, 13.6.88). Probably the main effect of the abolition of ILEA will be increased costs, pointless competition, and a significant redistribution of resources - in the first instance away from those in need, but also with a strong arbitrary element. The educational benefits are likely to be nil.

Re-organisation post-16

There is obviously a conflict between the goals of choice and economy. Circular 4/82 declared that the Secretary of State 'will not normally approve proposals which have as their consequence the closure or significant change of character of schools which, by demonstrating their success in the provision they make for sixth form education have already proved their worth'. The costs of this ideological commitment were eventually recognised. Circular 3/87 stated that he 'would not normally be prepared to approve the closure of a school of proven worth unless... the alternative proposals would secure at least the same quality and variety of education at lower cost'. But if educational beliefs sometimes override cost constraints, policy may not only be constrained by cost factors but wholly determined by them. In Hargreaves' view the introduction of middle schools was a result of the 'politics of administrative convenience' (in Cosin and Hales, 1983), as they made unnecessary the building of large new comprehensive schools. This 'severely restricted the possibilities for bringing about comprehensive school reform' (p218). On the other hand, in Sharpe's view (in Cosin and Hales, 1983), the scheme was administratively convenient but also the 'greatest single contribution to national educational developments in the post-war period'. Middle schools may in fact combine both educational and cost advantages, as they may facilitate large upper secondary schools with wide offerings for older children. A senior Scottish administrator would have preferred this option as 'it would have been easier to produce a really effective top school.... in those areas where there wasn't a strong tradition to stay on at school' (quoted in McPherson and Raab, 1988, p382). The comprehensive vision itself owes much to cost constraints, as many grammar schools were closed as a result of falling rolls rather than of educational judgement.

The same arguments apply to the establishment of sixth form and tertiary colleges. These have arisen in response to both falling rolls and change in educational thinking. While the size of the sixth form has grown substantially, rising from 8% to 18% of the school population in the 20 years after Crowther reported, the range of subjects had hardly widened. Nearly three quarters of students studied from a range of nine subjects (the figure had been 80% in 1960). Only 6% studied new subjects like computing or business studies (Edwards, in Ahier and Flude, 1983, p63). Despite the government's rejection of the recommendations of the Higginson Report, the Standing Conference on University Education has argued not only that broader subject matter is needed but that A-levels are overloaded with factual content which tends 'to blind the student to principles and concepts which might inform understanding' (the *Guardian*, 10.5.89). Institutions also need to change, preferably into a mix of sixth form, further education and training, as also proposed by Finegold *et al* (1990). The merging of sixth-form and FE would make the 16-19 age range fully comprehensive. Tertiary colleges would be the main means of achieving this. However, as with middle schools their adoption has been the product of administrative convenience, the first appearing in Exeter in 1972 as an economic rationalisation of sixth-form teaching. Thus 'what has often been advocated as the logical last step in comprehensive reorganisation was then given a severely utilitarian justification' (Edwards, in Ahier and Flude, 1983, p67).

Now the reverse applies. Utilitarian rationalisation is rejected as an impediment to the maintenance of expensive and inefficient sixth forms. Ranson (1990) details government spoliation of several reorganisation schemes, partly in favour of selection: in Wiltshire mushroom sixth forms were rejected 'because of the academic achievement of the two grammar schools' (p35); similarly in Devon. In 1987 the Secretary of State specifically rejected the abolition of selection in Conservative Gloucestershire, thus forcing even Tory authorities to keep faith. In non-selective areas such as Birmingham proposals for reorganisation have changed with the wind more than once. Although the secretary of state did approve replacement of some schools by sixth form colleges, under a Conservative administration the city was deliberately 'left with an amount of over-provision' (p42). In Manchester reorganisation plans have been gestating and changing for over five years.

In 1987 the government rejected ILEA plans to establish new tertiary colleges, while abolition dealt a further blow to tertiary development. The establishment of CTCs is yet a further spanner in the works. For instance, despite excess capacity, Wandsworth allowed a school previously closed to re-open as a CTC (Edwards, Gewirtz and Whitty, 1992, p101), presumably for the extra funding and to protect its sixth forms. In the authors' views, the CTC initiative 'was explicitly targeted at the very LEAs most likely to have their reorganization plans disrupted' (p89). Before it even became an LEA in its own right, a major part of Lewisham's development plan had become nugatory with the transfer of a Haberdashers school to CTC status (partly to protect its sixth form from tertiary reorganisation). The governing body's decision to seek CTC status was contested as far as the Lords. It should be noted that planning of post-16 education in London is already difficult enough with the level of private provision. According to one calculation, excluding those in FE colleges, 45% of 16-19s in the south-west and 39% in Greater London and the south-east are in fee-paying schools (*Guardian*, 14.1.91).

Not much after the abolition of ILEA, Leeds, also one of the country's biggest LEAs, put forward a plan for tertiary reorganisation. This was linked to the need to reduce spare capacity. While it could have simply closed a number of schools it chose to close all sixth forms and to establish in their stead, and in place of existing FEs, the largest tertiary college in the country (17,000 students); this would have been split into six sites spread around the city. While one reason was to make Leeds more attractive as a regional provider - since, 'under the "recoupment" system, Leeds is a substantial gainer' - the comprehensive ideals of the system were powerful.

> it unites the vocational and academic; it couples learning for a purpose and learning for its own sake; allows students to move between and among technological, art and science programmes. Socially it brings together the employed and unemployed, minority and majority groups, the disadvantaged and advantaged, blue collar and white collar workers, the young and old (Leeds Post-16 Development Proposal, pp 7 and 11).

The aim of extending post-16 education and of reducing wastage was related to the fact that 'many still seem to believe that education takes place in the sixth forms, training in the colleges and leisure pursuits in Continuing Education' (p12). Both retention of sixth forms and the formation of sixth form colleges or consortia were rejected for several clearly expounded reasons:

1. The decline in rolls had been too severe.
2. Few schools provide more than 10 A-levels (compared to 25+ for a tertiary college).
3. Small sixth-form classes increase pupil-teacher ratios lower down.
4. Closure of only some sixth forms would generate fierce local opposition to partiality.
5. Any compromise would make tertiary colleges unviable.
6. Greater flexibility was needed as a result of changing sources of funding (eg YTS).

While by now there were around 40 tertiary colleges in the country, the scheme was rejected by the DES. The main reason for rejection was because reorganisation required the loss of sixth forms. Most statutory objections were from the relatively well-heeled outer areas of Leeds. High schools themselves also opposed the change, though the initial proposal had expected this, as 'a sixth former is worth far more in terms of salary and promotion than a fifth former' (p14).

The replacement proposal after this rejection of the first scheme was for the abolition of all middle schools. This was apparently largely because post-16 colleges would in the future be difficult to establish after a break at 12 or 13. However, when the authority put forward its replacement proposal this was, astonishingly, with all reference to the very carefully worked out tertiary proposals removed. The proposal was now simply to cut capacity. Thus, instead of middle schools going in order to make a tertiary college more viable, they disappeared to make way for sixth forms. While it was stated that the tertiary college proposal might return once excess capacity was removed, this would depend on a review of sixth form viability. But the problem of reorganising twice, the trend towards stabilising rolls, government displeasure, and local opposition to the loss of sixth forms, now firmed up by the closures required in the second proposal, all make comprehensive tertiary reorganisation a distant prospect. A comprehensive and adult form of education at one end of the secondary scale has been lost without a gain at the other.

Conclusion

The government is teetering on the edge of enforcing opting-out. With the removal of all non-school post-16 education from LEA control it almost forcing itself into this position, as all LEA intervention, at least at the secondary level, becomes increasingly untenable. However, the government is hoist by its own petard of voluntarism, in the absurd position of virtually forcing schools to 'volunteer' to opt out - through offers of cash, or requiring in the 1993 Education Bill annual opt-out discussions by the governing body (followed by a report to parents of their reasons for rejecting an opt-out ballot). The 1993 Bill also proposes allowing special schools to opt out, thus creating unnecessary difficulties for LEAs who may have to bargain for places in special schools in unpredictable ways. The Bill also forces LEAs to share responsibility for the financial running of education with the body that funds grant-maintained schools, even if only one school opts out. As the General Secretary of the Society of Education Officers put it, 'it will be very difficult to work with them because they have a completely different agenda' (*TES*, 4.6.93).

Total opting out is obviously a contradiction in terms as it would remove the element of choice (between two different types of school), that the government claims to be essential. It is, in fact, unlikely that choice has ever been a true objective, as both the Education Department and the Treasury would find it hard to accept its inefficiencies. Choice cannot come cost-free. By contrast, central control, where this exists, appears to result in definite cuts, as in Northern Ireland (McKeown, 1991). There have been many reports of the government enticing opt-outs through promises of cash, for instance in Essex, where it is claimed that 22 of the 33 opted-out schools are to share £5.4m for capital expenditure, while the county has only £12m to spend on its own 695 schools. The ironies are, of course, profound. Essex is not well known for its generosity to education, but in this it has been respecting government wishes. The funding enabled a Tory MP in Chelmsford to express delight at their good fortune 'and he urged other schools to "Go for it" and opt out too' (*East Anglian Daily Times*, 23.1.93). Northampton is allocating £11,000 plus £20 per pupil for minor works - perhaps the first authority to delegate money for this purpose under LMS (*TES*, 12.2.93). This is not just a matter of degree of autonomy but of bidding up spending. But what competitive advantage will operate when all schools have opted out and cuts rather than added cash become universal?

Total grant-maintained status would also put the government in the uncomfortable position of reneging on its promises. Once the bogey of local government has been removed, who else is there to blame for problems but the government? Taking a swipe at local government has been easy. Full responsibility may not be. Even local government might gain from the new game of pass the buck. In the words of David Hart of the NAHT:

> Politicians are always adept at shifting the blame, and this is an Act where not only national but local politicians can shift the blame down to school level... The local politicians could turn round in the future and say, 'Well don't blame us, they were given the budgets, they were told they could do what they like' (quoted by Ball, 1990, p68).

Is it possible to take decentralisation further? The Adam Smith Institute has argued that councils should be single-tier and reduced in size, run as companies in which residents would own shares, and with councillors paid like directors of firms. Not long before this, the Institute of Economic Affairs had proposed 'the sale of most government and local government work' (*Guardian*, 17.9.88), with other services run by agencies. Shining clear in this vision is the total substitution of cost for policy considerations. 'Free of the normal constraints on local authority activities they would be able to operate commercially....' (Adam Smith Institute, 1989, p53). One day maybe we will see British local authorities funding private education in Japan.

Much left-wing critique, by contrast, continues to give LEAs substantial power, as without this the chance of a comprehensive education policy is reduced. For Brighouse and Tomlinson (1991) they are important to quality control. For Monck and Kelly *et al* (1992) they are necessary to effective school management. They rightly argue, in particular, that control over pay and staffing should be returned to LEAs. While they support LMS in principle, funding has always been shared between schools and LEAs and varying the share does not alter the principle (even if the practice varies). Many schools find budgetary delegation a burden rather than a boon, as it gives very little real freedom, especially in small schools. LMS should then be geared to what schools can best make use of and manage, not to the government's prejudices. The purpose of LMS is negative: the elimination of LEAs. Thus, while Monck and Kelly argue that LEAs are necessary to make LMS work, they are in reality arguing for a totally different policy.

It is indeed entirely arguable that true decentralisation requires a strengthening of local government. An alternative decentralisation, therefore, would be to break up much of central government, for instance hiving off Treasury functions to university economists, and passing a wide range of powers to local authorities, whether to unitary bodies or to a range of decentralised specialist services (where political power could be held at the regional level). Such an outcome is just as logical as the notion that the centre must acquire more power to be efficient, or that services should be fragmented to a market situation of post hoc choice, devoid of development or planning initiative.

The reduction or removal of LEA control has little to do with efficiency. Its function is a redistribution of welfare. Central to this is a segregation based on residential patterning: as suggested above, the concept of collective consumption at the local level must take into account its spatial distribution. Green-belt areas, parks, transport, playgrounds and other amenities, a clean environment, the quality of housing and education - all are spatially distributed, and this spatial distribution is competitive. In effect the government is attempting to end cross-residential subsidies so that the relatively well-off will be able to direct state resources more closely to their needs. In addition, the removal of control of all post-16 institutions from LEA control makes it impossible for any LEA to abolish its sixth forms in favour of separate post-16 institutions. Sixth forms favour middle-class students while tertiary colleges offer more extensive and balanced support. Only through the establishment of institutions like tertiary colleges can choice and opportunity be transferred to those who have most right to it: the students who pass through education.

9 Effective education

While an underlying theme of this chapter is *effective* education, the question is not how to make education effective but for what purposes or social groups education may be effective. In response there have perhaps been three main (chronological) paradigms:

1. Liberal-egalitarianism: effective education means expansion of (comprehensive) education to maximise working-class opportunity, assessed in mobility studies -sometimes disparagingly known as the 'political-arithmetic' approach, or alternatively as 'efficient egalitarianism' (Finegold *et al*, 1990).

2. The 'new' sociology of education, developed partly in response to the apparent failure of the above to achieve equality. It concentrated on curriculum and pedagogy rather than on organisation and outcomes. Effective education is ideologically sound pedagogy.

3. A right-wing reaction to both of the above, unconcerned with either equality or ideology. Effective education is effective schools. This account of education undermines assessment of the impact of educational structures and processes, as improvement is subsumed within the single institution, just as in other areas of right-wing thinking, efficiency is the firm, and morality is the family. Structures do not exist. Thus, while the 'good school' paradigm shares much of the political-arithmetic desire for measurement, it reverses the purpose.

The 'political-arithmetic' approach is fundamentally about class (or other social divisions). Inequalities between these have to be measured. A traditional Marxist dislike of this process derives in part from ambivalence towards the notion of working-class children becoming middle-class adults, but also from a legitimate wariness towards the concept of 'human capital' (central to the argument over skill shortages discussed in Part One).

> what must further be remarked about the theory of human capital is the direct appeal to pro-capitalist ideological sentiment that resides in its insistence that the worker is a *holder of capital* (as embodied in his skills and knowledge) and that he has the *capacity to invest* (in himself). Thus in a single bold conceptual stroke the *wage-earner*, who holds no property and controls neither the process nor the product of his labour, is transformed into a *capitalist* (Karabel and Halsey, 1977, p13; emphases in original).

A strict equation is made between personal and social rewards. 'It is now.... apparent to all that education pays, always in the long run, and often quite quickly' (Crowther Report, DES, 1963). Newsam had much the same approach, explicit in the report's title, *Half Our Future*. Expansion of opportunity should benefit both the nation and 'less able' (often working-class) children, as 'the future pattern of employment in this country will require a much larger pool of talent than is at present available; and that at least a substantial proportion of the "average" and "below average" pupils are sufficiently educable to supply that additional talent' (DES, 1963, p5). The 1963 Robbins report was released not by the Ministry of Education but by the Treasury (Hough, 1987).

The problem with the calculation of human capital, as with assessments of skill shortages, is that it can easily justify intensified tracking, whether on the basis of performance or aptitude. One outcome of such pressure is the attempt to establish a clear divide between academic and vocational or technical education, often on the assumption that 'half our future' must have a different future.

Technology, vocationalism and segregation

While suppressed working-class talent had to be released for the good of the nation, fear of a Pandora-box effect invited the channelling of this new talent in closely controlled ways. Growth may only be acceptable through segregation, and a vocational route was one expression of this. Sometimes this means that concern over segregation is transmuted to a choice between technical and non-technical routes. For instance, the Dainton Report called for a broad span of studies in the sixth forms so that 'irreversible decisions for or against science, engineering and technology, be postponed as late as possible' (DES, 1968, p87). In 1988 the Higginson Committee recommended expanding sixth-form study to five subjects, for much the same purpose. In 1982 the DES characterised O-level science syllabuses as 'overloaded, out of date and narrow, paying little regard to the relevance of science to industry or to adult life, and concentrating on abstract concepts from too early a stage' (quoted by McCulloch, 1986, p38).

However, unlike vocational education, technical education is not necessarily a source of inequality. This has been much discussed particularly in French educational sociology. The development of technological study is often a form of vocational inferiority designed to protect high status qualifications in traditional subjects or those related to the professions. However, as technology expands, elements of technical study are themselves partitioned off as a higher status route - medicine being the supreme example (Bourdieu and Passeron, 1977/90); though as there is often excess demand for these highly controlled jobs, it is possible that in time some areas of technical study are subject to increased access and therefore some deflation in status (Cherkaoui, 1982).

There is nothing lower-class about technical education: 'if, in the future, Oxbridge decides that BTEC qualifications should be included in the entry system, private schools will have to take the lead there as well if they are to retain their dominant position in the high status areas of higher education' (Salter and Tapper, 1985, p212). Vocational education, by contrast, is a traditionally distinct preparation for work. The interesting thing about British structures is that this distinction is postponed to relatively late (after age 16), but vocational routes are now being created within schools in order to prepare the less academically inclined for this highly abrupt juncture. This is not a powerful trend, on the other hand, and is contrary to the intention of the national curriculum, which is to maintain a generalist form of education. Indeed, the national curriculum can be seen as the culmination of a long-term trend towards integration pre-16. This is partly because separate routes were rejected by consumers of education as clearly inferior. At their demise only 11% of the relevant age group attended technical colleges. But generalist education also results partly from a humanist belief in the creation of all-rounder qualities. Perhaps this goes back to education's upper-class origins, when amateurism was decent and professionalism rather shabby. The expansion of education saw the expansion of this ethos, eventually including working-class children in its remit. Even more paradoxically, while socialist thinkers have for over a century strongly supported technical education, humanist education is now promoted as a weapon against incipient right-wing attempts to impose greater vocationalism on education. Thus an aristocratic worldview is used by the Left to defend working-class rights not to be pushed into a vocational ghetto, while the Right's national curriculum can masquerade as modernist, goal-directed education. This peculiar ambivalence to the use of vocational education within schools can be seen in the history of TVEI, the Technical and Vocational Education Initiative, established in 1982 to increase technological resources and innovative teaching practices for the 14-18 age range. In a sense it sought to incorporate the technical school *within* comprehensive schools. McCulloch (1986) places TVEI precisely in this context. The division in schooling between mainstream and vocational education had never really worked. 'It was this dichotomy that the TVEI was intended to resolve' (p39). Nevertheless, TVEI merely continues earlier ambiguities. One of the MSC-funded evaluation exercises (Barnes et al, 1987) found that 16 out of the 26 schools studied had 'contained' TVEI in such a way as to leave the main curriculum unaffected, while placements in clerical, manufacturing, maintenance, retail and caring occupations constituted the main pattern of work experience in the scheme. TVEI work experience opportunities have generally not often been matched to the 'hi-tech' focus of the TVEI schemes (NFER, 1987, pp118/9). It is also treated with suspicion by some parents who apparently see TVEI as a non-academic distraction (Barnes *et al*, 1987). The finding in Newcastle that 'TVEI pupils obtained worse examination results than non-TVEI pupils.... even after corrections were made for initial differences' (FitzGibbon *et al*, 1988, p49) may explain this. Certainly the initial hope that TVEI would encourage staying-on is not being fulfilled. In the earliest part of the pilot exercise about 70% of students on TVEI still left school at the minimum leaving age. As Fulton comments: 'It was surely unrealistic to suppose that the Initiative on its own, and without the help of maintenance allowances, could overcome all the longstanding pressures in favour of early leaving' (1987, p107).

Nevertheless, no reform has a single-sided effect. TVEI now receives some support as a bulwark against segregation. The government has certainly become rather cool towards TVEI. Despite spending over £1 billion on the initiative, in terms of its chief ideological premises it had failed - largely though its incorporation into professional modes: 'the new Right clearly finds it difficult to approve of the new subjects and the new styles of learning which TVEI courses have helped to pioneer' (Chitty, 1989, p176). 'Homespun TVEI' (Yeomans, 1989, p13) is now a rather quaint survival in the path of the juggernaut of the national curriculum.

The impact of the CPVE is similarly ambiguous. Introduced to provide post-16 study in schools where there was no wish to pursue A-levels, its origin in a section of the DES responsible for FE, and its placement under the vocational examining bodies, deliberately set this up as a non-academic stream, unlike the earlier Certificate of Extended Education, examined by the GCE and CSE boards. While the CPVE expands opportunity, the 'possibility arises of linking CPVE to TVEI courses and CGLI and B/TEC awards to bring into existence a differentiated or segmented school curriculum' (Radnor, Ball and Burrell, in Hargreaves and Reynolds, 1989, p104). More particularly, FE achieves 'a considerable "beach-head" in the schools'. The most significant question is how far projects such as the CPVE, or the Low Attaining Pupils Programme (LAPP), which tested new means for engaging the 'bottom 40%' through a greater 'practical slant', help the less academically able or instead merely protect the elitist academic nature of the A-level structure. It is of note that students themselves may reject this elitism. The government's continued rejection of reform of A-levels, eg through integrating vocational elements into its structure as proposed by Finegold et al (1990), has resulted in a completely separate route to a vocational A-level equivalent at General National Vocational Qualification (GNVQ) level three. When this proved a 'runaway hit with schools and sixth-formers' (TES, 30.7.93), probably exceeding the government's application target by 20,000 in its first year (partly because students appeared to favour continuous assessment, a broader range of study, and a modular approach), there were fears that the process was too fast and that too many academically able students were switching to GNVQs. It appears that half of applicants are 'good A-level material' (TES, 30.7.93). But then, of course, A-levels will become even more an elite qualification.

When the National Curriculum Council sought to develop a core skills package in order to bridge the academic/vocational divide, even some Conservative education ministers such as Mrs Rumbold recognised the importance of this programme (Graham and Tytler, 1993). Graham, as do Finegold et al (1990), sees core skills as both egalitarian and efficient. However, the concept is so woolly that its real application is difficult to determine. Institutions, not skills, are what count. The question is the degree to which GNVQs segregate access into FE, HE and work, not so much whether A-levels, GNVQs (and NVQs) segregate skills. While Chitty's fear that with developments such as the CPVE, YTS, and TVEI 'there seems little cause for optimism that the term "comprehensive education" will actually come to mean anything beyond the age of fourteen' (1989, p18) may be premature, the segregationist intention seems clear.

Efficient egalitarianism?

Comprehensive education in the USA divides secondary education into three tracks - academic, general and vocational - thus bringing a form of tripartite system within the school. Though the national curriculum may impede this, this may be the future of British education, which is encouraging vocationalism though within mainstream schooling. While Rhoades (1989) argues that vocational education in the USA reflects a general American belief that education should be relevant, and thus the 'tired but telling designations of "academic" and "vocational" subjects' may be overdriven, there is little doubt that the American system is inegalitarian. Natriello *et al* (1989) examined performance on standardized tests across two years in all three tracks on a very large sample, the first near the end of compulsory schooling. Whatever the causes, performance is rigidly contained within tracks over time. Murphy and Hallinger (1989) review studies which show that tracking depresses performance, offering differential curricular experience as the main cause. Despite American belief in mobility, tracking is subject to considerable 'lock-in', often for structural reasons such as resource controls on upper-track places. Tracking therefore promotes as well as reflects differences in performance. Page's qualitative study of teaching in the vocational track of an above average school found that teachers were committed, but also that vocational students tended to be marginalised. In the words of one teacher, 'I put worksheets in the principals' or counsellors' mailboxes, but they never ask me about it. As long as I *take care of* the classes, that's about it' (original emphasis, 1989, p208). It has been argued that the 'new basics' - an American approximation to the national curriculum - would eliminate this rigidity, but in Page's words, 'the remedy fails to take into account the institutional and cultural underpinnings of teachers' expectations' (p217). The fact that this 'entitlement curriculum' already has a powerfully skewed distribution - with (in 1983) one third of academic-track students meeting this curriculum but only 3% of vocational students (Murphy and Hallinger, 1989) - suggests that 'opportunity to learn' is an elusive concept.

Prais and Beadle (1991) view Britain's mainstream system as old-fashioned and cite several advantages to early vocational separation (such as a motivational effect on the less academically inclined). In much of Europe, schooling is indeed segregated on the basis of technical or vocational curricula. 'About a quarter of all 15 year-olds in France, the Netherlands and Germany are now in vocational streams' (Prais and Beadle, 1991, page iv). But these different systems are also closely geared to the preservation of structured inequalities. Germany reveals how the UK might have gone without comprehensivisation in its maintainance of a clearly articulated tripartite system: the *Hauptschule* (secondary-modern), the *Realschule,* an intermediate and largely vocational form like the British technical schools, and the *Gymnasium* (grammar school). This strongly entrenched system has seen only limited encroachment from comprehensives, still in effect an experimental form and taking only 5% of students overall - though this varies enormously according to regional political control, with Hesse having 15.6% of secondary intake in comprehensives in 1989, compared to 0.4% in Bavaria (Mitter, 1991, p159). In 1965 only 15% of 13 year-olds went to the *Gymnasium* and less than half of these got the *Abitur* (A-level) - up to 50% repeating a year to achieve this (Max-Planck-Institute, 1989).

The 'main school' (*Hauptschule*), however, is being abandoned in favour of the other two school types. In 1963, 70% of children went to the *Hauptschule,* 12% to the *Realschule,* 15% to the *Gymnasium.* By 1986 the figures were 38%, 29% and 28%, ie nearly equal proportions. Is this a great success or like everyone driving in the fast lane for fear of being overtaken? It is unclear whether education overall is being upgraded or whether 'grammar schools are becoming overly tolerant in selecting their candidates and are adopting structural as well as curriculum features previously associated with comprehensive schools' (Mitter, 1991, p163). Some conservative Länder have tried to stem the flow into the *Gymnasium* as 'the increasing enrolments were considered a threat to the quality of the education it offered' (Max Planck Institute, 1989, p122). Germany has in addition a variety of vocational upper schools and there have been plans to boost these, mostly through shifting the impact of falling rolls on to the general sector. However, their relatively low status stands in the way, with demand by both students and teachers actually reversing this effect. In 1985 spending on staff of nearly DM 31,700m in the general sector exceeded planned spending by nearly DM 2000m. In the vocational sector the actual figure of 5,500m *fell short of* the target by over 2,800m (Weiss and Weishaupt, 1989, p46). 'In view of the present high political priority of vocational education in FR Germany this result is surprising' (p49).

While the *Gymnasium* has become more popular the massive decline of the *Hauptschule* has left it as a sink school for poor rural catholics and the children of foreign workers in the cities. In Bavaria nearly half of the children go to the old and tiny (often religious) *Volkschule* or to the *Hauptschule*, while in industrial Bremen only a quarter do so (Hill, 1987). In 1980, 38% of the population in Germany attended the *Hauptschule* but the proportion of foreign children attending was 78%. Less than half get any qualifications. 27% of German children go to the *Gymnasium*, compared to 7% of foreign children (Max Planck Institute, 1989). The children of the foreign workers, predominantly Turks, have been the focus of considerable racism. In 1982 *der Spiegel* produced a headline: 'Wir können hier nicht halb Ankara bieten' (we can't invite half of Ankara here), at the same time quoting a teacher who went on to say that 'it is impossible to work with both groups'. The magazine went on to comment that 'on the playground one would think he is in deepest Dixieland' (quoted in Hill, 1987). These children now constitute about 10% of the school population, but effectively form a ghetto. Even apparently progressive aspects of education might add to this. For instance, mother-tongue teaching in Bavaria 'educates its foreigners to go home and resume their lives there' (Hill, 1987, p281). While in Germany what were 'in quantitative terms, the "main schools" will therefore increasingly become "remainder schools" for children of immigrants and members of marginal groups' (Mitter, 1991, p164), the *Realschule* and even the *Gymnasium* have become a route into quality apprenticeships or other vocational education. At the same time, the comprehensive, though limited, is becoming the respectable alternative to grammar schools, even in what was East Germany (Mitter, 1991, p164). The tracks have partly dissolved only to recrystallise in a different form.

The Netherlands has an even more fundamental division, with the lowest prestige schools labelled Junior Vocational schools themselves divided into occupational specialisations. It also maintains a distinction between academic and technical grammar schools. Such schools are entered from the age of 12. Italy has a rigid distinction between and within the academic and technical routes. The upper-secondary (14-18) schools (*liceo*, equivalent to the French *lycée*) have classical and scientific versions. For others leaving compulsory education at age 14 there is the option of a range of specialised technical institutes and vocational schools (*istituti professionale*). But the complex institutional separation in the post-14 secondary phase acts as a powerful filter. Only 62% of children enter this higher secondary stage. While entry to university from this route is possible, the success rate is appallingly low, with only about 10-13% passing (Meijer, 1991, p24.) In 1987, while only 25% of those reaching the end of compulsory schooling continued with academic courses, 32% entered technical institutes, 21% went into vocational schools, and about 10% took up state training courses or apprenticeships (Meijer, 1991, p15). The rigid tracking, apart from reducing opportunity from an early age, imposes high costs. For instance, only 25% of entrants to the vocational schools obtain a leaving diploma (p17). Italy has seen some of the biggest education reforms in recent decades, with around 90% of under-sixes in state nursery schools, the comprehensivisation of education up to the minimum leaving age of 14, and free access to university based on qualifications. Nevertheless, while attendance at university was about 25% of the relevant age cohort, by 1980 the success rate was only about 30% (Levy, 1992). Cobalti (1990) shows that the above reforms did not significantly alter the odds of transition from one level to another between social classes.

In France, the proportion of school-leavers going to university has increased more than four times since 1955. Cherkaoui (1982), examining the increase in *baccalauréat* successes, identifies three periods of growth: roughly the 1950s, 1960s and 1970s. The proportion of school-leavers getting the *bac* rose from 8% in 1950 to 16% in 1960 to 24% in 1970, hovering just above that thereafter. The cause of the latter stabilisation is not a decline in the pool of talent but appeared to be internal organisational adjustments which limited the deflation of credentials. While getting through the *bac* is an automatic ticket into higher education, the development of a two-track route to university (*à deux vitesses*), combined with the demands of the *grand école* - requiring a further two years of study on top of the *baccalauréat* - merely adds further hurdles to maintain elite distinctions.

Calls for comprehensivisation lower down have also been vitiated. The first attempt to establish comprehensives did not come until 1963, with the 11-15 *collège d'enseignement secondaire,* but this model was highly tracked and was replaced after 1977 with the *collège unique.* In principle, the comprehensive middle school is an undifferentiated route to the *lycée.* However, resistance by administrators, teachers and parents, severely restricted the comprehensive principle, a 'seemingly intractable collusion' (Weiler, 1988, p258) that has laid low the plans of both socialist and conservative governments. Schools are often comprehensive only on paper.

As for increased access to the *bac*, it would appear that this is taking place through a further segregation. The attempt to maintain the elite nature of French education while offering increased access was made through the establishment of technical grammar schools (*lycées d'enseignement professionels*) and technical A-level certificates (the *baccalauréat de technicien*), supplemented by the lower-level *brevet de technicien.* (Higher up came the development of technical universities, though these still attract not much more than 10% of students.) Growth is being managed through increased segregation, thus protecting differentials (Holmes, 1985). Segregation now reaches down into the comprehensive schools.

> the parting of the ways had to start in the very middle of the lower secondary level, and technical third and fourth years were started in 1985. This decision meant a radical alteration of the comprehensive principle, since at the end of the second year less able children tend to be advised to take these special courses, which it is hoped will remotivate them by offering practical instruction (Derouet, 1991, p126).

With growing choice this segregation is becoming generalised. 'There are growing disparities between the most sought-after schools, which pick the best pupils and attract the bulk of the money (with the blessing of the local authorities), and the mass of the schools that are dumping grounds for lower class children' (Derouet, 1991, p130). The process has in fact been very difficult to eradicate. The 1981 *Commission du Bilan,* for instance, spoke of 'new tracks of exclusion' which 'function essentially for the children who are socially already the most disadvantaged' (quoted in Weiler, 1988, pp257/8). For the less able, the cost of fighting the effect of this segregation is considerable. Even in the 1970s one third of children repeated a year to get as far as the *baccalauréat* and 10% repeat two years, with a small number repeating even more (Cherkaoui, 1982).

The growth of choice and parental involvement is as yet harder to map. France goes further than Britain in allowing parental involvement in streaming decisions. A study of the progress of 2,500 children (Duru-Bellat and Mingat, 1989) indicates that only 25% of streaming differences are explained by achievement (or age). While social class is not a significant determinant in itself it becomes so through parental involvement. Interestingly, this makes most difference to children of around average ability. For those with either a lot or very little ability, social class had little impact on streaming decisions through parental involvement. But for the huge swathe of middle rankers, parental class is important, with higher-class children over-represented in the higher streams. For those with poor parents, investment in an uncertain future of continued education may seem risky where earnings are important, and a lower stream is more acceptable. But for better-off parents with average children this risk is not a problem. For such people choice is easy.

Japanese education is supposedly based on free choice while in practice, as schools are finely graded according to their pass rates, they are highly selective. One of the oddest developments is the rise in status of the *kikokushijo,* the children of expatriate Japanese. Once considered slightly tainted and in need of help these children are now viewed as models to follow. Taught abroad - though often in Japanese schools - they have become an elite with their own educational facilities upon return, with the result that 'competition for places for non-*kikokushijo* has become increasingly fierce (Goodman, 1990, p229). While the UK may be following the USA in terms of vocational segregation within mainstream education, it is following the Japanese strategy of competitive education, with schools divided into a complex hierarchy of 'excellence' which segregates the local population into institutionalised streams. The Conservative government has chosen to segregate on the basis of prestige rather than of function. The reason for this is that segregation can be managed more efficiently within mainstream education, as demand for institutions providing low-status vocational education is always uncertain.

This does not mean there cannot be vocational-technical segregation based on high status. In Japan technical schools have been introduced in an elite form, along with further levels of differentiated entrance examination into HE, because 'conservatives saw the trends towards higher staying-on rates as constituting even greater cause for pursuing their long-cherished policy of diversification' (Schoppa, 1991, p45). CTCs are an attempt to follow this model. While the proposal seems to stand the national curriculum on its head, when Mr Patten 'looks forward to a day when parents can choose state schools that specialise in languages, science, or even teaching science in a foreign language' rather than selecting by area or ability (*Economist,* 25.7.92), the aim is no doubt a similar elite segregation.

Such developments must bring back into play earlier analysis of the effects of segregation. In Britain and the USA, the comprehensive/segregationist issue has been subject to intensive but inconclusive appraisal. The studies by Coleman in 1966 and later by Jencks (1972) were negative. The latter argued that schooling has limited impact on performance or on career once various background factors are controlled for. The critique is really of the use of education as a means of equalising opportunity. 'As long as egalitarians assume that public policy cannot contribute to economic equality directly but must proceed through ingenious manipulations of marginal institutions like the schools, progress will remain glacial' (p265).

This left-wing attack on the failure of education to reduce inequality merely gave a fillip to right-wingers who found any form of egalitarianism distasteful. Nevertheless, it is difficult to argue as a consequence of the belief that education is ineffective, that measurement of its effect should cease. The Right certainly does not believe it should - hence the ubiquity of national tests or other performance indicators. The real issue is not the fact but the purpose of measurement. The problem with Jencks' arguments is what counts as effective. 'Eliminating racial and socio-economic segregation in the schools might reduce the test score gap between black and white children and between rich and poor children by 10 to 20 percent' (p109). Perhaps it is a matter of taste, but only utopian predilections can reject such an improvement as worthwhile. If one adds any *increase* in segregation which may both add to inequality and reduce overall educational performance, then very substantial differences are brought into play by changes in educational organisation. There is a clear relationship between educational structures and class effects. Testing Turner's distinction between open and sponsored mobility, Morgan (1990) compares data on entry into higher education in the USA against England and Wales. Not just ability but class and parental education are relatively poor predictors of entry into higher education in the USA. The cost of standards is a very substantial class bias - leading Morgan to describe Britain's segregated system of higher education as akin to 'any centrally planned economy' (p53). It is possible that educational segregation maintains divisions not only between but within social classes. Spenner, Kerkhoff and Glass (1990) show that education in closed (selective) systems may affect not only immediate job status but selective entry into jobs which protect status through internal markets (though this might not be a long-term effect). Segregation may therefore serve not to produce work skills but to establish substantial work demarcations.

The analysis of Halsey, Heath and Ridge (1980), produced as part of the Oxford Social Mobility Project, and well after the American studies just mentioned, demonstrated clear class effects. The central historical focus of the former is the impact of the 1944 Education Act and the subsequent entrenchment of the tripartite system (though they included the remaining private sector along with grammar schools as selective schools). The timing of the study was perhaps unfortunate, coming before the full effects of comprehensivisation could be felt and therefore assessing a system apparently doomed. Nevertheless, with current pressure to return to segregation, the results of the survey are again highly relevant. The Act 1944 was fundamental in opening up opportunities for working-class children. A crucial measure of this is the number of children staying on past the minimum leaving age. The proportion of higher ('service') class boys staying on increased by 50% over the period but the increase was 200% for an intermediate class and yet larger, 240%, for the working class (Halsey *et al*, 1980, p136). Continued progress towards erosion of differentials depends on continued expansion: 'the service class has set a pattern of increasingly extended secondary schooling, following a path towards saturation.... which is trodden later first by the intermediate and finally by the working class' (p146). However, this does not mean Britain has become significantly more egalitarian. The second major finding is that the expansion through tripartism added a brake to equalisation. Looking at examination success the authors find that once IQ and any cultural effects of the family are controlled for, the main source of differential progress is the type of institution attended, and this attendance is itself based on differential class access to types of school

186

(private schools, 'good' grammar schools) - based presumably on income and residential advantages. Working-class children attending such schools tend to do as well as middle-class children, while middle-class children at lower-level schools perform about the same as working-class children. But the middle class has better access to superior schools (schools that are effective suppliers of credentials). Similarly to Jencks (1972) and also to Bowles and Gintis (1976), Halsey *et al* conclude that 'IQ is a relatively unimportant determinant of the type of school one goes to, or of the length of one's school career' (1980, p163). The critical determinant is social background, but this is mediated by the type of school attended. (The authors say nothing about the effect of the actual school.)

One of the problems of this study is that it measures mobility between points within the system (sons against fathers) at the same time that the system itself is changing. The determining impact of the labour market on education was discussed in Part One, but here it need only be noted that value added to (or subtracted from) social status through education must be deeply affected by direct changes in the demand for labour. If the working class has been declining, this does not represent a 'success' for education so much as an exogenous change which has to be controlled for in any assessment of mobility due to education itself. On one count (Price and Bain, in Halsey, 1988, p164), in 1951 manual workers comprised 72.5% of the workforce, while by 1981 this had become 56.4%. Similar concerns have been expressed about health inequalities. There are undoubtedly considerable class inequalities in respect of access to health facilities (Goodin and Le Grand, 1987), of illness and life expectancy (*The Black Report*, Townsend and Davidson, 1982), and there are strong links between deprivation and health inequalities (Townsend, Phillimore and Beattie, 1988). However, the argument in the *Black Report* that health inequalities have widened over time is more controversial. The apparently declining health of working-class people, relatively speaking, might partly be the result of the decline of the working class, which may leave the less healthy as well as the less well-off behind.

The results of Halsey, Heath and Ridge have been re-examined by Blackburn and Marsh (1991), controlling for both changes in the class structure (viewed as a continuum) and in the number of selective places available. These had already been increasing prior to the 1944 Act. The main finding is that a 'pre-existing trend of growing inequality was initially reversed by the Act but then inequality rose again to a higher level than before' (p526). The strengthening of inequality was not caused by the Act but by the growth in selective places and by the baby boom, which accentuated competition for places on traditional class lines. However: 'If the 1944 Act had not been in place when the baby boom generation became adolescents, class inequality would almost certainly have been very much higher' (p530).

In sum, there are very clear relationships between social divisions and the organisation of educational provision. Mapping these is critical. Observation that change over a fairly short period has limited impact on reducing inequality, whether cognitive or pecuniary (eg Jencks, 1972), ignores the fact that inequality itself increases by increments and that without reform its hold would be even more powerful. Effective education is fair education.

Working-class education

Merely counting the numbers of working-class youngsters who become middle-class was for many, of course, hardly the way forward. 'Is the sociology of education obsessed with mobility and status attainment? Then the new sociology discovers as its topic educational knowledge and the reproduction of social classes' (Wexler, 1987, p6). It is a common enough argument that education may enhance rather than mitigate inequality, and may even reproduce inequality and the processes on which it is built. At its most extreme, the 'children of managers and professionals are taught self-reliance within a broad set of constraints, the children of production line workers are taught obedience' (Bowles, 1971, p39). In the well-known theory of Bowles and Gintis (1976), there is a 'correspondence' between the social relations of production and the social relations of education. Both data and theory in this paradigm have been subject to considerable criticism (eg Demaine, 1981): it treats the working class as homogeneous and fails to see the educational divisions that are built upon gender and colour. It understates the impact of mobility and radically oversimplifies forms of pedagogy. Indeed, much of the rightward shift in education is premissed on the notion that 'good' education is rigorous and much working-class education 'progressive' or over-individualistic. In addition:

> Education, indeed, has been seen as hostile to industry and commerce and
> to its materialistic values. Rather than preparing people for production,
> education has often been seen as providing the antidote to its dehumanizing
> and vulgarizing effects (the Leavisite movement is a major example)
> (Moore, in Cole, 1988, p77).

More generally, is education functional for capitalism in the way specified by Bowles and Gintis? The following comparison of quotations from articles by Bowles and by the most prestigious of structural-functionalists, Talcott Parsons, arguing that class differences are not central to society, accentuates the incongruity.

> An ideal preparation for factory work was found in the social relations of
> the school: specifically, in its emphasis on discipline, punctuality,
> acceptance of authority outside the family, and individual accountability for
> one's work (Bowles, 1971).

> First, from the functional point of view the school class can be treated as
> an agency of socialization.... The socialization functions may be summed
> up as the development in individuals of the commitments and capacities
> which are essential prerequisites of their future role-performance (Parsons,
> 1959)

In their efforts to explain the stability of capitalist societies Marxists tend to reify their integrative mechanisms. Schooling fails many, but in so doing it prepares its subjects for failure in life. One response is the notion of resistance, but this is a rather minor qualification. Even in the case of Willis (1982) rebellion is functional for capitalism, as the 'lads' lark about at school to get through the school day, end up in poorly paid jobs, and lark about at work to get through the working day.

An incisive view of the Bowles and Gintis theory comes in a different form of social control argument, that of the CCCS (1981). This contains a coherent understanding of change in education, and in fact periodises the work of Bowles and Gintis as an element of a general disaffection with education; economic decline has disillusioned both Right and Left. But theories such as that of Bowles and Gintis were perhaps even more pessimistic than those on the Right, leaving a 'sense of near closure' (CCCS, 1981, p187). Education is no longer a liberator but entraps. Like Bowles and Gintis, however, the CCCS argue that 'the needs of capitalist industry do exercise a major influence on the character and structure of the education system' (CCCS, 1981, p31), but their view of education is as a site of struggle over time between forces for and against 'popular education'. The Labour Party has traditionally represented working-class demands for a popular, non-elitist education but supplied instead a statist, top-down form.

> Labour, in effect, attempted to serve two masters: popular interests and those of capital. It attempted, in a way that very much conforms to classic Marxist definitions of 'social democracy', to harmonize the needs and politics of antagonistic classes (p163).

As the end of economic growth began to bite, disillusion took hold. The Right began a 'back to the basics' movement, associated with an almost frenzied attack on progressive and comprehensive education. The ensuing moral panic over education led to repression and popular education became a distant dream.

The most critical problem with this is the false idealisation of 'popular' education. Little attempt is made to relate any such conception to survey data, and it is impossible to prove its existence from the evidence presented - mainly political and related documents. No adequate proof is given of a popular drive towards a specifically working-class education. Indeed, historically it seems difficult to know what it means. The following is from Marx's quotation of extracts from the Report from the Select Committee on Mines, 1866. The questions at issue are child labour in the mines and miners' demands for the compulsory education of their children. (Marx cites the witnesses as workers in coal mines.)

> Q: Do you not think it would be a very hard case, where a parent had been injured, or where he was sickly, or where a father was dead, and there was only a mother, to prevent a child between 12 and 14 earning 1s.7d. a day for the good of the family?... Are you prepared to recommend legislation which would prevent the employment of children under 12 and 14, whatever the state of their parents might be?
> A: Yes....
> Q: Does there appear to be any desire on the part of the employers that the boys should have such hours as to enable them to go to school?
> A: No; the hours are never shortened for that purpose....
> Q: Would you call for the interference of Parliament?
> A: I think that if anything effectual is to be done in the education of the colliers' children, it will have to be made compulsory by Act of Parliament....
> Q: Would you lay that obligation upon the colliers only, or all the workpeople of Great Britain?
> A: I came to speak for the colliers....
> (Marx, 1976, pp627-629)

Here the state is required to establish popular education even if the real cost (loss of earnings) has to be borne by the miners' families. Resistance comes from employers unwilling to lose the exploitative rates child labour enables. The 100 years since has been spent in the expansion of educational access for all and, whatever its limitations, retrospectively recasting working-class demand for education as a demand for something other than state intervention seems peculiarly unhelpful. And the critique of the state chimed with right-wing antagonism to state intervention.

The demand for community control of education is extremely limited. Restlessness often acts within a broad parameter of inequality. For instance, growing demands in recent years by black people for separatist schools could be seen as a demand for a more equal system but are in effect a demand for improved access within an inherently unequal system. Surveys consistently reveal widespread support for private education. 64% of one sample favoured a private educational service, while as many as 73% were 'tolerant of' contracting out of state education (Taylor-Gooby, 1985, p46). This is so even amongst working-class people. 53% of working-class people in the sample analysed by Heath, Jowell and Curtice favoured private education. The writers treated the 'aristocracy of labour' - foremen and technicians - separately. 71% of this group favoured private education (1985, p18).

In a second version of these arguments the CCCS (now DCS) acknowledge the above weaknesses. Yet, even if the earlier critique of state education 'will sound dangerously similar to the New Right case' (Johnson, in DCS, 1991, p32) and 'seemed to play into enemy hands' (p33), it is unfortunate that those on the Right who helped promote a moral panic over education could cite left-wing writings as support for their cause. The paradox continues. In the new version, as the Left sees the Right establishing a strong state in support of the market, it also reverses earlier belief in popular education in favour of state control. If, as with Green (in DCS, 1991), the 'arguments for a decentralized system appear very sound and more or less unimpeachable from a socialist perspective' this can still mean many things.

> Local control can mean control in the hands of either local authorities or teachers, or, in some version, parents. Local authority control is not necessarily any more democratic than central government control.... teachers do have their own, often contradictory and sectional interests, and the notion of control by the experts is a fabian doctrine with fairly questionable democratic credentials. Direct popular control by parents at the local level has never yet existed and there is certainly no sound theory upon which to judge its viability (pp18/19).

The problem here is the unwillingness to distinguish between policy and practice. The failure to adopt a national curriculum until the late 1980s is described as the result of laissez-faire, yet this is completely inappropriate. The curriculum was provided through public provision, consisting of a high level of investment in teacher training and considerable input into dissemination through such bodies as the Schools Council. The curriculum was indirect and decentralised, not laissez-faire. The purpose was positive, not one of disregard: teachers are generally better able to assess student needs than are civil servants. Senior civil servants may have liked to use the term laissez-faire to describe their own lack of control, but one should be wary of giving this usage ideological support.

At the same time the equation is continued between ideology and educational effects, for instance where vocational initiatives are seen 'to provide an effective, streamlined and adequately motivated labour force for a dynamic capitalism' (Avis, in DCS, 1991, p133), or where 'the CPVE is constructed as a form of anticipatory socialization' (p124). We are back to the tired Olympian view of Bowles and Gintis. Even resistance is fatigued.

> Mary: I'm sick to death of education at the moment.
> Val: You feel cut off from the rest of the world, don't you.

Such quotations certainly do not prove an untapped reservoir of popular demand for a critical curriculum no longer defined by its 'separation from the social world' (p213). There is no demand for popular control of education. While conflict and resistance both occur, so does compliance, and even complaisance (eg Baxter, 1988). The distribution of such responses may be random, fleeting, and contradictory even within the same individual.

A third left-wing approach to the notion of control, the no-longer 'new sociology of education', is closely related to the ideological concerns of Bowles and Gintis, though it is again more positive, as exposure of the 'hidden curriculum' means that teachers are no longer 'inevitably subsumed as agents of ideological determination' (Chitty, 1989, p53). Perhaps a working-class education could be developed. If the linguistic codes of working-class children - particularistic and context-bound - are seen to represent difference rather than deprivation, the answer may be to make education conform with working-class needs, though others see this as suppression of working-class opportunity.

> This points to severe limits on a policy - easily derived from Bernstein's prescription - which sees as the main solution to educational poverty the use of subcultural orientations which include diffuseness of thought, context-bound expression, low educational levels, poor conceptual development, absence of generality in thinking.... An alternative policy is the development of an educated working class, whatever dangers this may bring for capitalism (Levitas, 1974, pp149-152).

The new sociology proposes as solutions to the problem of class differentials not compensatory education, which implies working-class deficiencies, but a revolution in the classroom. However, the concept of deficiency is unnecessary. Instead of talking about cultural resources, the theme of Bernstein, Bourdieu, and the new sociology, it makes more sense to talk of resource cultures. General environmental degradation; poorly resourced schools; parental experience of low pay, menial work and unemployment; knowledge of inequalities in education and employment - all these ensure some fit between cultural expectations and available resources without use of the background culture of any specific group as an intervening variable. Even government seems to understand this. While it can easily cope with the problematic of culture - 'Recent evidence suggests that youngsters take their decisions about whether or not to aim for higher education well before they reach the age of 18; and that social, cultural and peer-group influences are crucial factors in those decisions' - it also recognises the significance of resources and physical environment. The participation of young people 'will by the 1990s be as much affected by the gathering impact of policies in the fields of housing, health and the social services generally as by educational policies' (DES, *Higher Education into the 1990s*, 1985).

Perhaps partly because of this, the new sociology of education, believing that change in the classroom could change society, but ignoring the reality of structural factors and resources in influencing the relationship between education and class, now seems naive. In the end it is necessary to recognise 'the exploratory, tentative and, on occasions, contradictory nature of our writings' (Whitty, 1985, p81). More recent adaptations also seem doubtful. Spours and Young, for instance, propose a new approach under the rubric of Vocational Aspects of Academic Learning (VAAL), which might for instance encourage teachers to 'examine the ways [in] which particular industrial processes were socially shaped'. Yet the conversion of vocationalism to 'to interrogate the world of work' (1988, p11), however worthwhile, is clearly not going to help anyone get a job; whatever its virtues and (rather vague) promises, it is unlikely to be an especially marketable approach now or in the future.

The new sociology relied overmuch on change through support of single institutions. Paradoxically, in taking seriously the notion that individual schools can provide the basis for change, it makes the right-wing paradigm, support of the 'good school', perfectly natural.

> By accepting the meta-framework of realism, they accepted also the hegemonic class's misleading definition of the socially formative power of schooling. New sociology rejected the false promise of the claim, but not the assumption of the school's efficacy (Wexler, 1990, p171).

The myth of the 'good school'

> So pass I hostel, hall, and grange;
> By bridge and ford, by park and pale,
> All-arm'd I ride, whate'er betide,
> Until I find the holy Grail.
> (from Tennyson's *Sir Galahad*)

Even if he established a new cause, Kenneth Baker makes an unlikely Sir Galahad, and the modern holy Grail, a rather mystical conception of the 'good school', is located in middle-class suburbia. It also requires little adventuring to find.

> There is no secret about what makes for a good and popular school: a strong head teacher with a clear sense of purpose, supported by parents and governors alike in the direction he wants to take the school; teachers who are keen to teach and who provide the very best encouragement for children to learn; good discipline and a character with which children can identify and which means that learning can take place in an ordered background; and schools which reinforce the values which parents wish their children to have. Grant-maintained schools will be free to develop these qualities (Lawlor, 1988, p28).

This guidance from the Centre for Policy Studies should be helpful in informing choice, even if replacing grant-maintained with non-GM schools in the last sentence would not alter the statement's sense. Any parents still in doubt can seek advice from the GM helpline advertised in the national media: 'To be able to decide whether GM status is right for your child's school, you need the facts.' It would be a remarkable achievement indeed if a helpline could help you decide whether your own school would be better under local or central government control. Mystification as well as measurement is part of the new paradigm. In fact, the performance indicators which provide the basis for bringing the school to book are often symbolic only, this being most obvious with the 'Citizens Charter' and the rather silly 'Charter Mark', supposedly an award for good public-service performance. A mere 100 'Charter Marks' are available for public-service organisations, including schools, and a mere 80 schools applied in the first year of its life, yet the whole of the education system is treated like a primary school at a prize-giving, the headteacher-cum-prime minister awarding platitudes and fatuous gold stars. In the meantime, teachers and headteachers grapple with their everyday difficulties.

Performance indicators are really political indicators. When the *Daily Express* (21.1.87) reported on an academic study comparing various ways of ranking LEA performance (with exam results as the indicator), it argued that 'those which go in for anti-sexist and anti-racist initiatives in a big way score badly', particularly commenting on Brent and Haringey, which came in positions 88 and 91 respectively out of 96. ILEA was criticised despite a comfortable rank of 56. Oddly, the paper failed to point out that Conservative Bromley came bottom, with Norfolk at 93 and Essex at 92. And while Harrow came top, Liverpool came fourth, Coventry fifth, and Manchester tenth. Radically left-wing Ealing came in 18 positions above radically right-wing Kent. While teachers in disadvantaged areas struggle to do their best for their students, the *Daily Mail* (19.9.87) devotes half a page to an all-girl grammar school which produced 28 grade-A passes in a GCSE French exam, which, oddly, 'is another endorsement for the traditional policies of the 800-pupil school' rather than a reflection of a highly selective intake.

Academic and official support for the notion of the 'good school', even if far more subtly defined than above, is also a problem, in particular as it diverts attention from the impact of school *type* (the creation of socially homogeneous schools through some sort of selection or self-selection process), the chief concern of the 'political-arithmetic' approach, towards schools wholly removed from their organisational context, ie their place within local and national structures of opportunity. ERA defines a good school by absolute test and exam results. An earlier official definition by HMI (in its report *Ten Good Schools*, DES, 1975) had been subjective and took no account of intake, but in its attempt to define elements of good organisation taking into account relations with the local community, was more sophisticated than the current concentration on comparison of test or exam results. One of the first academic studies to look at the impact of the school through the use of statistical analysis (Reynolds, in Hammersley and Woods, 1976) produced correlations between certain variables which suggested a school effect. All the schools were from a single, apparently socially homogeneous area and were similar in ability intake. Ranking schools on the basis of where they sent their students upon leaving, higher ranking schools tended to have better attendance and low teacher turnover, to require school uniforms and to have prefects. They also placed little reliance on corporal punishment. The suggestion, therefore, was that good schools are those that have an ethos of discipline, responsibility, and commitment. But, apart from the lack of multivariate analysis, the study failed to separate endogenous from exogenous variables. For instance, delinquency is treated as a school effect (largely resulting from inadequate truancy policies), but it is exceedingly unlikely that schools *cause* or are responsible for a failure to control delinquency. At the same time, intakes are differentiated by crude class indicators. Yet intakes from generally poor areas will still differ by the social characteristics of their particular catchment areas, some of which will be more delinquent. This also explains why the poor performing schools also have strong control mechanisms. The study therefore simply inverted causality. As with other studies discussed below, the residual effects of schools cannot be used to explain differences in performance when the adequacy of data on social background can never be reliably ascertained.

Nevertheless, analysis of this area is getting more worthwhile and more sophisticated, for instance in the analysis of the British sample within the Second International Mathematics Study (Cresswell and Gubb, 1987). Overall it would seem that student and home variables, school type and the degree to which the curriculum is covered ('opportunity to learn') are the most critical variables. Nevertheless, about half of all variance in one sample cannot be explained by the variables used, and it is of note that the study showed that school type (eg grammar against comprehensive) has a substantial impact once other factors are controlled, explaining more variation in performance than individual school factors.

Two of the most well-known studies which look at this issue are Rutter (1979) and Smith and Tomlinson (1989). If earlier findings (eg Jencks, 1972) appeared to show that education has had only limited impact on inequality, Smith and Tomlinson comment that Jencks' conclusion 'was a direct response to the compensatory education programmes that were favoured in the 1960s' (p19), rather than an assessment of the efficacy of schools in adding to knowledge and understanding (though their own study set out largely as a study of the efficacy of education in respect of colour and ethnicity). However, assessment of inequality *is* an assessment of institutional differences. While occasional schools might appear to be different, *on average* this is limited. 'Stating it slightly differently, we can say that if all high schools were equally effective (or ineffective) inequality between twelfth graders would fall less than one percent' (Jencks, 1972, p90), and change in average performance would not be very different. The data are also incapable of revealing how far choice may be zero-sum *between institutions*. The study of single institutions takes the evaluation of outcomes out of context - the context of what is happening in and between all schools in an area. To be effective, the focus of such studies should surely be the area (all schools within this), not the school as such. And analysis should surely be of more schools. Rutter *et al* looked at a mere 12 schools, Smith and Tomlinson at 18. The strategy is to compare exam or test results late on in secondary schooling with test results at the start, supplementing the data in different ways - eg by surveys of the students, parents and teachers, as well as by reference to administrative records. However, there must be some statistical doubts about the representativeness of these school samples, even when the number of children is large. Double the number of schools might be inadequate, and there may be particular problems when one school appears to explain a large part of the institutional-level variation (Goldstein, 1987, p26), as occurs in the Smith and Tomlinson study where one school is truly heroic.

The new paradigm meshes very well with an important social and political agenda. During the expansionist period it was perhaps correct to assess the impact of growth. With expansion at an end it seems reasonable to look at the quality of current provision. What is it, if anything, that makes one school better than another, and what impact does this have on achievement? *The School Effect* (Smith and Tomlinson, 1989), in fact fails to answer the former question but has important things to say in response to the latter. While differences between schools are 'small compared with the enormous differences between individuals' (p301), it 'turns out that family background factors explain a relatively small proportion of the variance in *progress* between individual children' (p22). While there is a 'very strong tendency for the level of attainment to be stable over time for the same child' (p23), where there is progress it seems this can be put down to the school rather than to social background. Rather surprisingly perhaps, this even appears to work in the first two years. For instance, taking a male originating from the British Isles, from a skilled working-class family, and achieving an average first-year score in maths, he could get a maths score in the second year ranging from 27.2 in the lowest school to 35.6 in the highest (p172), the mean for all children being 31.4. Schools seem to make a difference.

By the time fifth-year exam performance is taken into account this is more substantial. Allocating points for grade achieved, and taking the same person referred to above (achieving an average reading score in his second year), his total exam points could vary from 0.8 to 13.2, depending on the school attended. Even excluding the exceptionally high-scoring school, the remaining range represents 'a difference between schools of about four grade C passes at O level, or eight lower grade results' (p268). The same child might get three effective passes in one school but seven in another. 'Making schools more effective must, therefore, be a high priority for any present-day government' (p300). Some credence is given to government intentions to compare schools on the basis of crude exam and test results. While they argue that absolute exam results could be highly misleading, they are so convinced that 'school differences are large enough to transcend, to a considerable extent, the large differences between schools in the background and initial attainment of the children going to them' (p277), that such publication would in general be meaningful.

But how meaningful would they be? Smith and Tomlinson do acknowledge that even if parents received and understood highly sophisticated information on progress, the pressure would be on schools with poor *intakes*, and these 'would not generally be the least successful schools' (p304). Even if the school effect were as powerful as suggested, there is probably nothing that local choice could do to take advantage of this, or to encourage equalising tendencies between these. The study compared 18 schools, but who has such choice? If this depended on two or three randomly grouped schools in most of the sample, there really would be very limited rational basis on which to make a choice. Grouping schools into rough local authority areas, and looking at exam results for the average attainer, in one area of three schools the exam range is only 1.2 points. It is also far from apparent, as was suggested in the last chapter, that parents make the use of attainment results that the government thinks they should. 'Overall satisfaction with the school and the assessment of standards of behaviour are very little related to the child's attainment' (p67). In the Rutter study 'the parental subscription rate was not significantly associated with any of the four outcome measures, nor.... with the overall school process measure' (p161). On the other hand, once background variables such as social class are controlled for, the picture may change. Then 'the parental assessment of the child's attainment is fairly strongly related to the child's actual attainment' (Smith and Tomlinson, p179). Choice is as much a class as an educational discriminator.

The data also have problems of interpretation. As one example, there is only limited evidence from the data of stability in performance between schools over time. The following reproduces the most extreme discrepancies in Smith and Tomlinson's rankings (pp172 and 284) of predicted second-year improvement (in maths tests) against predicted fifth-year improvement (in exam results over second year reading scores). Each column represents a school's ranking.

year two	3	8	9	12	14	16	17
year five	11	15	17	4	3	2	9

In over a third of the schools, progress in maths between years one and two would be a very poor indicator of likely general improvement by year five. It is obviously possible for some secondary schools to serve their intake more than their leaving cohort, or vice versa, but it is extremely unclear how to judge this differential performance.

A second problem with the actual data is that school effects may be area effects (ie over and above aggregation of individuals' class background). One potentially important variable is the rate of social change, especially inward and outward migration. Falling rolls, as discussed in the previous chapter, have an important negative effect on intake, resources, teaching provision, and confidence. The reverse applies to schools in growing areas. In fact, Smith and Tomlinson produce turnover figures which may support this notion and themselves point out that 'there may be some association between good examination results (after controlling for background factors and earlier attainment) and low pupil turnover' (p280). Over the period of the study the six best schools on average retained 74% of their students. The six worst schools retained 64% (p299.). The latter could, of course, reflect flight from inadequate schools, though legislation giving full effect to this was not yet in place. The Rutter study, by contrast, found no area effect. However, balance of intake, clearly area-related, did. The higher the percentage of more able children (relative to school intake) the smaller the probability of delinquency, the better the attendance, and, to a lesser degree, the higher the average academic attainment (p158). An average child is likely to do better in schools with above average students and worse in schools with below average students. Gray, Jesson and Sime's (1990) analysis of 290 schools (using different data-sets), a far larger school sample than in the above studies, also found a school effect, but this was less than that of Smith and Tomlinson. However, they also argue that some of this is explained by unknowns such as the historical status of schools attracting types of people whose characteristics are inadequately picked up by the crude class indicators used in most value-added studies. The authors develop an aggregate (as opposed to individual) social background measure which reduces apparent inter-school differences by over 25%. After social background (10-20%) and prior attainment (60%), schools may explain only 1-5% of the residual variance between individuals, and this is less than 2% of the *total* variance. This seems to produce results not dissimilar to those of Jencks (1972), mentioned above.

This effect also tends to be underplayed compared to the effect *on* (rather than *of*) ability differences. There are major variations between schools in terms of how they appear to serve their ability intakes: 'both high- and low-attaining pupils benefit from going to the better schools: but the high-attaining pupils benefit more' (Smith and Tomlinson, p269). While the exam scores in Smith and Tomlinson ranged by over 12 points for the average-ability, British (skilled manual) child, taking a socially similar child of well above average ability produces a range of nearly 18. However, for the well below average equivalent the range is less than five (and in fact less than two once a single outlier is removed). While Smith and Tomlinson show that many schools do consistently well or badly for most abilities, 'even a very good school cannot do much, within the framework of the current exam system, to help a child with a low reading score to get any kinds of results' (p269). This is important in light of the claim by the government, and much right-wing propaganda, that comprehensive and progressive education have severely limited the progress of the less able. To enable less able children to achieve in exams would require the incorporation of exam material and styles to suit their abilities, but this of course would be seen as a lowering of standards. Whatever the school effect, class remains a powerful factor. Controlling for second-year attainment, 'middle class pupils do considerably better in the exams than working class pupils' (Smith and Tomlinson, p266). This may have been worth two grade-C O-levels.

A third major problem with the empirical nature of the school effect paradigm, at least in the case of Smith and Tomlinson, is the admission that 'we have not been able to achieve our original objective of explaining why some schools are more successful than others' (p280). The Rutter study looked at several items such as the use of praise, use of homework and so on. Combined into a scale these produced a substantial correlation with the outcome measures, but in Smith and Tomlinson's view the inclusion of multiple explanatory factors simply creates a 'cognitive snowstorm' (p25). Nevertheless, the resultant simplification into two sources of effect - on the one hand a bundle of individual characteristics such as class and gender, on the other the impact of the school as a whole - means that it is impossible to say *why* the school has an effect. It is merely a statistical residual, describing some of the apparent variation in outcomes that standard regression analysis would assume is random. The findings show that some of this apparently random individual variation is in fact systematic between-school variation. However, this can be caused by any number of school characteristics such as the head teacher, individual teachers, a specific exam policy, the degree of child-centredness, or any combination of these and other factors. Both studies choose 'school ethos' as the explanatory variable, but this catch-all is of little help. It is as likely to be a result as a cause of the other factors just mentioned, and begs more questions than it answers. Much of this ethos depends on intake in the first place: surveys of values in schools have long shown, amongst other things, that working-class children may have difficulty in adjusting to schools with a specifically middle-class ethos (eg Jackson and Marsden, 1966), or that for children in grammar schools 'the holding of school-approved values was associated with the sons of parents who had been to grammar schools' (King, 1969, pp155/6); or, in Bourdieu and Passeron's terms, there are significant differences between social groups in the way that '*cultural capital* and *class ethos*' can be 'converted and cashed' (1977/90, p87).

Finally, the concentration on *schools* reifies a complex of processes. A school is a head, one or more deputies, a set of teachers, facilities, a history, a support system, an intake, a group of parents, a relationship with other schools, and so on. Smith and Tomlinson do at least point out that 'the actions that have to be taken to transform an ineffective school into an effective one, or to maintain the performance of an already effective one.... may not be the same' (p26), but there is a whole complex of issues concerning the dynamics of change (eg changes in intake, staffing, policies etc) which is, oddly, not well reflected in these longitudinal studies. Measuring increases in performance over time actually fails to tell us what happens between times. Any one or combination of the above factors may help or impede general progress, and it is these, the subject of many small-scale studies (eg Ball, 1987), which count. One obvious contender here are the different subjects or departments within schools. While there may be good and bad schools, parts of schools may also be good or bad. Smith and Tomlinson did not look systematically at variation within schools, though they did compare performance in subjects, noting 'that academic success in secondary schools needs to be studied by subject, or by subject groups, rather than overall' (p276). Comparing predicted exam scores in maths and English (p295) shows some close relationships but about a third of schools showed wild divergences, these being the following pairs of rankings:

| **English** | 18 | 10 | 2 | 15 | 3 | 7 |
| **Maths** | 8 | 2 | 9 | 1 | 18 | 14 |

In addition, the studies seem unclear to what extent effective teaching counts as a factor endogenous to schools. Even the ability 'to become outstanding teachers' is not, in Rutter's terms, 'an unalterable characteristic', as 'it was very much easier to be a good teacher in some schools than it was in others. The overall ethos of the school seemed to provide support and a context which facilitated good teaching' (p139). However, this makes a false distinction between teaching qualities innate to the individual and those inculcated by the school. Teaching skills depend on a multiplicity of factors such as career progression (eg incentives to perform), the extent of 'burn-out', the impact of problems represented by specific children, whether similarly motivated teachers arrive or leave the school, and so on. Their ability is certainly not an 'unalterable characteristic', but nor is it something necessarily dependent on a nebulous 'school ethos'. No worthwhile ethos can survive in the first place without good and committed teachers. To put this another way, there is simply no such thing as a 'good school', and seeking to mystify education through statistics which can only posit ethos as the source of good schooling, is no help.

Revaluation of education

One of the most significant distortions of the good school myth is that the past does not exist, while the present stretches into the future unconstrained. Performance at one precise time is assumed to dictate a school's entire future potential. Paradoxically, this concentration on process continues the new sociology of education's tendency 'to espouse "practice", but outside of any historical specificity' (Wexler, 1987, p86). One of the most important historical specificities is *how* ability is measured, and indeed how the process of measurement is itself negotiated. Finally, therefore, to return to the question of standards, pursuit of effective education, despite the rhetoric, often seems a concern for *high* rather than good standards, ie with raising the bar of the high jump rather than getting more people over it. This is apparent in the rejection of the expansion of A-levels and in attacks on 'over-generous' GCSEs. There are powerful political limits to any attempts at an upward recalibration of qualifications, but there seems little doubt that many on the Right have sought this; the entire panoply of tests is itself a recalibration of the student's educational experience: measurement, not improvement, is now the purpose of education.

This process is obviously linked to increased pressure towards institutional segregation. The long-term educational outcome might be an upper class using exclusively private education and universities; a lower middle class and upper working class attending the better state schools outside local government control, then going to university or college, and a bottom third of poor working-class people attending 'sink' schools and then going on to either low paid jobs or compulsory Youth Training placements. A further result would be the *creation* of an underclass - not in the sense of some inherent inability to break out of long-term poverty, but of a form of closure enforced from outside. An underclass may be created by government action, for instance if in education it succeeds in forcing the poor into a ghetto. Such separation would also serve to protect the educational achievement of the rest of the population from competition.

The underlying reason for this pressure for change is probably cycles in economic well-being. If in booms qualifications become less relevant both for employers and employees, as the former have to lower the cost of entry to employment and the latter have no need to invest more to get in, in a period of high unemployment the credentials that education provides become supremely important. The role of the government here is vital as it controls the flow of education. Under pressure to expand education (because all people want improved chances), but recognising that overall expansion will increase the chances for all and not solely for its own potential constituency of support, it makes the system more competitive instead. Those with immediate advantages of income, background, or residence will gain.

Thus education is being recalibrated. It is, of course, a common argument that education is highly inflationary, whether as a result of a bidding-up between competing groups for credentials (Collins, 1979), or between institutions competing to provide education (Archer, 1982). Similar to Collins' argument is that of Dore: 'The paradox of the situation is that the worse the educated unemployment situation gets and the more useless educational certificates become, the *stronger* grows the pressure for an expansion of educational facilities' (in Cosin and Hales, 1983, p51). These are of course antithetical arguments. In Collins' and Dore's view it is the 'pull' of the public which creates educational inflation. In Archer's case the pull is institutional, with education sometimes imposed on the public - 'both the victims of the expanding context and the source of their own victimization through their collective responses towards the system' (Archer, 1982, p48). Either way, those at the bottom of the pile are chasing a moving target. Of course, the inflation argument is somewhat simplistic, but it does indicate that growth or change in educational output can have an alternative interpretation, and it is apparent that in a period of economic flux the political grasp over such interpretations is increasing.

These changes have to be seen in the context of electoral change in the post-war period. The most obvious is the decline in the size of the working class, and the concomitant fall in Labour's share of the vote, and more generally of a class de-alignment in voting behaviour. A comparison of two electoral samples 20 years apart shows the following changes.

Table 9.1:   Class composition of the electorate, 1964 and 1983

	1964	1983
Salariat	18	27
Routine nonmanual	18	24
Petty bourgeoisie	7	8
Foremen and technicians	10	7
Working class	47	34
	100%	100%
	N = 1475	3790

Source: Heath, Jowell and Curtice (1985), p36

Himmelweit (1985) points to the strength of instrumental attitudes as the basis of political voting, arguing a loss of class loyalty. Heath, Jowell and Curtice argue that both the 'expressive' and the 'instrumental' theories tell part of the truth. The latter underplays the proven existence of substantial class and party loyalties. The former underplays how parties are affected by changes in the class structure and then adapt policies to meet their perceptions of these. If 'social class, housing, education and other aspects of social structure constitute the sources of group interest', these interests 'provide a potential for political action' (Heath, Jowell, and Curtice, 1985, p10). The authors' survey of attitudes not surprisingly finds that the salariat and the petty bourgeoisie strongly agree with right-wing alternatives concerning nationalisation, income distribution, job creation schemes, trade union legislation and private education. However, private education is the issue most strongly supported b / routine non-manual workers, while 53% of working-class people are marginally in favour. Such structural change has a major impact on relative advantages conferred by education. The findings of Blackburn and Marsh (1991), discussed above, that changes in the class structure, demography, and supply of education all have profound implications for the understanding of inequality, are important also in understanding demand for education. For instance, when growth in the number of selective places 'was outstripped by the "baby boom" population.... the effective value of social advantage became greater' (p529).

While there is a tendency to think of the value of education as a constant, the environment which gives education its worth is constantly changing. One major change is the probability of unemployment: 'one could say that the return of mass unemployment, in the British context at least, has had the general effect of "raising the stakes" in the mobility "game"' (Goldthorpe and Payne, 1986, p18). The DE/PSI study of young adults and long-term unemployment (White and McRae, 1989) compared two cohorts of young people, one entering the job market before the recession of the early 1980s, the other during the recession. 30% of the 1975-78 entrants (the first cohort) had a job lasting at least three years, while a negligible number of the 1980-83 entrants had. The average percentage of time spent in employment for the group entering the market before the recession was 67%, compared to 15% of the later group. Starker contrasts are hard to imagine. Are we to assume that the later group had suddenly become demotivated? Or that they had suddenly reached a much lower level of skills? In fact the group entering the market in the later, recessionary period was the better qualified. For instance, 24% had A-E O-level grades compared to 18% of the earlier sample, and 8% had A-levels compared to the previous 3% (p67). For the second cohort the ratio of school success to employment success was on the average extremely unfavourable, and it is during this period of decline in the purchasing power of qualifications that much educational change has been determined. It is well known that qualifications as a rule buy more income, but this is a trend association which ignores a deeper dynamic caused by economic fluctuations. Business cycles deeply affect judgements of the value of education.

Qualifications change their value for different groups. The actual impact of educational deflation or inflation is indicated in a German study of attitudes to examinations. Analysing responses in a 1982 survey to a question which asked whether 'everyone has the possibility to be educated according to their aspirations and abilities?', showed that the proportion of respondents believing this to be the case had declined from 73% in 1963 to 50% in 1979. Meulemann argues that it was Germany's success which was the source of this increase in cynicism. The decline of faith in education occurred despite the fact that it was precisely this period that saw Germany's major educational expansion. More qualifications merely flood the market. 'The increase in competition makes certificates simultaneously more important and more worthless.' Viewing these results in a different way Herbert and Sommer (in Sommer and Waldburg-Zeil, 1984) split the sample into two age cohorts, one educated before the big expansion in education, the other having passed through it. They then split each group into two: those with *Hauptschule* certificates (perhaps comparable to the old CSE) and those with higher level qualifications. The group with the lowest proportion of positive responses relative to 1963 was the young and more educated group, suggesting that belief in the deflated value of credentials applies most to those who had the highest expectations of gain from them. Increased access is a threat and leads to devaluation of the worth of qualifications to both employers and job-seekers. The notion of effective education is highly dependent on its social and economic context.

Conclusion

The search for effective education continues, but with highly divergent views not only of the meaning of effectiveness but the best means to achieve this. The current paradigm of the 'good school' has extremely limited credentials and is undoubtedly designed to resegregate education in order to protect the competitive advantage of different social groups threatened by a mix of growth and intermittent recession. While selection may not always be overt, as rolls rise it will increasingly be the case, as in Japan, that the school will choose the child, and not the reverse. In Japan, the child goes through a 'sausage-slicing' process where schools select on the basis of the part of the normal curve achieved. British tests provide the basis for this. Whether or not school organisation or ethos can create significant value added, the most important input *from the school's point of view* is not teachers, nor ethos, nor the head, nor local financial control, but its children. It may be the case that with a given intake better teachers can get better results but, with a given set of teachers, improving the intake will increase output far more. The pressure on schools to compete for more able students will be massive, and this will become circular. The higher the proportion of able students it has, the more it will attract.

The notion of the 'good school', or even the more general concept of effective education, is unhelpful: not because good schools do not exist, but becasue there is no ideal-typical good school; each is highly context-bound. Thus even general accounts of what good schooling means, such as Brighouse and Tomlinson (1991), cannot lead very far. If there is any task to perform in pursuit of effective organisation, it is simply to ensure that specific weaknesses are dealt with. This is most certainly not a reason to search out the 'bad school', which is merely the ghost image of the mythological 'good school'. Indeed, as Ball points out, the 'bad school' is a central part of the new discourse of power. 'Effectiveness researchers both construct a concept of the ineffective or sick school and draw upon the use of confessional techniques (an admission of transgressions and a ritual of atonement) as a mechanism for the return to health or to a state of grace' (1990, p90).

Schools may certainly have problems. This may be an inadequate teacher who, for instance, ends up teaching the wrong age group or cannot cope with difficult students. One central solution is to return power to LEAs, as redeployment is the best answer. The straitjacket that reduction in LEA power has produced merely freezes incompetence. Other problems may be a loss of confidence as rolls fall, or particular resource inadequacies, a lazy headteacher, or financial problems resulting for instance from a poorly run decentralised contract. The solutions to such problems require intelligence and goodwill, and it is precisely these qualities that are made difficult by current legislation, which prefers central bureaucracy to goodwill and standard rules to intelligence.

Conclusion

Recent change in education is built on various myths: standards are falling, the UK suffers from endemic skill shortages, teaching lacks discipline, LEAs exercise too much control over school action but too little over quality, schools can be defined as uniquely good or bad. These myths have received support from a variety of political and social quarters, not only from the Right. The proposed solutions have generated new myths which also receive widespread support. Few deny the importance of raising standards, increasing skills, extending choice, or supporting the good school. Yet these goals are such vacuous generalities as to be unarguable. The real issue is not standards, nor choice, and so on, but the use these concepts are put to. Their use thus far is either to extend control (eg through the national curriculum) or to fragment alternative agendas (eg the use of choice to break LEA planning targets). It is important, therefore, not to reconvert these vacuous symbols to better use but to undermine them. Most of the current reform structure should be scrapped, as its rationale is at best extremely tenuous: little is an inevitable response to an underlying problem. For instance, the 'rationalisation' of the curriculum could have followed a number of different paths, from complete control of what teachers do, through providing the basis of comparative tests, to ensuring minimum attention to critical areas of teaching. In trying to do all three, chaos ensues. Moreover, the rationalisation of the curriculum does nothing to rationalise education but may merely standardise absurdity. Under Baker and MacGregor elements of this had already twisted and turned in several directions. Even this was not the end for the poor institutions, such as the National Curriculum Council, set up to make it seem as if order was being imposed. 'Delivery or ridicule faced NCC and SEAC at every turn' (Graham and Tytler, 1993, p113). Kenneth Clarke then sought to be the new Canute in commanding that history exclude modern events (perhaps, for instance, to prevent it analysing the chaos of the national curriculum). After wanting it to stop at 1945 he settled for history ending 20 years before the present (though updated only every five years). Thus for some time students will presumably learn about the Cold War but not be told it has ended. Graham and Tylter complain about this 'major... political intrusion' (p70), but it is difficult to see why, as this is central to current irrationalisation. A national curriculum is a political curriculum, and has to be, particularly in a highly centralised country where executive power goes largely unchecked. In the case of the music curriculum, Graham and Tytler approvingly note that the 'jazz-loving Secretary of State was delighted at the inclusion of Waller and Ellington' (p81). We must be pleased that thousands of students may learn to share his tastes, though this is ironic in view of years of right-wing onslaught against 'popular' music. But Ellington does, of course, keep out music that young people may actually like and understand.

The national curriculum has been an appalling waste of public money, but it would cost very little to scrap, even if the continued circulation of some of its content as advisory and practical material, the maintenance of a requirement to retain technology teaching, and action to make good teacher shortages in critical areas, are undoubtedly worthwhile goals in themselves. However, one of the central purposes of the national curriculum is to aid institutional segregation. A comprehensive structure of education based on a differentiated curriculum is now being replaced by a comprehensive curriculum with a differentiated structure. Equality in one area provides the basis for inequality in another. Many on the Left, of course, seek comprehensiveness in both structure and content, as this eliminates all possibility of tracking. However, students do vary in ability, aptitude and aspirations; an enforced single curriculum is simply a control mechanism, like the medicines Victorians rammed down children's throats for their moral rather than their physical well-being.

Institutional comprehensiveness must remain the chief goal of change in education, as the evidence of the impact of segregated structures on both performance and justice is extremely clear. In addition, large, comprehensive institutions extend choice to students while small, supposedly 'good' institutions close this off. We must allow students to determine their own futures, and with this the future of education. Attempts to constrain such choices, at least at the later ages, are probably good for no-one. After 16, effective choice may only be achievable in large institutions such as tertiary colleges. These receive widespread support, though sometimes with an implicit element of compulsion. It is not persuasion that is needed, however, so much as opportunity. Young people must make their own decisions between education, work, or any combination of these.

There is also no reason why the fundamental principle of large within-institution choice should not be extended downward into most secondary schooling. This is not just a matter of ensuring that all students engage with vocational or 'practical' education, but of offering significantly different curricular programmes within institutions (produced on a modular basis rather than associated with tracking). This would again require the scrapping of the national curriculum. It would also require the removal of legislation which undermines the stability of institutions, as it takes time to build up effective provision. At the secondary level this can be enhanced through an enforced process of school closures (that is, on the basis of a rational distribution of schools rather than on the whimsy of school choice). This would enlarge schools and therefore grant more choice to students. Combined with protection of the rights of parents to have their children attend the nearest school, or for new entrants to follow siblings, parental choice would no longer become a determinant of educational provision.

Quality must thereafter derive from LEA support and through close and regular assessment from a reconstituted HMI. The machinery for this has always existed but central government has shown no interest in making it work. Having failed to do this, it abolishes both of these control mechanisms as a means of shifting the blame from its own failure. One final reform would be a major decentralisation of power from the centre to the periphery. Once a new tertiary structure is in place, and excess capacity eliminated, the sole function of the centre would be to provide funding, to monitor provision, and to encourage research into opportunities and outcomes. The latter by itself would at least do much to inhibit the dishonest propaganda that the government has made use of to establish its new agenda.

The saddest thing about current change is that the government has no explicit vision of an educational future, other than that expressed through the bureaucratically imposed targets of the national curriculum. How many schools will opt out? No-one knows. What will be the effect of choice and decentralisation on standards and fairness? No-one knows. Vision has been replaced by control. The existence of every marginal school, the content of what every child learns, and the pay and conditions of every teacher, now depend on detailed central decisions. None of this provides the stability which education increasingly needs. When the Conservative government brought in economic reforms to end once and for all Keynesian stop-go policies, the level of political intervention required to maintain equivalent reforms in education has introduced stop-go and little else. The last few years have seen a phenomenal welter of changes in how schools operate, as the centre thinks up some new gap that needs to be filled or new use that education can be put to.

Faced with the absurdity of this situation, the edifice has already begun to crumble. In August 1993 the government announced the abolition of publication of league tables for seven and fourteen year-olds, proposed to simplify both the national curriculum and tests, and to allow research into the use of value-added in measures of school performance. The revolution is beginning to look shabby. One long-term lesson that must be learned is that prejudice and moral panic are not sound bases for reform in education. Sneering at teachers or other professional people in education is not an especially intelligent way of securing their co-operation in reform.

There are still tasks to be achieved, but these are much more self-contained and pragmatic than the grandiose but ramshackle structure introduced through and since ERA. Building up post-16 education through tertiary colleges, the integration of vocational education more closely into the mainstream, ensuring adequate resources for critical elements of the curriculum, improving the means of redeploying or removing highly inadequate teachers, extending nursery provision - all these receive fairly widespread if not universal support. The critical issue, though, is how these changes vacillate between comprehensive and segregationist structures. Thus, post-16 education may be extended through broad and open provision or through intensified separation between the academic and the vocational. In comprehensive structures teachers may be subject to support in the case of failure, with some chance to improve. In a segregationist system they will be forced into 'sink' schools where they can do most harm.

The battle for and against segregation continues. It has been argued above that much demand for change in education is still fundamentally about this issue rather than about standards or skill shortages, both of which are used to justify reform for *and* against segregation. Nor do these supposed problems dictate either a centralising or decentralising strategy. Such decisions will always remain a purely political choice. The arguments are part of a repeated cycle which is intensified by economic cycles that in turn make education more (or less) critical to certain social groups. There is no underlying trend in British education which suggests it fails to perform adequately. Even the constraints imposed by a relatively laissez-faire political system are probably exaggerated, but if the Right has made dreadful mistakes, the Left too should be wary of grandiose change.

Bibliography

Adam Smith Institute (1989), *Wiser Counsels*, London

Adler, M., Petch, A., and Tweedie, J. (1989), *Parental choice and educational policy*, Edinburgh University

Ahier, J. and Flude, M. (1983), *Contemporary education policy*, Croom Helm, London

Alexander, R., Willcocks, J. and Kinder, K. (1989), *Changing primary practice*, Falmer

Allmendinger, J. (1989), 'Educational systems and labour market outcomes', *European Sociological Review*, 5, 3, 231-250

ALTARF (1984), *Challenging Racism*, All London Teachers Against Racism and Fascism, London

AMA (1988), *The organisation and management of equalities policies* (mimeo)

Amano, I. (1990), *Education and examination in modern Japan*, University of Tokyo Press

Anderson, A. (1987), 'Adult training', *Education and Training UK*, Policy Journals

Appignanesi, L. (ed) (1989), *Postmodernism*, Free Association Books, London

Archer, M. (ed) (1982), *The sociology of educational expansion*, Sage, London

Audit Commission (1984), *The impact on local authorities' economy, efficiency and effectiveness of the block grant distribution system*, HMSO

Audit Commission (1987), 'The management of London's authorities', *Occasional Paper 2*, HMSO

Audit Commssion (1988), 'Surplus capacity in secondary schools', *Occasional Paper 6*, HMSO

Audit Commission (1993), *Adding up the sums: schools' management of their finances*, HMSO

Bacon, R. and Eltis, W. (1978), *Britain's economic problem: too few producers*, Macmillan, London

Ball, Stephen (1987), *The micro-politics of the school*, Methuen, London

Ball, Stephen (1990), *Politics and policy making in education*, Routledge, London

Ball, Stephen (1990a), *Foucault and education*, Routledge, London

Ball, W. and Solomos, J. (1990), *Race and local politics*, Macmillan, London

Banham, J. (1989), 'Building a stronger partnership between business and secondary education', *British Journal of Educational Studies*, 37, 1, 5-16

Barber, M. and Brighouse, T. (1992), *Partners in change: enhancing the teaching profession*, IPPR, London

Barker Lunn, J.C. (1970), *Streaming in the Primary School*, NFER, Slough

Barnard, G. and McCreath, M. (1970), 'Subject commitments and the demand for higher education', *Journal of the Royal Statistical Society*, 133, 3, 358-408

Barnes, D. *et al* (1987), *The TVEI curriculum: 14-16*, Training Agency

Barnett, C. (1986), *The audit of war*, Macmillan, London

Barr, N. (1993), 'Alternative funding sources for higher education', *The Economic Journal*, 103, 418, 718-728

Barrs, M. (1990), *Words not numbers: assessment in English*, NATE

Barthes, R. (1967), *Elements of semiology*, Hill and Wang, New York

Bassett, K. (1980), 'The sale of council houses as a political issue', *Policy and Politics*, 8, 3, 290-307

Baudrillard, J. (1990), *The revenge of the crystal*, Pluto, London

Baxter, A. (1988), 'Their fault or ours? The contraction of work and the "radicalisation" of young people, *British Journal of Education and Work*, 2, 1, 25-38

Bell, D. (1976), *The cultural contradictions of capitalism*, Heinemann, London

Ben-Tovim, G., Gabriel, J., Law, I. and Stredder, K. (1986), *The local politics of race*, Macmillan, London

Benn, C. and Fairley, J. (1986), *Challenging the MSC*, Pluto, London

Bernstein, Basil (1971), *Class, codes and control*, Routledge and Kegan Paul, London

Bernstein, Basil (1972), 'Education cannot compensate for society', in Rubinstein, D. and Stoneman, C. (eds), *Education for democracy*, Penguin, Harmondsworth

Bevan, S. and Varlaam, C. (1987), 'Political pressures and strategic aspirations in the youth training scheme, *Education and Training UK*, Policy Journals

Bird, E., Schwarze, J. and Wagner, G. (1992), 'The changing value of human capital in Eastern Europe', *Discussion Paper 55*, German Institute for Economic Research, Berlin

Blackburn, R. and Marsh, C. (1991), 'Education and social class: revisiting the 1944 Education Act with fixed marginals', *British Journal of Sociology*, 42, 4, 507-536

Blondel, D. (1991), 'A new type of teacher training in France', *European Journal of Education*, 26, 3, 197-205

Blunkett, David, and Jackson, Keith (1987), *Democracy in crisis*, The Hogarth Press, London

Blyth, W. and Derricott, R. (1977), *The social significance of middle schools*, B.T.Batsford, London

Boddy, Martin, and Fudge, Colin (eds) (1984), *Local socialism*, Macmillan, London

Bondi, Liz (1989), 'Selecting schools for closure', *Journal of Education Policy*, 4, 2, 85-102

Bondi, Liz (1991), 'Choice and diversity in school education: comparing developments in the United Kingdom and the USA', *Comparative Education*, 27, 2, 125-133

Booth, T. and Coulby, D. (ed's) (1987), *Producing and reducing disaffection*, Open University

Bosche, Susanne (1983), *Jenny lives with Eric and Martin*, Gay Men's Press, London

Boudon, R. (1973), *Education, opportunity and social inequality*, John Wiley, New York

Boulton, P. and Coldron, J. (1989), *The pattern and process of parental choice*, Sheffield City Polytechnic

Bourdieu, P. and Passeron, J-C. (1977/1990) *Reproduction in education, society and culture*, Sage, London

Bowles, S. (1971), 'Unequal education and the reproduction of the social division of labour', *Review of Radical Political Economics*, 3, Autumn

Bowles, S. and Gintis, H. (1976), *Schooling in capitalist America*, Routledge, London

Boyd, W. (1991), 'Choice plans for public schools in the USA', *Local Government Policy Making*, 18, 1, 20-27

Boyson, Rhodes (1972), *Education: threatened standards*, Churchill Press, London

Boyson, Rhodes (1975), *The crisis in education*, The Woburn Press, London

Brandt, G. (1986), *The realization of anti-racist teaching*, Falmer Press, London

Braverman, H. (1974), *Labour and monopoly capital*, Monthly Review press, New York

Brighouse, T. (1991), 'The uncertain future of local education authorities', *Local Government Policy Making*, 18, 1, 8-13

Brighouse, T. and Tomlinson, J. (1991), 'Successful schools', *Education and Training Paper 4*, IPPR

Britton, Martin, and Rosen (1966), 'Multiple impression marking of English compositions', *Schools Council Examinations Bulletin, No.2*, HMSO

Broadfoot, P. (1986), 'Assessment policy and inequality', *British Journal of Sociology of Education*, 7, 1

Broadfoot, P. (1990), 'Research on teachers: towards a comparative methodology, *Comparative Education*, 26, 2/3, 165-168

Brown, P. and Ashton, D. (ed's) (1987), *Education, unemployment and labour markets*, Falmer Press, London

Bush, T., Kogan, M. and Lenney, T. (1989), *Directors of education*, Jessica Kingsley, London

Butcher, H. and Rudd, E. (1972), *Contemporary problems in higher education*, McGraw-Hill, London

Callinicos, A. and Harman, C. (1987), *The changing working class*, Bookmarks, London

Carter, Ronald (ed) (1990), *Knowledge about language*, Hodder and Stoughton, London

Castells, M. (1977), *The urban question*, Edward Arnold, London

Castells, M. (1983), *The city and the grassroots*, Edward Arnold, London

Cawson, A. and Saunders, P. (1983), 'Corporatism, competitive politics, and class struggle', in King, R. (ed), *Capital and Politics*, Routledge, London

CCCS (Centre for Contemporary Cultural Studies) (1981), *Unpopular education*, Hutchinson, London

Cherkaoui, M. (1982), *Les changements du systeme educatif en France 1950-1980*, Presses Universitaires de France

Chitty, C. (1989), *Towards a new education system: the victory of the New Right?*, Falmer Press, London

CLEA (Council of Local Education Authorities) (1987), *The report on the first Standing Conference on education*, CLEA, London

Cline, P. and Tony Graham, P. (1991), 'School-based management - an emerging approach to the administration of America's schools', *Local Government Studies*, July/August, 43-50

Clune, W. and Witte, J. (ed's) (1990), *Choice and control in American education* (vol.1), Falmer, London

Cobalti, A. (1990), 'Schooling inequalities in Italy', *European Sociological Review*, 6, 3, 199-214

Cockburn, Cynthia (1977), *The local state*, Pluto Press, London

Cockcroft, C. (1982), *Mathematics counts* (Cockcroft Report), HMSO, London

Cohen, P. and Bains, H. (ed's) (1988), *Multi-racist Britain*, Macmillan, London

Cole, Mike (ed) (1988), *Bowles and Gintis revisited*, Falmer Press, London

Collins, B. and Robbins, K. (ed's) (1990), *British culture and economic decline*, Weidenfeld and Nicolson

Collins, R. (1979), *The credential society*, Academic, New York

Coombs, P. (1968), *The world educational crisis*, Oxford University Press

Coombs, P. (1985) *The world crisis in education*, Oxford University Press

Cosin, B. and Hales, M. (ed's) (1983), *Education, policy and society*, Routledge, London

Cox, B. (1991), *Cox on Cox*, Hodder and Stoughton, London

Cox, C.B. (1972), *Critical Quarterly*, 14, 1

Cox, C.B and Boyson, R., *Black Paper 1977*, Temple Smith, London

Cox, C.B. and Dyson, A.E. (1968), *Fight for education*, Critical Quarterly Society, London

Cox, C.B. and Dyson, A.E. (1968), 'A word in the desert', *Critical Quarterly*, 10, 1/2

Cox, C.B. and Dyson, A.E., *Black Paper Two*, Critical Quarterly Society, London

Cox, C.B. and Dyson, A.E., *Black Paper Three*, Critical Quarterly Society, London

Cox, C. and Marks, J. (ed's) (1982), *The right to learn*, Centre for Policy Studies, London

Cox, Theo (1979), 'A follow-up study of reading attainment in a sample of eleven-year old children', *Educational Studies*, 5, 1, 53-59

Cresswell, M. and Gubb, J. (1987), *The Second International Mathematics Study*, NFER-Nelson, Windsor

Crouch, C. and Marquand, D. (1989), *The new centralism*, Basil Blackwell

Curran, J. *et al* (1987), 'Media Coverage of London Councils: Interim Report', Goldsmith's College (mimeo)

DCS (Department of Cultural Studies) (1991), *Education Limited*, Unwin Hyman, London

Dearlove, John (1973), *The politics of policy in local government*, Cambridge University Press

Demaine, Jack (1981), *Contemporary theories in the sociology of education*, Macmillan, London

Dennison, S. (1984), *Choice in education*, IEA, London

Department of Employment (May 1992), *Labour Market Quarterly Review*

Department of Trade and Industry (1989), *Information technology*, HMSO

Derouet, J-L. (1991) 'Lower secondary education in France', *European Journal of Education*, 26, 2, 119-131

DES (1963), *Half our future* (Newsom Report), HMSO

DES (1968), *Enquiry into the flow of candidates in science and technology into higher education* (Dainton Report), HMSO

DES (1975), *A language for life* (Bullock Report), HMSO, London

DES, HMI (1978), *Mixed ability work in comprehensive schools*, HMSO

DES, HMI (1981), *Curriculum 11-16: a review of progress*, HMSO

DES, HMI (1983), *Curriculum 11-16: towards a statement of entitlement*, HMSO

DES (1985), *Better schools*, HMSO

DES (1985), *Education for all* (Swann Report), HMSO

DES (1985), *The development of higher education into the 1990s*, HMSO

DES, HMI (1986), *Education in the Federal Republic of Germany*, HMSO

DES (1987), *Teachers' pay and conditions*, HMSO

DES, TGAT (1987), *The national curriculum 5-16: a consultative document*, HMSO

DES, APU (1988), *Language performance in schools*, HMSO

DES (1988), *Report of the Committee of Enquiry into the Teaching of English Language* (Kingman Report), HMSO

DES (1988), *Education statistics for the United Kingdom*, HMSO

DES, HMI (1988), *Secondary schools: an appraisal*, HMSO

DES (1988), *Advancing A levels* (Higginson Report), HMSO

DES (1989), *Discipline in schools* (Elton Report), HMSO

DES (1990, HMI) *Teaching and learning in New York City schools*, HMSO

DES (1990), *English in the national curriculum* (Cox Report), HMSO

DES (1990) (with DTI, DE), *Highly qualified people: supply and demand*, HMSO

DES (1991), *Education statistics for the United Kingdom*, HMSO

DES, HMI (1991:a), *Aspects of vocational education and training in the Federal Republic of Germany*, HMSO

DES, HMI (1991:b), *Aspects of upper secondary and higher education in Japan*, HMSO

DES, HMI (1992), *Education in England 1990-91*, HMSO

DES (1993), *School teachers' review body: second report* (Day Report), HMSO

DEYA (1983), *Youth policies, programs and issues*, Department of Education and Youth Affairs, Canberra

Digby, A. and Searby, P. (1981), *Children, school and society in nineteenth-century England*, Macmillan

Dolton, P., Makepeace, G. and Treble, J. (1992), 'Evaluating YTS using YCS', mimeo, Department of Economics, University of Hull

Donnison, David, and Ungerson, Clare (1982), *Housing policy*, Penguin, Harmondsworth

Douglas, J.W.B. (1964), *The home and the school*, MacGibbon and Kee, London

Dunleavy, P. (1980), 'The political implications of sectoral cleavages and the growth of state employment', *Political Studies*, 28, no's 3/4

Duru-Bellat, M. and Mingat, A. (1989), 'How do French Junior Secondary Schools operate?' *European Sociological Review*, 5, 1, 47-64

Dyson, A. (1970), 'Culture in decline', *Critical Quarterly*, 12, 2, 99-104

Dyson, K. and Humphreys, P. (1988), *Broadcasting and new media policies in Western Europe*, Routledge

Echols, F., McPherson, A., and Willms, J. (1990), 'Parental choice in Scotland', *Journal of Educational Policy*, 5, 3, 207-222

Eckstein, M. and Noah, H. (1989), 'Forms and functions of secondary school-leaving examinations', *Comparative Education Review*, 33, 3, 295-316

Edwards, Viv (1983), *Language in multicultural classrooms*, Batsford, London

Edwards, J. (1987), *Positive discrimination, social justice, and social policy*, Tavistock Publications, London

Edwards, R. (1988), 'Equality Strategy: why we need to consider labour market issues', *British Journal of Education and Work*, 2, 1, 17-24

Edwards, T., Gewirtz, S., Whitty, G. (1992), 'Researching a policy in progress: the city technology colleges initiative', *Research Papers in Education*, 7, 1, 79-103

Elias, P. and Blanchflower, D. (1987), 'Who gets the good jobs?', Institute for Employment Research, University of Warwick (mimeo)

Fainstein, S., Gordon I., Harloe, M. (1992), *Divided cities*, Blackwell, Oxford

Finch, A. and Scrimshaw, P. (ed's) (1980), *Standards, schooling and education*, Hodder and Stoughton

Finegold, D. and Soskice, D. (1988), 'The failure of training in Britain', *Oxford Review of Economic Policy*, 4, 3, 21-50

Finegold, D. *et al* (1990), 'A British *Baccalauréat*', *Education and Training Paper 1*, IPPR, London

Finniston, M. (1980), *Engineering our future*, Department of Industry

FitzGibbon, C. *et al* (1988), 'Performance indicators and the TVEI pilot', *Evaluation and Research in Education*, 2, 2, 49-60

Flew, A. (1987), *Power to the parents: reversing educational decline*, The Sherwood Press

Flynn, N, Leach, S. and Vielba, C. (1985), 'Abolition or reform', *Local London Briefings 2*, George Allen

Forrester, A., Lansley, S., and Pauley, R. (1985), *Beyond our Ken*, Fourth Estate, London

Foster, Hal (1983), *Postmodern Culture*, Pluto, London

Foster, Peter (1990), *Policy and practice in multicultural and anti-racist education*, Routledge, London

Fowler, W. (1988), *Towards the national curriculum*, Kogan Page, London

Franklin, Bob, and Parton, Nigel (ed's), (1991) *Social work, the media and public relations*, Routledge

Fuhr, C. (1989), *Schools and Institutions of Higher Education in the Federal Republic of Germany*, Inter Nationes, Bonn

Fullan, M. (1991), *The new meaning of educational change*, Cassell, London

Fulton, O. (1987), 'The technical and vocational education initiative', *Education and Training UK*, Policy Journals

Gale, B. (1991), 'Giving schools and colleges greater choice: Cambridgeshire's approach to delegating funding for education support services', *Local Government Policy Making*, 18, 2, 30-39

Galton, M. and Willcocks, J. (1983), *Moving from the primary classroom*, RKP, London

Garrish, S. (1986), 'Centralisation and decentralisation in England and France', *SAUS Occasional Paper 27*, University of Bristol

Gaziel, H. (1989), 'The emergence of the comprehensive middle school in France', *Comparative Education*, 25, 1, 29-40

Giddens, A. and Held, D. (ed's) (1982), *Classes, power, and conflict*, Macmillan, London

Gipps, C. and Goldstein, H. (1983), *Monitoring children*, Heinemann, London

Gilroy, D. (1992), 'The political rape of initial teacher education in England and Wales', *Journal of Education for Teaching*, 18, 1, 5-22

Gilroy, Paul (1987), *There ain't no black in the Union Jack*, Hutchinson, London

Golding, P. and Middleton, S. (1982), *Images of welfare*, Martin and Robertson, Oxford

Goldsmith, M. (ed) (1986), *New research in central-local relations*, Gower, Aldershot

Goldstein, H. (1987), *Multilevel models in educational and social research*, Charles Griffin, London

Goldstein, H. (1991), 'Assessment in schools', *Education and Training Paper 5*, IPPR, London

Goldthorpe, J., Llewellyn, C. and Payne, C. (1980), *Social mobility and class structure in modern Britain*, Clarendon Press, Oxford

Goldthorpe, J. and Payne, C. (1986), Trends in intergenerational class mobility in England and Wales, *Sociology*, 20, 1-24

Goodin, R. and Le Grand, J. (ed's) (1987), *Not only the poor*, Allen and Unwin, London

Goodman, R. (1990), *Japan's 'international youth'*, Clarendon Press, Oxford

Gordon, Paul and Klug, Francesca (1986), *New Right New Racism*, Searchlight

Gottdiener, M. (1987), *The decline of urban politics*, Sage, London

Gough, Ian (1979), *The political economy of the welfare state*, Macmillan, London

Graham, D. and Tytler, D. (1993), *A lesson for us all*, Routledge, London

Gray, J. and Jesson, D. (1987), 'Exam results and local authority league tables', *Education and Training UK*, Policy Journals

Gray, J., Jesson, D., Pattie, C. and Sime, N. (1989), 'Youth Cohort Study: Education and training opportunities in the inner city', Department of Employment Training Agency

Gray, J., Jesson, D. and Sime, N. (1990), 'Estimating differences in the examination performance of secondary schools', *Oxford Review of Education*, 16, 2, 137-158

Green, Andy (1992), 'The role of the state and the social partners in VET systems', mimeo

Gyford, John (1984), *Local politics in Britain*, Croom Helm, London

Gyford, John (1985), *The politics of local socialism*, George Allen and Unwin, London

Gyford, J. and James, M. (1983), *National parties and local politics*, George Allen and Unwin, London

Habermas, J. (1976), *Legitimation crisis*, Heinemann, London

Halsey, A. (ed) (1988), *British social trends since 1900*, Macmillan, London

Halsey, A., Heath, A. and Ridge, J. (1980), *Origins and destinations*, Clarendon Press, Oxford

Halstead, M. (1988), *Education, justice and cultural diversity*, Falmer Press, London

Hambleton, R. and Hoggett, P. (1987), *Decentralisation and diversity: localising public services*, SAUS, University of Bristol

Hammersley, M. and Woods, P. (ed's) (1976), *The process of schooling*, Routledge

Hampton, William (1987), *Local government and urban politics*, Longman, London

Hargreaves, A. and Reynolds, D. (1989), *Education policies: controversies and critiques*, Falmer Press,

Hart, P. (1990), 'Skill shortages in the United Kingdom, *NIESR Discussion Paper 169*, London

Hart, P. and Shipman, A., 'Skill shortages in the United Kingdom: the lessons from case studies', *NIESR Discussion Paper 169*, London

Hart, P. and Shipman, A. (May 1991), 'Financing training in Britain', *National Institute Economic Review*, 77-85

Harvey, David (1990), *The condition of postmodernity*, Basil Blackwell, Oxford

Haywood, R. (1989), 'Look over your shoulder, Mr Baker: the Norwegian connection', *Journal of Education Policy*, 4, 2, 163-169

Heath, A., Jowell, R. and Curtice, J. (1985), *How Britain votes*, Pergamon, Oxford

Hess, G. (1992), 'Chicago and Britain: experiments in empowering parents', *Journal of Education Policy*, 7, 2, 155-171

Hill, A. (1987), 'Democratic education in West Germany: the effects of the new minorities', *Comparative Education Review*, 31, 2, 273-287

Hillgate Group (1987), *The reform of British education*, London

Himmelweit, H., Humphreys, P. and Jaeger, M. (1985), *How voters decide*, Open University Press

Hindess, B. (1983), *Parliamentary democracy and socialist politics*, Routledge and Kegan Paul, London

Hirst, P. and Zeitlin, J. (ed's) (1989), *Reversing industrial decline*, Berg, Oxford

Hiskett, M. (undated), *Schooling for British Muslims*, Social Affairs Unit, London

Hoggett, Paul, and Hambleton, Robin (eds) (1987), 'Decentralisation and democracy', *SAUS Occasional Paper 28*, University of Bristol

Holbrook, D. (1964), *English for the rejected*, Cambridge University Press

Holliday, I. (1991), 'The New Suburban Right in British local government', *Local Government Studies*, Nov -Dec, 45-62

Holmes, Brian (ed) (1985), *Equality and freedom in education*, George Allen, London

Home Office (1988), *A scrutiny of grants under Section 11 of the Local Government Act 1966*, HMSO

Hopkins, D. and Leask, M. (1989), 'Performance indicators and school development', *School organisation*, 9, 1, 3-20

Horio, T. (1988), *Educational thought and ideology in modern Japan*, University of Tokyo Press

Horton, T. (ed) (1990), *Assessment debates*, Hodder and Stoughton, London

Hough, J. (1987), *Education and the national economy*, Croom Helm

Howarth, M. (1991), *Britain's educational reform*, Routledge

Hughes, A. and Trudgill, P. (1979), *English accents and dialects*, Edward Arnold, London

Hunter, Ian (1988), *Culture and government*, Macmillan, London

Husen, T. (1979), *The school in question*, Oxford University Press

Iben, M. 'Attitudes and mathematics', *Comparative education*, 27, 2, 135-149

IEA (1992), *The state of the economy*, London

ILEA, *The English curriculum: gender, material for discussion*

ILEA, *The English curriculum: race, material for discussion*

ILEA (1984), 'Towards new policies on attendance' (mimeo)

ILEA (1984), *Improving secondary schools* (Hargreaves Report)

ILEA (Research and Statistics) (1985), *Socio-economic background, parental involvement, and children's achievements in junior schools*

ILEA (1986), 'Towards new policies on attendance' (mimeo)

ILEA, Research and Statistics (1986), *1985 attendance survey*

ILEA, Research and Statistics (1987), *The London reading test*

ILEA, Research and Statistics (1987), *Ethnic background and examination results*

ILEA, Research and Statistics (1987:a) *Actual and predicted examination scores*

Illich, I. (1970), *Deschooling society*, Penguin, Harmondsworth

Indian Workers Association (Southall), *Black inner city uprisings: the regeneration of racism*

Ingham, M. (1985), 'Industrial Relations in British Local Government', *Industrial Relations Journal*, 16, 1

ISIS (1989), *Choosing your independent school*, Independent Schools Information Service

Jackson, Brian and Marsden, Dennis (1966), *Education and the working class*, Penguin

Jeffcoate, R. (1979), *Positive image: towards a multiracial curriculum*, Writers and Readers Publishing Cooperative, London

Jencks, C. (1972), *Inequality: a reassessment of the effect of family and schooling in America*, Basic Books, New York

Jones, Ken (1989), *Right turn: the Conservative revolution in education*, Hutchinson, London

Jordon, Steve (1986), 'Pedagogy and profiling on YTS: some problems in the sociology of the new vocationalism, Institute of Education, University of London (mimeo)

Karabel, J. and Halsey, A. (ed's) (1977), *Power and ideology in education*, Oxford University Press

Keddie, Nell (ed) (1973), *Tinker, tailor... the myth of cultural deprivation*, Penguin, Harmondsworth

Kellett, A. (1992), *Basic Broad Yorkshire*, Smith Settle, Otley

Kelly, E. and Cohn, T. (1988), *Racism in schools - new research evidence*, Trentham Books, Stoke-on-Trent

Kerchner, C. and Mitchell, D. (1988), *The changing idea of a teachers' union*, Falmer Press

Kimber, R. and Richardson, J. (ed's) (1974), *Pressure groups in Britain*, Dent, London

King, Ronald (1969), *Values and involvement in a grammar school*, Routledge, London

Kogan, M. and D. (1983), *The attack on higher education*, Kogan Page, London

Labour Housing Group (1984), *Right to a home*, Spokesman, Nottingham

LAMP (Low Attainers in Mathematics Project) (1987), *Better mathematics*, HMSO

Lawlor, Sheila (1988), *Opting out*, Centre for Policy Studies, London

Lawrence, Bernard (1972), *The Administration of education in Britain*, B.T. Batsford, London

Lawton, D. (1968), *Social class, language and education*, Routledge and Kegan Paul

Lawton, D. and Chitty, C. (ed's) (1988), *The national curriculum*, Bedford Way Papers/33, Institute of Education, London

Layfield (1976), *Local Government Finance* (The Layfield Report), HMSO

Le Corbusier (1946/70), *Towards a new architecture*, The Architectural Press, London

Lee, D., Marsden, D., Rickman, P., Duncombe, J. (1990), *Scheming for youth*, Open University Press

Le Grand, J. (1982), *The strategy of equality*, George Allen and Unwin, London

Leonard, M. (1988), *The 1988 Education Act*, Basil Blackwell, Oxford

Levitas, Ruth (1986), *The Ideology of the New Right*, Polity, Cambridge

Levitas (1974), *Marxist perspectives in the sociology of education*, Routledge and Kegan Paul, London

Levy, C. (1992), 'The politics of the higher educated in Italy' (mimeo)

Lieberman, Ann (ed) (1990), *Education reform strategies*, Falmer Press

Lightfoot, M., and Rowan, P. (1988), 'ILEA: Unsuitable Case for Treatment?', *Ginger Paper 3*, Education Reform Group, London

LINC (1991), *Language in the National Curriculum: Materials for Professional Development*

London Research Centre (1986), *Review of London's needs*

Loughlin, M., David Gelfand, M., and Young, Ken (1985), *Half a Century of Municipal Decline*, George Allen and Unwin, London

Lowe, Stuart (1986), *Urban social movements*, Macmillan, London

Lumb, S., Mason, R. and Price, G. (1991), 'Technology teacher training: the North-West Consortium Articles Teacher scheme in England', *European Journal of Education*, 26, 3, 207-219

Maclure, J. (1968), *Educational documents*, Methuen, London

Marcuse, H. (1964/1972), *One dimensional man*, Abacus, London

Marenbon, J. (1987), *English our English*, Centre for Policy Studies, London

Marquet, P-B. (1978), *L'enseignement ne sert à rien*, Les editions ESF

Marsland, D. (ed) (1987), *Education and youth*, Falmer Press, London

Marx, Karl (1976), *Capital*, Penguin, Harmondsworth

Mason, G., Prais, S. and van Ark, B. (1990), 'Vocational education and productivity in the Netherlands and Britain, *NIESR discussion paper 191*, London

Matthews, R., Feinstein, C. and Odling-Smee, J. (1982), *British Economic Growth*, Clarendon Press, Oxford

Max-Planck-Institute (1980), *Bildung in der Bundesrepublik Deutschland*, Ernst Klett, Stuttgart

Max-Planck-Institut (1989), *Between elite and mass education*, State University of New York Press

McCulloch, G. (1986), 'Policy, politics and education: the Technical and Vocational Education Initiative', *Journal of Education Policy*, 1, 1

McKeown, P. (1991), 'Removing Education from Local Government - Lessons from Northern Ireland', *Local Government Studies*, July-August, 51-65

McNamara, D. (1992), 'The reform of teacher education in England and Wales', *Journal of Education for Teaching*, 18, 3, 273-285

McNay, I. and Ozga, J. (ed's) (1985), *Policy-making in education*, Pergamon, Oxford

McPherson, A. and Raab, C. (1988), *Governing education*, Edinburgh University Press

Meijer, K. (1991), 'Reforms in vocational education and training in Italy, Spain and Portugal', *European Journal of Education*, 26, 1, 13-26

Mellor, Hugh (1985), *The role of voluntary organisations in social welfare*, Croom Helm, London

Merson, Martin (1989), 'Teacher match and education policy', *Journal of Education Policy*, 4, 2, 171-184

Micklewright, J., Pearson, M., and Smith, S. (1989), 'Unemployment and early school leaving', Queen Mary College (mimeo)

Miles, Robert (1989), *Racism*, Routledge, London

Minford, P. (1991), *The supply side revolution in Britain*, Edward Elgar, Aldershot

Mitter, W. (1991), 'Comprehensive schools in Germany', *European Journal of Education*, 26, 2, 155-165

Monck, E. and Kelly, A. (1992), *Managing effective schools*, IPPR, London

Morgan, H. (1990), 'Sponsored and contest mobility revisited', *Oxford Review of Education*, 16, 1, 15-27

Morris, M. and Griggs, C. (ed's) (1988), *Education - the wasted years?*, Falmer Press

Mulhern, F. (1979), *The moment of 'Scrutiny'*, London

Munsey, Brenda (ed) (1980), *Moral development, moral education, and Kohlberg*, Religious Education Press, Birmingham, USA

Murphy, J. and Hallinger, P. (1989), 'Equity as access to learning', *Journal of Curriculum Studies*, 21, 2, 129-149

Murray, C., Maguire, M. and Ashton, D. (1988), 'Youth lifestyles, employment and the labour market', *British Journal of Education and Work*, 2, 2, 28-49

National Writing Project, Staffordshire (May 1988), 'Writing and the world of work', *Newsletter No.2*, School Curriculum Development Committee

Natriello, G., Pallas, A. and Alexander, K. (1989), 'On the right track? Curriculum and academic achievement', *Sociology of Education*, 62, April, 109-118

Naylor, Fred (1989), *Dewsbury: The school above the pub*, The Claridge press, London

NEDO (1987), *IT Futures...IT Can Work*, HMSO

Newton, K. and Karran, T. (1985), *The politics of local expenditure*, Macmillan, London

NFER (1987), *The TVEI experience*, Manpower Services Commission

Noah, H. and Eckstein, M. (1989), 'Tradeoffs in examination policies', *Oxford Review of Education*, 15, 1, 17-27

Nuttall, D. (1986), *Assessing educational achievement*, Falmer Press, London

OFSTED (1993), *English: key stages 1, 2 and 3*, HMSO

O'Hear, P. and White, J. (1991), 'A national curriculum for all', *Education and Training Paper 6*, IPPR

Oulton, N. and Steedman, H. (1992), 'The British system of youth training: a comparison with Germany, NIESR, mimeo

Packard, V. (1957/81), *The hidden persuaders*, Penguin, Harmondsworth

Page, Reba (1989), 'The lower-track curriculum at a "heavenly" high school, *Journal of Curriculum studies*, 21, 3, 197-221

Parsons, T. (1959), 'The school class as a social system', *Harvard Educational Review*, XXIX (Autumn), 297-318

Pedley (1969), *The comprehensive school*, Penguin, Harmondsworth

Peters, R.S. (1970), *Ethics and education*, George Allen, London

Poppleton, P. (1990), 'The survey data', *Comparative Education*, 26, 2/3, 183-191

Poppleton, P. and Pullin, R. (1992), 'Distant voices: English teachers views on change in initial teacher education, *Journal of Education for Teaching*, 18, 2, 115-129

Prais, S. (May 1991), 'Vocational qualifications in Britain and Europe: Theory and Practice', *National Institute Economic Review*, 86-93

Prais, S. and Beadle, E. (1991), *Pre-vocational schooling in Europe today*, NIESR, London

Punter, D. (ed) (1986), *Introduction to contemporary cultural studies*, Longman, London

Purvis, J. and Hales, M. (ed's) (1983), *Achievement and inequality in education*, Routledge/Open University

Raffe, D. (1987), 'YTS and Scottish School-leavers', *Education and Training UK*, Policy Journals

Raffe, D. (ed) (1988), *Education and the youth labour market*, Falmer Press, London

Raggatt, P. and Weiner, G. (ed's) (1985), *Curriculum and assessment*, Pergamon, Oxford

Ramdin, R. (1986), *The making of the black working class in Britain*, Gower

Ranson, S. (1990), *The politics of reorganizing schools*, Unwin Hyman, London

Ranson, S. *et al* (1985), *Between centre and locality*, George Allen, London

Ranson, S. and Tomlinson, J. (1986), *The changing government of education*, George Allen and Unwin

Rees, T. (1988), 'Education for enterprise', *Journal of Education Policy*, 3, 1, 9-22

Rees, G., Tweedale, I., Rees, T. and Read, M. (1988), 'Adult training policy and local labour markets', *British Journal of Education and Work*, 2, 1, 1-15

Rees, G., Williamson, H. and Winckler, V. (1989), 'The "new vocationalism": further education and local labour markets', *Journal of Education Policy*, 4, 3, 227-244

Regan, D. (1987), *The local Left*, Centre for Policy Studies, London

Reid, Ivan (1978), *Sociological perspectives on school and education*, Open Books, Shepton Mallet

Reid, W. and Walker, D. (1975), *Case studies in curriculum change*, Routledge, London

Rex, John (1983), *Race relations in sociological theory*, Routledge, London

Rex, John (1986), *Race and ethnicity*, Open University Press, Milton Keynes

Rhoades, G. (1989), 'Conceptions and institutional categories of curriculum', *Journal of Curriculum Studies*, 21, 1, 11-35

Rhodes, R. (1981), *Control and power in central-local government relations*, Gower, Farnborough

Ridley, N. (1988), *The local Right*, Centre for Policy Studies, London

Rigg, M., Elias, P., White, M. and Johnson, S. (1990), *An overview of the demand for graduates*, PSI/Institute for Employment Research

Ringer, B. and Lawless, E. (1989), *Race-ethnicity and society*, Routledge, London

Robertson, John (1981), *Effective classroom control*, Hodder and Stoughton, London

Robey, D. (ed) (1973), *Structuralism: an introduction*, Clarendon Press

Rose, R. (1980), *Politics in England*, Faber, London

Rosen, Connie and Harold (1973), *The language of primary school children*, Penguin, Harmondsworth

Ross, A. and Tomlinson, S. (1991), 'Teachers for tomorrow', *Education and Training Paper 7*, IPPR, London

Rowbotham, S., Segal, L. and Wainwright, H. (1979), *Beyond the fragments*, Merlin Press, London

Runnymede Trust (1989), *The MacDonald Report*

Rutter, M., Maughan, B., Mortimore, P. and Ouston, J. (1979), *Fifteen thousand hours*, Open Books, Wells

Salter, B. and Tapper, T. (1985), *Power and policy in education: the case of independent schooling*, Falmer

Saunders, Peter (1979), *Urban politics*, Hutchinson, London

Schools Council (1981), *Education for a multiracial society*, School's Council Publications

Schoppa, L. (1991), *Education reform in Japan*, Routledge

Schwab, J. (1989), 'Testing and the curriculum', *Journal of Curriculum Studies*, 21, 1, 1-10

SCIP (1991), Mini-Enterprise in Schools, Schools Industry Curriculum Partnership 1991/92, (pamphlet)

SCPR (1992), *British Social Attitudes: cumulative sourcebook*, Gower

Scruton, Roger (1980), *The meaning of Conservatism*, Penguin, Harmondsworth

Scruton, Roger (1988), *Conservative thinkers: essays from the Salisbury Review*, The Claridge Press, London

Seifert, R. (1987), *Teacher militancy*, Falmer Press, London

Seldon, A. (1986), *The riddle of the voucher*, IEA, London

Sexton, S. (1987), *Our schools: a radical policy*, IEA, Warlingham

Sharpe, L. (ed) (1979), *Decentralist trends in western democracies*, Sage, London

Shilling, C. (1989), 'The mini-enterprises in Schools Project, *Journal of Education Policy*, 4, 2, 115-124

Shipman, A. (undated), *Skills shortages in Britain and West Germany*, NIESR discussion paper 192

Shipman, Marten (1984), *Education as a public service*, Harper and Row, London

Shrimpton, Jean (1964), *The truth about modelling*, W.H. Allen, London

Simon, B. (1988), *Bending the rules*, Lawrence and Wishart, Lawrence

Singh, G. (ed) (1982), *The critic as anti-philosopher: essays and papers by F.R. Leavis*, Chatto and Windus

Sivanandan, A. (1986), *From resistance to rebellion: Asian and Afro-Caribbean struggles in Britain*, IRR

Smellie, K. (1968), *A history of local government*, George Allen and Unwin, London

Smith, D. and Tomlinson, S. (1989), *The school effect*, PSI, London

Sommer, W. and Waldburg-Zeil, A. (1984), *Neue Perspektiven der Bildungspolitik*, Weltforum Verlag, 1984

Spenner, K., Kerckhoff, A. and Glas, T. (1990), 'Open and closed education and work systems in Great Britain', *European Sociological Review*, 6, 3, 215-236

Spours, K. and Young, M. (1988), 'Beyond vocationalism: a new perspective on the relationship between work and education', in *British Journal of Education and Work*, 2, 2, 5-14

Stal, F. and Thom, F. (1988), *Schools for barbarians*, The Claridge Press, London

Stanworth, P. and Giddens, A. (ed's) (1974), *Elites and power in British society*, Cambridge University Press

Statham, J., Mackinnon, D. and Cathcart, H. (1989), *The education factfile*, Hodder and Stoughton, London

Steedman, H. (1992), 'Mathematics in vocational youth training for the building trades in Britain, France and Germany, *NIESR discussion paper 9*, London

Steedman, H., Mason, G. and Wagner, K. (May 1991), 'Intermediate skills in the workplace: deployment, standards and supply in Britain, France and Germany', *National Institute Economic Review*, 60-76

Stewart, John (1983), *Local Government: The conditions of local choice*, George Allen and Unwin, London

Stibbs, Andrew (1979), *Assessing children's language*, National Association for the Teaching of English and

Ward Lock Educational, London

Stibbs, Andrew (1987), 'Language and multicultural education', *English in Education* (NATE), 21, 2, 27-34

Stoker, Gerry (1988), *The politics of local government*, Macmillan, London

Stradling, R., Noctor, M. and Baines, B. (1984), *Teaching controversial issues*, Edward Arnold, London

Taylor-Gooby, P. (1985), *Public opinion, ideology and state welfare*, Routledge, London

ThinkLinc No 6 (newsletter), Linc Centre, Leeds, Autumn, 1991

Thompson, Denys (1964), *Discrimination and popular culture*, Penguin, Harmondsworth

Thornthwaite, S. (1990), 'School Transport and the Education Reform Act', *Local Government Studies*, July -August, 15-23

Tomlinson, H. (ed) (1992), *Performance-related pay in education*, Routledge, London

Townsend, P. and Davidson, N. (ed's) (1982), *Inequalities in health*, Penguin, Harmondsworth

Townsend P., Phillimore, P. and Beattie, A. (1988), *Health and deprivation*, Croom Helm, London

Tracy, M. and Morrison, D. (1979), *Whitehouse*, Macmillan, London

Travers, T. (1986), *The politics of local government finance*, Allen and Unwin, London

Troyna, Barry (ed) (1987), *Racial inequality in education*, Tavistock, London

Troyna, B. and Williams, J. (1986), *Racism, education and the state*, Croom Helm, London

Turner, Bryan (ed) (1990), *Theories of modernity and postmodernity*, Sage, London

Twitchin, J. and Demuth, C. (1985), *Multi-cultural education*, BBC, London

Urry, J. and Wakeford, J. (ed's) (1973), *Power in Britain*, Heinemann, London

Verhoeven, J. (1992), 'Key issues in educational policy for secondary schools in federated Belgium', *Journal of Education Policy*, 7, 1, 99-107

Wain (1972), *Critical Quarterly*, 14,1

Wainwright, Hilary (1987), *Labour: A tale of two parties*, The Hogarth Press, London

Waites, B., Bennett, T, and Martin, G. (ed's) (1982), *Popular culture*, Croom Helm, London

Walker, Stephen and Barton, Len (ed's) (1987), *Changing policies, changing teachers*, Open University Press,

Wallace, C. and Cross, M. (1990), *Youth in transition*, Falmer Press, London

Weale, M. (1993), 'A critical evaluation of rate of return analysis', *The Economic Journal*, 103, 418, 729-737

Weiler, H. (1988), 'The politics of reform and nonreform in French education', *Comparative Education Review*, 32, 3, 251-265

Weiler, H. (1990), 'Curriculum reform and the legitimation of educational objectives: the case of the Federal Republic of Germany', *Oxford Review of Education*, 16, 1, 15-27

Weiss, M. and Weishaupt, H. (1989), 'Economic austerity in West German education?, *Journal of Education Policy*, 4, 1, 39-51

Wexler, P. (1987), *Social analysis of education*, Routledge, London

White, M. and McRae, S. (1989), *Young adults and long term unemployment*, PSI, London

Whiteley, Winifred (1969), *The uneducated English*, Methuen, London

Whitty, Geoff (1985), *Sociology and school knowledge*, Methuen, London

Wiener, M. (1985), *English culture and the decline of the industrial spirit, 1850-1980*, Penguin

Williams, K., Williams, J. and Thomas D. (1983), *Why are the British bad at manufacturing?*, Routledge

Williams, Raymond (1962/76), *Communications*, Penguin, Harmondsworth

Williams, Raymond (1961/65), *The long revolution*, Penguin, Harmondsworth

Williams, Raymond (1989), *The politics of modernism*, Verso, London

Willis, Paul (1977), *Learning to labour*, Gower, Aldershot

Wilson, N. (1992) 'The new national curriculum: a socialist view', SEA

Winkley, D. (1991), 'The LEA and the primary school', *Local government policy making*, 18, 1, 14-19

Wojciechowska, A. (1989), 'Curriculum reform in mathematics', *Journal of Curriculum Studies*, 21, 2, 151 -159

Wright, Nigel (1977), *Progress in education*, Croom Helm, London

Yeomans, D. (1989), 'TVEI: policy, practice and prospects', *British Journal of Education and Work*, 3, 3, 6-15

Young, Ken (1975), *Local politics and the rise of party*, Leicester University Press

Young, Ken (1983), *National interests and local government*, Heinemann

Young, M (1971), *Knowledge and control: new directions for the sociology of education*, Collier-Macmillan

Young, M. (1972), 'On the politics of educational knowledge', *Economy and Society*, 1, 2

Index

R

R